THE IMAGE OF JASON IN EARLY GREEK MYTH

This book looks to construct a detailed portrait of the myth of the Greek hero, Jason. This involves examining all extant evidence, both literary and iconographical, for this hero up until the end of the fifth century B.C. It is at this point, the last quarter of the fifth century, which marks a change in Jason's depiction with later sources showing his need to rely on the figures around him for his success.

A crucial part of this evidence is iconographical in nature, and this examination will reveal that there are many aspects of the tale that only survive in this form, making it a particularly valuable source, and one which has often been underestimated by previous scholars. This work will examine the evidence from the earliest references in order to understand the depictions of Jason which would have been familiar to, and would have resonated with, the Greeks in earlier societies. This hero can justifiably be placed alongside other great Greek mythological figures such as Perseus, Theseus and Herakles. This work aims to provide a much-needed cohesive study of his earliest depictions, noting the interaction of visual evidence with literary sources in the creation of a portrait of the character.

Simon Spence, taught and studied at University College Dublin, where he completed his M.Litt., and at the University of Nottingham where he completed his Ph.D. Today he works in Dublin, Ireland.

THE IMAGE OF JASON
IN EARLY GREEK MYTH

An examination of iconographical and literary
evidence of the myth of Jason up until
the end of the fifth century B.C.

by Simon Spence

First published 2010

© Simon Spence

This book was printed and bound by CreateSpace

ISBN: 978-1449593575

For Aideen

Contents

Abbreviations

Aesch.	Aeschylos
Ant.	Sophokles' *Antigone*
Astr.	Hyginus' *De Astronomia*
ApB	Apollodoros' *The Library*
AR	Apollonios Rhodios
AJA	*American Journal of Archaeology*
BICS	*Bulletin of the Institute of Classical Studies*
CA	*Classical Archaeology*
Cho.	Aischylos' *Choephoroi*
Eum.	Eumelos' *Korinthiaka*
EGM	*Early Greeky Mythography*, R. Fowler
Fab.	Hyginus' *Fabulae*
G & R	*Greece and Rome*
Hek.	Fragments of Hekataios in *Early Greek Mythography*
Hes.	Hesiod
Hist.	Herodotus' *Histories*
Il.	Homer's *Iliad*
Kaibel	Fragments of Epicharmos cited according to G. Kaibel, *Comicorum Graecorum Fragmenta* 1
LIMC	*Lexicon Iconographicum Mythologiae Classicae*
Med.	Euripides' *Medea*

Met.	Ovid's *Metamorphoses*
MW	Fragments of the Hesiodic corpus cited according to R. Merkelbach and M.L. West, *Fragmenta Hesiodea*
N²	Fragments of Euripides cited according to A. Nauck, *Tragicorum Graecorum Fragmenta*
Nau.	*Naupaktia*
Nem.	Pindar's *Nemean Odes*
Od.	Homer's *Odyssey*
Ol.	Pindar's *Olympian Odes*
Paus.	Pausanias
Pher.	Pherekydes
PMG	Fragments of the Greek Lyric Poets cited according to D.L. Page, *Poetae Milici Graeci*
Py.	Pindar's *Pythian Odes*
R.	Radt, *Tragicorum Graecorum Fragmenta*
Σ	Scholia
TAPA	*Transactions of the American Philological Association*
Th.	Hesiod's *Theogony*

Note on Spelling of Names

For the purpose of this book, I have chosen to use transliteration rather than Latinization. There are two notable exceptions to this; the Latinized "Jason" and "Medea" have been used in preference to "Iason" and "Medeia." Choosing to use the latter would have adversely changed the title of the book and it was felt that given the prominence of Medea in the discussion, the Latinized form was more appropriate.

Introduction

'Jason is clearly one individual whose heroic
character is transformed very significantly through
time within the literary tradition.'[1]

    When considering any myth, a select number of sources will stand out and dominate our perception of the story. The purpose of this book is to re-examine the evidence and assess the portrayal of the early myth of Jason, one of the oldest and best known heroes of Greek mythology, in order to redress this imbalance, and to present what would have been the earliest versions of the tale, before a few ancient texts came to guide our perceptions of the hero along a particular path. Portraits of Jason after the fifth century present a character who is reliant on the characters around him for his successes, and even feeble in some depictions. This is in marked contrast to earlier portraits of a dynamic and talented leader. My approach will involve the study of all the early extant evidence, both from literary sources and from archaeology, with a view to producing a fresh examination of all surviving material. This will then allow us to evaluate the contribution of iconography to this myth, looking at what visual art brings to our understanding of the figure of Jason and his story. It is my intention to demonstrate the extent to which iconography complements, contributes to, and even supersedes the literary sources on occasion, and to illustrate how valuable such evidence is to our overall view of the myth.

    This is something which has not been done to any significant extent in previous scholarship, in two respects. In the first place, it is rare that we have a cohesive and chronologically based discussion of any mythical character, with scholars frequently taking the easier approach of adopting whatever portrait of the character in question that is best known, without stopping to analyse whether this is in fact a faithful

---

[1] Mackie pp. 3-4.

representation. In the second place, scholars have as yet been slow to acknowledge the role played by iconographical evidence in this quest to compile a 'pure' version of the myth, or of the character in question. While many authors have spent time discussing the place of vase painting and sculpture in the ancient world, there has been less tendency to look at the iconographical evidence in conjunction with literary evidence, and to explore their mutual relationship. This is what I intend to do in this work, with particular reference to the character of Jason and his famed quest for the Golden Fleece.

In fact Jason as a character himself, has been surprisingly neglected until now, with most authors simply dealing with him as he occurs in relation to other matters. For example Hugo Meyer's *Medeia und die Peliades* provides an important collection of material on a character that is central to the Jason myth, but its focus is firmly on the figure of Medea, and Jason is mentioned only in this context. It has been rare that other scholars engage with early extant references to Jason, and C. J. Mackie in 2001 is one of the first to re-examine the material available, especially vase painting, and to conclude that the early Jason was a distinct and different character to the one that we see in later sources.[2] Mackie's work is an important start, and I believe that it is a useful contribution to a wider need to re-address the myth of Jason. It is however, limited in its scope due to the size of the article, and there is much more that can be covered in this quest to know the early Jason.

Two other recent works stand out as attempting to redress this balance, and to deal more extensively with the character of Jason. Timothy Gantz's *Early Greek Myth* is a comprehensive and detailed overview of most early Greek mythology and includes a useful study of Jason and the Argonauts. Gantz includes valuable iconographical

---

[2] Whereas I am referring to the early Jason up until the end of the fifth century, Mackie for the purposes of his article, appears to identify the "early" Jason as the figure of epic poetry and early art and he places Pindar, Euripides and Apollonios Rhodios in a group as late sources. p. 4.

evidence in his discussion, but his bias is still more focused on literary evidence. Given the wide ranging nature of his study, it is also impossible for him to discuss the iconographical pieces in detail, and his work, while useful, is more of a catalogue of available material than an analysis of it, or of how different sources might interact in the creation of a character portrait.

Jenifer Neils is another scholar who has worked to bring iconographical evidence more to the fore when discussing this hero Jason. Her entry in LIMC sets out to gather and record as many artistic pieces as possible, and combined with work from other authors on Medea, Pelias, and Phineus among others, LIMC provides an indispensable source book for the myth of Jason and its visual representations.

What I am seeking to accomplish here is to provide an examination of a single hero in depth, and to redress the imbalance between literary and iconographical sources in previous academic discussions of Jason. The material found in *Early Greek Myth* and LIMC provides solid and rich groundwork for any examination of myth. I hope to build on this by taking what is found in both of these collections of sources, expanding on it by referring to further material, and providing a detailed assessment of the role played by iconography in enhancing the knowledge we have from literature.

My approach to providing this reassessment of the available evidence and of the character of Jason is to concentrate on what I have called the 'early myth'. For the purposes of this work the term 'early' refers to evidence that can be dated prior to the end of the fifth century B.C. The term has been used to varying degrees by recent authors. John Boardman's *Early Greek Vase Painting*, uses iconography from the dark ages down to the sixth century B.C.,[3] whereas Timothy Gantz's *Early Greek Myth* includes material down to the end of the fifth century

---

[3] Boardman (1978), p. 7.

and even beyond to Apollonios Rhodios' *Argonautika*, and Apollodoros, where he feels it is appropriate.[4] This work will instead cover the period from the earliest extant material beginning in the eighth century and carry through to 400 B.C. While my dates differ slightly from those adopted by others, I have a particular reason for this, that will allow me to address an issue of importance that relates to general perceptions of the myth of Jason. The end of the fifth century marks a turning point in the portrayal of this character, and so my choice of this date as my finishing point, is designed to incorporate the work of Euripides, especially his *Medea*, and some of the subsequent iconography which appears to be influenced by this play. Jason in Euripides' *Medea* is a less positive character to the image seen in earlier works, both literary and iconographical. Following on from the *Medea* however, we begin to see more presentations of Jason as a character who relies on the figures around him for his success, as demonstrated in Apollonios' *Argonautika*.[5] Throughout this work when referring to the early myth of Jason I wish to include all evidence that can be dated up until 400 B.C.

---

[4] Gantz freely admits that his date is arbitrary but believes in including later sources where evidence exists that they draw from earlier works. p. xvii.

[5] R.L. Hunter describes Jason in the *Argonautika* as demonstrating 'the ambivalent insecurity of Orestes in Euripides' *Elektra* and, to a less extent, Aeschylus' *Choephoroi*. Both Orestes and Jason require support and encouragement to accomplish difficult but necessary tasks which have been imposed upon them by oracular command.' (1988; p. 452).

Uncovering the Early Jason

The approach that this work will take is to follow the myth of Jason, working through each episode in the story in turn, so that a comprehensive study of his character and its portrayal in the various sources can be established. For each section, all available material has been gathered and presented. Our starting point in most cases tends to be the existing literary evidence, followed by an examination of the iconographical evidence that still remains to us. Having assembled and discussed the significance of the sources, I will then assess the role of Jason himself, in order to gain an understanding of his myth and how it changes over time. I will also specifically explore the role iconography plays in this portrayal, as its influence has often been underestimated before now. Each episode of the myth will differ in terms of the quantity of source material available and what proportion of this is literary or iconographical. So it will also be important to understand why a particular aspect of the myth does or does not attract the attention of the visual artist.

As part of this approach to the evidence, it will be useful on occasion to make comparisons to other contemporary heroes. The myth of Perseus is a particularly useful myth when assessing Jason, as there are many similarities in both the structure of his story and in the details of his myth. Given that the popularity of the Perseus myth is at its height in vase painting during the sixth century, there are many parallels between Jason's quest for the fleece and Perseus' journey to slay the Gorgon Medusa. For similar reasons we can also draw comparisons with heroes such as Theseus, Bellerophontes, Herakles and Orestes, as each of these can contribute to our understanding of the hero in mythology.[6]

---

[6] Buxton points to the patterns that emerge in myth and how these stories tend to have a remarkable number of similarities. He uses the myth of Jason as an illustration of this (p. 75ff.).

Transformation in the character of Jason - the role of Euripides

As I have mentioned, the date chosen for the end of this assessment of Jason is 400 B.C.   This date covers a point of transformation in the depiction of the hero, as in 431 B.C. Euripides' *Medea* portrayed the figure of Jason in tragedy. We know that Aeschylus and Sophocles also produced plays about the Argonauts during the fifth century, but Euripides offers us the first complete surviving portrayal of the character. Part of this book will look at the transformation in the depiction of the hero Jason after the production of the *Medea*, which can also be traced in the vase paintings of the end of the fifth century, with the role of Medea becoming more prominent than was the case up until this point. For the most part in early myth Medea plays the role of 'hero-helper', although she is more ruthless and assertive than many other female characters who play a similar supporting role. This role dated back to the earliest sources where a local princess falls in love with the visiting hero and leaves her family to join him on the journey home. The same is the case for Theseus and Ariadne, Perseus and Andromeda, and as part of this work I will look at how Medea moves beyond this role of 'hero-helper' to adopt a more active role, and how this affects the portrayal and perception of Jason as a result.

Part of the significance of this is that many modern authors appear to choose the Euripidean portrayal of Jason as the basis for his image in early myth as a whole. Moses Hadas and H. A. Shapiro are two such examples of modern authors who see Euripides' Jason as a reflection of his portrayal in early myth, ignoring those depictions of the hero in art and literature that differ from the Euripidean version. It will be important to look at how secondary literature treats Jason and having re-examined the sources, whether this is a fair reflection of the early myth.

The Source Material - Literary and Iconographical

Before beginning to trace the development of the myth of Jason in literature and iconography, I feel that it is useful to provide a guide to the main sources which I will be referring to in the course of this work. My intention is not to provide a detailed analysis of these sources, since such an approach is covered in other areas of scholarship. Instead, I wish to simply identify the way in which these sources can contribute to our search for the earliest and purest version of the Jason myth.

The earliest complete works in literature come from the epic poets of the late eighth and early seventh centuries B.C. Both the *Iliad* and the *Odyssey* are generally believed to date to the second half of the eighth century, with the *Iliad* possibly predating the *Odyssey* by about a quarter of a century.[7] Snodgrass has done much to assess the way in which the Homeric epics were known to early Greek artists and he throws some doubt on how widespread knowledge of the Homeric epics was up until the mid sixth century. He believes that the availability of Homer's *Iliad* and *Odyssey* in the ancient world was relatively poor until the sixth century,[8] when, as Karl Schefold puts it, 'there is a renaissance of the epic in the first third of the sixth century,' and this 'corresponds to the epic narrative style in vase painting.'[9]

Aside from the date at which the works of Homer may have had an impact on other artists, his epics demonstrate the wealth of

---

[7] Snodgrass discusses the dating of the Homeric epics, and draws attention to recent debates as to their chronology, saying "There has been some agreement that the Iliad, at least, may have reached its final Homeric form as early as the mid-eighth century...but in the last few years, at least in Anglo-Saxon scholarship, there has been quite strong support for dating Homer and the Iliad appreciably later than this." p. 12-3. However, Snodgrass concludes his discussion of modern critical views of Homer, correctly in my view, by saying that he "personally would not support the recent move to bring down Homer's date." p. 13.

[8] Ibid., p. 164.

[9] Schefold (1992), p. 4.

stories which were available at the time. Many of these tales would have existed in oral form long before this age and part of Homer's usefulness is that his epics record some of the earliest stories in myth and demonstrate to us a range of the earliest known tales. Both Homer and Hesiod draw on stories known to the wider world, and at times they do not even need to recount all of the detail to remind their audience of the story. Easterling and Knox give two such examples of a myth which is alluded to by Homer, but its full content is not related (p. 106).[10] The first is that of Oidipous, of which a summary is given in *Odyssey* Book 11 (271-80):

> And I saw the mother of Oedipodes, beautiful Epicaste, who did a monstrous thing in the ignorance of her mind, wedding her own son; and soon the gods made these things known among men. Nevertheless, in lovely Thebes, suffering woes, he ruled over the Cadmeans by the dire designs of the gods; but she went down to the house of Hades, the strong warder, making fast a deadly noose from the high ceiling, caught by her own grief; but for him she left behind countless woes, all that a mother's furies bring to pass.[11]

Easterling and Knox correctly suggest that this brief look at the Oidipous myth 'must recall a more extended treatment elsewhere' (p. 106). The same is true for other Homeric passages. *Iliad* IV (364-410) points to the story of Seven Against Thebes and the Epigoni. Agamemnon provokes Diomedes by describing the superior bravery of Diomedes' father, Tydeus. The passage does not make a full reference to the Oidipous myth, but is used by the poet as a reference point. The wider tale would appear to be well known to the audience, otherwise a more detailed description would be required. *Iliad* XXIII (677-80), also points to the

---

[10] In Chp. 4, 'The Epic Tradition after Homer and Hesiod' (*The Cambridge History of Classical Literature I: Greek Literature*).

[11] Homer's *Odyssey*, translated by A.T. Murray, and revised by George E. Dimock, vol. 1: p. 421.

myth when it says that the boxer Euryalos, came to the Thebes for the funeral games held after the death of Oidipous.

However the story of Oidipous can be seen in a wider context, as the *Theogony* (326) mentions the Sphinx as being the bane of the Thebans, and *Works and Days* (156-65) mentions the story of Seven Against Thebes.

These Homeric and Hesiodic references show that the poets did not need to explain all aspects of these well known stories. This is a very a good comparison to what happens with the Argonautic myth. The main basis for arguing that there was an early, pre-Homeric Argonautic epic, comes from one of these references in the *Odyssey*. At *Odyssey* XII (70) the Argo is said to be 'known to all', and this surely points to some treatment of the Argonautic myth in the eighth century.

G.L. Huxley is in little doubt of the existence of a pre-Homeric *Argonautika*. He believes that 'Homer reminds us of his source when he describes the wandering rocks, between which, before Odysseus came, only Argo had passed, with Hera's help because she loved Jason.[12] Huxley also points to Kirke from the *Odyssey* belonging to the Argonautic myth as she is the sister of Aietes.

Huxley's main argument falls into three parts. The first is that there are specific references to the Argonautic myth in the *Odyssey*, and by extension this may be based on the presence of an eighth century *Argonautika*, an epic poem which Homer used as the basis for many aspects of Odysseus' adventures. The second part is the general appearance of references in Homer, as the *Iliad* also makes links to Jason and Hypsipyle, with mention of their son Euenos (12.467-9 and 23.747-8). The final part is Huxley's belief is that the Argonautic myth would have found popularity in an age of exploration and with 'the

---

[12] Huxley, p. 60.

citizens of maritime states during the first stage of colonial expansion in the eighth century B.C.' [13]

While I certainly agree with Huxley's supposition, I also believe that it is difficult to judge the extent to which such an Argonautic myth influenced epic poetry of this age.   Where Huxley argues for the existence of an *Argonautika* and demonstrates its influence upon Homeric epic, Heubeck refers to the early epic in relation to the *Odyssey* Book 10. He suggests that the character of Kirke may have been mentioned in the *Argonautika* as the early epic dealt with Aietes, Kirke's brother, and Medea, both of whom were linked to 'magic arts'.[14] He also speculates that the   poet of the *Argonautika* may have given the character of Kirke her name, genealogy, and country, transferring her from a figure of Greek folktale to a character of epic. Although there is no definitive evidence to prove Heubeck's point, it does show how there is a belief that Homeric epic does draw from an earlier Argonautic epic when dealing with the wanderings of Odysseus. He also believes that in looking at the journey made by Odysseus that he 'is therefore following in the footsteps of Jason',[15] and that the patterns of the tale in the *Argonautika* formed a framework used by Homer for the *Odyssey*.

It is therefore a common theme of Homeric epic to see how the poet used well known myths by alluding to them but assuming prior knowledge by his audience. As with the example of Oidipous, the story of the Argo is a familiar tale. Given this it is also clear that the events and the wanderings of Odysseus are also influenced by the voyage of the Argo. This is important for the myth of Jason as the Argonautic voyage is mentioned in the *Odyssey* and described as being 'known to all' (*Od.* 12.69).

---

[13] Huxley, p. 60.

[14] Heubeck, pp. 51-2.

[15] Ibid., p. 52.

Hesiod's work is generally regarded as being dated to 700 B.C., a short time after Homer.[16]   The *Theogony* and the *Works and Days* are believed to be his works.   What makes Hesiod stand out as being useful as a source, is his knowledge of mythology.   Combined with the work of Homer, Hesiod's two sources provide a wealth of references to early myth, and although Hesiod is not regarded as a comparable author to Homer in terms of his style,[17] he provides many useful insights to the stories and myths.   Poems such as the *Ehoiai* (*Catalogue of Women*), or the *Megalai Ehoiai* are most likely not to be by Hesiod, despite being attributed to him in older scholarship.   These are more likely to have been from the early sixth century. Nevertheless, they can provide useful information for various aspects of our study.

A further work, mostly lost save for some fragmentary evidence, is the *Naupaktia*. This was a poem recited at Naupaktos, and the work is generally ascribed to a native of Miletos.[18]   It too is dated to the eighth century, and although for the most part we only have small fragments from the *Naupaktia*, and third party references to the *Argonautika*, they both provide useful insights showing us how these poems demonstrate a widespread knowledge of the myth at this time. They also establish Jason as a figure of the epic cycle and one of the oldest figures in myth.

One other possible source from epic literature is Eumelos, although the date and ownership of his work, the *Korinthiaka*, is widely debated.   Pausanias says that Eumelos was son of Amphilytos and of the family of the Bacchidae, but doubts whether the *Korinthiaka* can be ascribed to this Corinthian poet, stating:

---

[16] West (1988, p. viii) in fact argues that Hesiod pre-dates the Homeric epics, but Snodgrass's arguments for the retaining of the 'traditional' dates for Homer's *Iliad* and *Odyssey* counter this stance. See further, Snodgrass (1998, pp. 13 ff.).

[17] Ibid., p. vii.

[18] Huxley provides a detailed discussion on the origin of this poem. See p. 68 f.

> Eumelos...who is said to have composed the epic
> poem, says in his Corinthian History (if indeed the
> history be his)...(Paus 2.1.1).[19]

Pausanias believed that there was only one poem that could
be attributed to Eumelos with any degree of certainty:

> In the reign of Phintas the son of Sybotas the
> Messenians for the first time sent an offering and
> chorus of men to Apollo at Delos. Their processional
> hymn to the god was composed by Eumelus, this
> poem being the only one that is considered genuine
> (Paus. 4.4.1).[20]

If we take the processional hymn and try to date Eumelos,
then we do indeed find him working in the eighth century. West points to
Paus. 2.1.1 and dates Eumelos to 'before the Messenian War, so
sometime in the mid eighth century,'[21] as the Messenian War is dated to
ca. 730 B.C. Having established the date of Eumelos, the question of
the date of the *Korinthiaka* remains. It is this poem that I will discuss in
this book as it contains a umber of key references to the myth of Jason.

Huxley believes that the poem can be dated to the second
half of the eighth century B.C. and certainly ties the *Korinthiaka* to
Eumelos.[22] For example, when he discusses Pausanias and his telling
of the story of Jason and Medea's children in Corinth (Paus. 2.3.11), he
believes there is no reason to doubt that it is genuinely Eumelian.[23]
Huxley also distinguishes between the fragments attributed to Eumelos
that he believes are genuine, and those which were less securely
ascribed. For example three fragments of the *Europia* are assigned to

---

[19] Trans. W. H. S. Jones and H. A. Ormerod (Pausanias vol. I, p. 247).

[20] Ibid., Pausanias vol. II, p. 353.

[21] *Greek Epic Fragments: from the seventh to the fifth centuries B.C.* (2003), p. 26.

[22] Huxley, p. 61 ff.

[23] Ibid., p. 65.

Eumelos in a scholium to *Iliad* 6.131, but Huxley believes there are poor foundations for this.[24]

Finally, West takes Eumelos to be an early epic source, but casts doubt on the date of the *Korinthiaka*.[25] He points out that 'it may be that Eumelus' name was remembered in connection with the processional and then attached to the epics because no other name of a Corinthian poet was available.'[26]

For the purposes of this book I have continued to make the basic assumption that the *Korinthiaka* and the work of Eumelos dates to before the end of the fifth century, and whether or not this material dates to the eighth (Huxley) or sixth century (West), we can be relatively certain that it crosses with this period of the early myth of Jason.

Our next group of sources for the myth of Jason are the lyric poets. The authors we will be referring to date from the seventh century onwards. For the most part evidence for lyric poetry remains in fragments, and when looking for the evidence concerning Jason, we find references from Simonides, Ibykos, Mimnermos and Pindar. Pindar is an exception to these fragmentary sources and one which I will deal with in further detail below.

Mimnermos, like Homer and the author of the *Naupaktia*, came from Ionia on the eastern edge of the Aegean. There appears to have been a rich tradition in poetry from this region, and Mimnermos is said to have lived in Smyrna during the seventh century B.C.[27] Simonides came from Ceos, an island off the coast of Attica, and worked during the end of the sixth century through to the start of the fifth century B.C. His work included poems related to the Persian Wars, and he was

---

[24] Huxley, p. 75.

[25] West (2003), p. 26ff.

[26] Ibid, p. 27.

[27] See Mulroy, p. 43.

believed to have retired to Sicily in his later years.[28]   The last in this particular group of lyric poets is Ibykos, who can be dated to the last half of the sixth century B.C., and therefore roughly contemporary with Simonides.

For most of the evidence from lyric poetry we have fragments, usually cited by later authors.   However, one of the major sources in this account of Jason is Pindar, since his *Pythian* 4 is an ode that deals entirely with the voyage of the Argo. He, like Hesiod, was born in Boeotia, and lived from around 518 B.C. to approximately 438 B.C., and appears to have been composing up until the third quarter of the fifth century.   *Pythian* 4 is an ode which was presented in 462 B.C., and was used to try to persuade king Arkesilas IV of Kyrene to allow one of his citizens to return from exile. Pindar uses Jason as a model of diplomacy, tact and leadership, and therefore flatters Arkesilas by drawing links between the king and the hero. His less positive portrayal of Pelias could even serve as a warning to Arkesilas of the kind of behaviour he should try to avoid.

The final literary sources to whom I will refer extensively in this discussion, all from the fifth century, are the three tragedians, Aischylos, Sophokles and Euripides, and the mythographer Pherekydes. Little is known about Pherekydes, except that he was an Athenian who worked in or around the mid fifth century B.C.   Fragments of his work, however, provide many useful pieces of evidence for the myth of Jason, and indeed other aspects of Greek myth.

Aischylos is dated to 525/4-456/5 B.C., and is thought to have produced somewhere between seventy and ninety plays. Related to the Jason myth he produced a *Phineus* in 472 B.C., and probably a tetralogy based on the story of Lemnos and the relationship between Hypsipyle and Jason.

---

[28] Mulroy, p. 185.

Sophokles lived a remarkably long life from approximately 496 to 406 B.C. He was said to have written about a hundred and twenty plays, and again in relation to Jason we have evidence for the existence of plays such as the *Women of Kolchis*, the *Root-cutters*[29] , the *Women of Lemnos*, and *Peliades*.

Euripides was born around the 480s B.C., and lived in Athens for most of his life. He moved to Macedon in 406, and died there soon after (406-405 B.C.). Our primary focus in this work will be the *Medea* of 431 B.C., although there is also evidence from lost plays such as his *Peliades* (455 B.C.) and *Hypsipyle*, which will be helpful to our purpose.

Finally, we must also mention literary scholia, which can be useful, if unpredictable, sources of evidence. These were commentaries penned by ancient scholars, and often appear in extract, or condensed form in the margins of the texts they were studying. In some cases what remains are only fragmentary notes or jottings. Many scholia are based on archaic or classical sources for myth, but it can be difficult to place them correctly. Nevertheless, although we cannot always accurately date the scholia, or corroborate their sources, they can be very enlightening as we learn of references from authors whose works may be lost.

Turning to iconography, evidence which can be used and related to specific mythological scenes first emerges in the seventh century. This was also a time when labelling of visual representations of figures on such artefacts was begun, and so scenes on vase painting can be specifically connected to the myths of the age. Generally art is divided into five categories along the lines of date: Geometric (c. 900-700

---

[29] Although the remaining fragments of the *Root-cutters* do not deal directly with Jason himself, the reference (fr. 534 R) to Medea and her skill with herbs shows a clear connection with the story of Jason. It may be that Medea is gathering the herbs to either create the potion used to protect Jason against the fire-breathing bulls in Kolchis, or on the return to Greece, to rejuvenate Jason or his father, Aison.

B.C.), the Orientalising period (c. 725-600 B.C.), Archaic (c. 600-480 B.C.), Classical (c. 480-323 B.C.) and Hellenistic (from c. 323-30 B.C.).[30] The timeframe which we will have most cause to refer to in the course of this work will mainly cover the Archaic and Classical periods. Evidence from vase painting and sculpture rarely portray a myth consistently over a long period of time, so we will be able to trace evidence of change in some of our visual sources. While iconographical evidence can cover a variety of artistic material from vase painting to sculpture to coins, it will emerge that the vast majority of our surviving sources in the case of Jason come from vase painting. We will have cause to refer to a few works of sculpture, but most extant representations of the hero are in the context of paintings on pottery.

Subjects in art change as myths fall in and out of favour at different periods. The Archaic period tends to be one where the great creature-slayers are favoured. Images of Perseus and the Gorgons, Herakles and the many creatures he encountered, Bellerophontes and the Chimaira, and Theseus and the Minotaur all enjoy favour in the black, and later in the red, figure vase painting of this period. In the fifth century we see the influence of tragedy on images in vase painting as there appears to be an interest in myths which were produced on stage, and it would seem that a dramatic production could lead to new elements of the story achieving notice and interest in visual representations.[31]

The shape and use of vases also has an impact on their usefulness as sources. Although visual art rather than the archaeological detail of these pieces is the subject of this work, it is worth noting a few points about how vases were used. For instance, lekythoi were commonly used as funerary vessels and so the fact that many of the depictions of Medea's rejuvenation of the ram appear on these may

---

[30] Sparkes provides a useful breakdown of these periods, and the main features of each, pp. 3-27.

[31] Shapiro looks at the connections between literature and vases, ch. 4, p. 121 ff. See also Woodford (2003, pp. 105 ff.) for further discussion of how vase painters were inspired by productions on stage.

tie into their use. In a more general sense, scenes on vases demonstrate how the myths were an aspect of everyday life. We have artistic representations of mythic events appearing on vessels that were used for a variety of purposes, from domestic storage to entertaining, to cooking and transporting. Sparkes suggests that in monetary terms pots were relatively inexpensive items for the Greeks due to the low cost and ready availability of clay, and the vast number of different vessels produced.[32] They would therefore have permeated every rank of society, as would the mythical scenes depicted on them. This in turn would mean that there would have been a widespread knowledge of at least some aspects of the myth of Jason, given the portrayals on a variety of different artefacts.

Jason and the Golden Fleece

I will now begin the process of examining these sources by moving through the various stages of the myth. In order to show the contribution made by such a detailed examination to our understanding of the myth however, it is worth recapping on the general framework of the story - the version that is most quickly thought of in relation to Jason. In Iolkos king Aison is usurped by his brother Pelias, and his son Jason is sent away for safe keeping. Years later Jason returns to the city to claim the throne from Pelias. The tyrannical king agrees, but demands that Jason win the Golden Fleece from Kolchis first. Jason gathers the heroes of Greece and sails to Kolchis where he wins the fleece with the help of the local princess. He departs with Medea, bringing her back home. On their return, Medea kills Pelias using her herbs and magic, and the couple are exiled to Korinth. Although it is a Euripidean invention, Jason's move to abandon Medea to marry another local princess, and her subsequent murdering of their children in revenge, is now one of the more recognisable elements of the story.

---

[32] Sparkes, pp. 142-3.

We can now begin our more detailed study of these events, beginning with Jason's parentage, and continuing until his old age and death as portrayed in Euripides. This will allow us to compile what I hope will stand as a definitive study of the character of Jason, and of his adventures and accomplishments, prior to the shift and transformation begun in Euripides' portrayal. And as we progress we will begin to see the importance of combining literary and iconographical evidence in constructing a comprehensive body of knowledge, highlighting the gaps that have previously gone unnoticed or un-remarked by many other modern authors.

1

Iolkos to Lemnos

Background: Iolkos, Aeson and Pelias

Jason's home in Northern Greece provides the framework and focus for his entire story. As in the case of many Greek heroes, the myth has its basis in family conflict, and in many of our sources the need for Jason to be raised away from his home is significant. As with Perseus, who was raised away from his birthplace with his mother, Danae, or Orestes, who was brought up away from Mycenae, Jason's early years are interrupted by a family tension. The conflict with Pelias is central to the tale, and is the cause of his expedition to Kolchis. Establishing what status Pelias had in Iolkos, whether or not he was the rightful king of the city, and how Jason and his father Aison fit into this, is therefore significant in our attempt to understand this myth, and organise its component parts.

Aison generally appears in the story only in relation to Jason. There are no substantive stories of Aison's early life, and all we have are references to his parents and birth. According to the *Odyssey*, Aison was the son of Tyro and Kretheus. Tyro also bore children to Poseidon, one of whom was Pelias;

> But she conceived and bore Pelias and Neleus, who both became strong henchmen of great Zeus; and Pelias dwelt in spacious Iolkos and was rich in flocks, and the other dwelt in sandy Pylos. But her other children, she, the queenly among women, bore to Kretheus: Aeson, and Pheres, and Amythaon, full of the joy of chariot battle (*Od.* 11.254-59).

Hesiod's first surviving reference to Aison is found in the *Theogony* (*Th.* 993), where it is simply says that he is the father of

Jason. According to the *Nekuia*,[33] as we have seen Aison's father was Kretheus and his mother was Tyro, while Tyro also bore Pelias and Neleus to Poseidon, (Σ *Od.* 12.69)[34] which makes Pelias and Aison half brothers. In *Pythian* 4, we also see Jason describe his father as being the son of Kretheus (*Py.* 4.153).[35]

The main thrust of the story of Pelias and Aison focuses on their later years. Evidence concerning Aison falls into two categories. In the first, we are given to believe that he dies when Jason is only a child, whereas in the second, he is depicted as living to witness his son's return to Iolkos and the challenge to Pelias. With regard to the first of these variants, two scholia refer to Aison's death. Scholia to the *Odyssey* (Σ *Od.* 12.69) say that Aison died when Jason was only a child and so Pelias took on the role of guardian until Jason had grown up and was ready to assume his rightful place. Scholia to the *Theogony* concur with this, saying that Aison dies and Pelias steps into the role as king. However, the more familiar of the stories is the version presented by Pindar. According to Pythian 4, Aison has lived on into old age, and he is presented as appearing in the market place when Jason returns to Iolkos to face Pelias;

> When [Jason] entered his home, his father's eyes
> recognised him and then tears burst forth from under
> his aged eyelids as he rejoiced in his soul to see his
> extraordinary offspring, fairest of men. (*Py.* 4.120-3).

Of these two tales of Aison, the second version where he lives into old age, appears to find more favour in the extant evidence. In vase painting Aison is depicted as being rejuvenated by Medea after

---

[33] Gantz p. 172.

[34] Also Hes. fr. 38 MW.

[35] Jason speaks to Pelias about his ancestry and his father's role in the kingdom saying, '...as for the sceptre of sole rule and the throne upon which Kretheus' son once sat and rendered straight justice to his people of horsemen, these you must give up without grief on both sides...' (*Py.* 4.152-55).

Jason returns successfully from Kolchis, a subject I will return to in Chapter 4.

We now turn to look briefly at the nature of the relationship between Jason and Pelias. If Aison dies when his only son is young, and his half brother Pelias steps in and takes over as a caretaker ruler until such time as Jason is able to govern for himself, then any claim made to the throne by Pelias would be unjust. If Pelias had seized the throne from Aison by force, as suggested by Pindar (*Py.* 4.106-15), there would be a justification for Jason's actions in challenging his position. Given that Pindar is our sole source for this version of events however, it is worth considering the context of *Pythian 4*. Pindar is composing the ode in an attempt to persuade King Arkesilas IV of Kyrene to allow the exiled Damophilos to return to the city. In the ode, Pindar implies a comparison between Arkesilas and Jason, and emphasises Pelias' unreasonable nature by suggesting that he usurped a throne that was not rightfully his. In doing so, Pindar enhances Jason's qualities and his skill at using wise and soothing words, and therefore obliquely compliments Arkesilas (for example, 101 and 138).

As for Jason's mother, six names are offered for this character. The earliest extant evidence for this comes from Hesiod (Hes. fr. 38 MW), where Jason is said to be the son of Polymede. However, two other sources give us an alternative name, since according to both the scholia to the *Odyssey* (Σ *Od.* 12.69), and the mythographer Pherekydes (Pher. fr. 104c), Jason's mother was called Alcimede. We also find the names Eteoklymene (Stesichoros *PMG* 238), Amphinome (Diodoros 4.50.2), Polypheme (Herodoros fr. 40 Fowler), and Theognete (Andron fr. 5 Fowler).

The identity of Jason's mother does not affect the overall story as she plays only a minor role, even less significant than that of Aison. The scholia to the *Odyssey* say that she sent Jason away when Aison died, as her son was only an infant, and she feared for his safety.

The first complete reference to Jason's mother's part in the action is from Pindar's *Pythian* 4., where Pindar says, Jason's parents feared for their son's safety and held a mock funeral once he was born, in an attempt to feign his death. They then secretly sent their child away to Cheiron so that he could be raised safely in the mountains;

> Lawless Pelias gave in to his white wits and usurped
> it [the throne] by force from my justly ruling parents,
> who, as soon as I saw the light, fearing the violence
> of the overbearing ruler, made a dark funeral in the
> house, and added women's wailing as if I had died,
> but secretly sent me away in my purple swaddling
> clothes, and, entrusting the journey to the night,
> gave me to Cheiron, son of Kronos, to raise (*Py.* 4.
> 109-115)

In a slightly different manner, Perseus too leaves his home city for his upbringing, as his grandfather Acrisios sends the young infant and his mother Danae to what he assumes will be certain death. The reason for Akrisios' concern was that the oracle said that death would come to him from an offspring of Danae. This tale may be as early as Hesiod, as one fragment says that Perseus (and probably Danae too) was put into a chest and thrown out to sea (Hes. fr. 135 MW).

As to Jason's other family members, we are more accustomed to hearing of him in isolation. However, at least one source indicates that Jason may have had a sister. A fragment from the lyric poet Ibykos states that Jason had a sister called Hippolyta (Ibykos 301 PMG)[36] who we can only presume to be the daughter of Aison since there is no evidence of an alternate candidate. There is no evidence of this sister playing any substantial role in the tale, such as Elektra did in the story of Orestes, and when Pindar describes the return of Jason to Iolkos, he describes the reaction of Aison, but makes no mention of any

---

[36] '...for according to Ibycus Jason had a sister Hippolyta.'

other family members.[37]   Only later sources state that Jason had a brother called Promachos (A.p.B. 1.9.27 and Diodoros 4.50-1).

As for the family of Pelias; he appears to have more than one child. In the *Odyssey*, Homer says that Tyro "conceived and bore Pelias and Neleus" (*Od.* 11.254). As seen Hesiod, Pelias was the brother of Neleus and son of Poseidon (Hes. fr. 38 MW). According to the *Iliad* he was the father of the ill-fated Alkestis, future wife of Admetos (*Il.* 2.711-5), who ended up volunteering for death in her husband's place, and later in the fifth century Pindar also mentions this fact (*Py.* 4.138). Hesiod adds Pasidike to Alkestis as one of Pelias' children (Hes. fr. 37.16-22 MW).

As we saw in the *Odyssey*, Pelias was born and lived in Iolkos (*Od.* 11.253-5). However, the *Odyssey* doesn't give us any insight into a conflict between Aison and Pelias.

The oracle which causes Pelias so much trouble and anxiety is given to him when Jason is only a child. The earliest extant literary source for this is quite late in the timeframe we are looking at here. It is in the fifth century that Pindar says that the oracle at Delphi tells Pelias that death will come from someone of his own race, and warns him to look out for anyone appearing to him wearing a single sandal (*Py.* 4.75-8). Pindar's version then follows on to describe Jason's entrance, wearing only one sandal, and his claim of the throne that belongs to his father (*Py.* 4.79ff). Pherekydes differs in his telling of the myth, since he says that Jason is merely a citizen of Iolkos, while Pelias is the king. Pelias holds a sacrifice and the citizens, including Jason, arrive to attend. Pherekydes says that Jason came in from the fields after ploughing and

---

[37] It may be argued that Medea plays for Jason the same role that Elektra plays for Orestes. Elektra's participation in the death of Aigisthos is similar to Medea's role in the death of Pelias. However, although Elektra is a vocal supporter to Orestes, she takes no part in the action. For Jason it appears that Medea is the one who co-ordinates the death of Pelias.

arrived in the palace with only one sandal (Pher. fr. 105). In Pherekydes'
version therefore, Jason is not educated away from Iolkos, and there is
no challenge to the king for the throne. It is quite different to the version
in Pindar, where the hero claims the throne from the current king and
accepts the king's challenge to fetch the golden fleece as a test to prove
his abilities. In Pherekydes, Jason has lived peacefully in Iolkos under
Pelias' rule, and only comes to the king's attention by virtue of his single-
sandaled state. Pindar and Pherekydes follow the same version of the
story in relation to the motif of the single sandal, and the need to send
the hero away from Iolkos on an expedition, but they offer different
reasons for Pelias' actions in dispatching Jason on such a quest.

Therefore, the intentions of Pelias are somewhat ambiguous.
Is he deliberately requesting that Jason undergo dangerous tasks in a
hope to see him fail and possibly killed, or is he simply reacting to the
oracle and trying to prevent the inevitable - namely his own death? This
lack of clarity regarding his motives is also tied into his position as king
and whether he is actually a legitimate ruler. In Hesiod, Pelias is called
the 'great king' (*megas basileus: Th.* 995) and this may indeed indicate
that Pelias is the rightful ruler. As we have seen, the scholia to the
Odyssey say Jason as a child was rushed away from Iolkos for fear of
his life (Σ *Od.* 12.69), and Pindar states clearly that Pelias seized the
throne from Aison (*Py.* 4.109-116), and that the usurper never learned of
Jason's birth. It also appears that in *Pythian* 4, Pelias is unaware of
Jason's existence until the hero's return to Iolkos.

This may be a trend going back to Hesiod and Mimnermos,
both of whom describe Pelias as *hubristês* (*Th.* 996; '[Jason] suffered for
the arrogant Pelias': Mimnermos 11 W[38]). In the end there is no early
evidence prior to 400 B.C. of the killing of Aison by Pelias, and the
literary sources are unclear on Pelias' connections to the throne.
Furthermore, it is only from the time of Pindar onwards that the idea of

---

[38] Translated by West, p. 29.

Pelias seizing the kingship starts the chain of events which sees Jason challenge him for the throne.

Instead, earlier evidence shows that Pelias feared for his life due to the oracle and he sought to prevent it, in a similar way to Akrisios in the story of Perseus who exiled his grandson after learning her may be a threat to his life.[39]   The earliest strand to this story of Pelias in extant literature shows him as an evil tyrant who makes excessive demands on Jason by asking him to voyage in search of the golden fleece (*Th.* 992-1002; Mimnermos 11 W).   Connected to this is the evidence from scholia to the *Odyssey* (Σ *Od.* 12.69), and scholia to the *Theogony* (Σ *Th.* 993), where Pelias becomes king when Aison dies, but is only expected to remain in power until Jason comes of age and can assume the role himself.   Given that this version is from scholia, it is difficult to date its source, but it could be seen to connect to our earliest evidence as Pelias, once he has become king, may be unwilling to relinquish power.

However, sources from the fifth century onwards give two further strands: that of Pelias seizing the throne by force from Aison (*Py.* 4.110), or an oracle predicting that a threat would come from the man wearing one sandal (Pher. fr. 105).

Unfortunately there is no extant visual evidence supporting Pelias' killing of Aison and Aison only appears in vase-painting as a part of his rejuvenation by Medea later in the myth [see below, Chapter 4]. Possibly the main reason for this lack of iconography relating to Pelias, Aison and the throne of Iolkos is the absence of a particular scene from

---

[39] Pherekydes says that Akrisios locked his daughter in a bronze chamber when he heard the news that if she become pregnant, her son would pose a threat to his life. Zeus visits Danae in the form of golden rain so as to be able to flow into the underground chamber. This leads to her becoming pregnant and giving birth to a son, Perseus. Once Akrisios learnt of this news he locked them in a chest and they were set out to sea (3F10).

the narrative that could be captured. For instance, no literary evidence remains from the period prior to the end of the fifth century to point to the killing of Aison by Pelias. And yet this would be a potentially interesting subject for an artist as we can see with Klytaimnestra's murder of king Agamemnon. The death of the king has a long tradition in art. An early example is a terracotta plaque from Gortyn which shows the killing of the king by Klytaimnestra and Aigisthos and is dated to 630-610 B.C.[40] A later example is an Attic red-figure kalyx-krater, showing Agamemnon at the centre of the scene with Aigisthos to his right, with sword drawn, and Klytaimnestra running up behind Aigisthos with an axe.[41] The vase is dated to 470 B.C. and the representation of the scene does not change dramatically from the first example.

The depiction of Jason with the single sandal is also a part of the tale which may be of interest to iconography, although it is disappointing that so few examples have survived, with only two examples surviving prior to 400 B.C. [Fig. 1 and Fig. 24].[42] The scene discussed in Pindar when Jason confronts the king, might also be the type of subject that would be of interest to an artist, but we have no extant examples of this episode. This part of the myth is somewhat confused as there are a number of variations on the relationship between Jason, Aison and Pelias. If Pherekydes says that Jason was a citizen of Iolkos, then the versions showing Jason's return to the city with one sandal may not have been widely known enough to warrant depictions in art.

The first extant piece of visual evidence for this period of Jason's life is a coin dating to 470 B.C. [Fig. 1], and showing the head of Jason on one side and the single sandal on the other. Both Pindar (*Py.*

---

[40] Heraklion Archaeological Museum 11512. Shapiro (1995), image no. 87.

[41] Boston, Mus. of Fine Arts 63.1246. Shapiro (1995), image 89.

[42] Kirk believes that this is in fact an early aspect of the tale based on the fact that the single sandal may be a folktale motif (p. 162).

4.71-8), and Pherekydes (Pher. fr. 105), mention the single sandal in Jason's encounter with Pelias. Pherekydes says that Jason journeyed from his work in the fields where he was ploughing, and having crossed a river, he forgot about his left sandal, and appeared in front of Pelias at the temple of Poseidon wearing only one shoe. On the other hand, Pindar has Jason arrive back in Iolkos after being raised and educated by Cheiron. The young hero enters the city wearing one sandal, but Pindar doesn't elaborate on how he lost the other shoe, instead focusing on the oracle and the significance of this symbol for Pelias. Later evidence from Apollodoros has Jason losing the sandal as he hurries across the river Anauros on the way to attend Pelias' sacrifice to Poseidon, and so Apollodoros uses the same version as Pherekydes (ApB 1.9.16). Possibly Pindar left out this part of the story, as his audience would have already been aware of the tale and of how Jason lost the sandal. The coin with Jason's head and the sandal [Fig. 1] is of a similar date to Pherekydes' version of the myth.

Combining the evidence from Pherekydes with the visual evidence, we see that the single sandal as a motif for Jason is well established before the end of the fifth century. Our earliest example of the single sandal is from an attic dinos dated to 570-560 B.C. [Fig. 24]. The scene on this vase shows the Kalydonian Boar Hunt, where Meleagros has called together many of the Greek heroes to help him to rid his land of this dangerous creature. Jason is one of these men, and he appears on two vases before the end of the fifth century attacking this animal with the other hunters. Although I will deal with the Kalydonian Boar Hunt later in this book, the earliest example shows Jason wearing one sandal, and this is our earliest extant example - literary or visual. It does raise questions as to why Jason is wearing one sandal at this stage in the myth, as the Kalydonian Boar Hunt is usually said to occur on Jason's return to Greece, having won the golden fleece. However, the symbol may be of more importance to the artist of the dinos vase than the sequence into which it should be placed. This may be a type of

synoptic scene, a technique which is identified by Shapiro.[43] This is a
scene in art where a number of episodes or sequences from a myth are
condensed into one image. The purpose here is to show the boar hunt,
but since Jason has no identifiable physical traits in art, the artist may
have chosen to select a symbol that a viewer can identify despite the
problems of chronology. The use of the sandal may be inappropriate if
we invoke the rules of time and order of our myth, but the symbol of the
sandal is closely associated with Jason and helps the viewer to
differentiate him from the other heroes present.

The Education of Jason

As we have seen, Pherekydes has stated that Jason
remained in Iolkos when Pelias was king. However, according to Hesiod
(fr. 38, 40 MW), and Pindar (*Py.* 4. 109-116), Jason was taken away from
Iolkos and raised by Cheiron.

Cheiron was the traditional teacher and mentor to the young
heroes, but from the evidence Jason was one of the earliest examples of
a boy being raised on Mt. Pelion by the centaur. In Hesiod's reference to
Cheiron's education of Medeios, Jason's son, there may be an unstated
connection to Jason's own earlier education:

> The son of Aeson took from Aeetes the daughter of
> that Zeus-fostered king by the design of the gods,
> the eternal fathers, after completing the many
> oppressive ordeals enjoined upon him by the great
> overbearing king, the brute Pelias, who was wicked
> and stern in action. Having completed them,
> Aeson's son reached Iolcus after long sufferings,
> bringing the curly-lashed girl on his swift ship, and
> made her his fertile wife. And surrendering to Jason
> shepherd of peoples, she bore a son, Medeios,

---

[43] Shapiro (1995), p. 4.

whom Chiron the son of Philyra brought up in the mountains in fulfilment of the great Zeus' purpose (Hes. *Th.* 992-1002).[44]

As a further example of Cheiron's skill as teacher, Hesiod says that he raised Achilleus. In the *Iliad*, Eurypylos speaks to Patroklos and asks him for assistance:

> ...lead me to my black ship...wash the black blood from it with warm water, and sprinkle on it soothing herbs of healing power, which men say you learned from Achilles, whom Cheiron taught, the most just of centaurs. (*Il.* 11.828-32).[45]

At a much later date we also have evidence of Cheiron educating heroes such as Asklepios (ApB 3.10.3), Herakles (Σ Theokr. 13, 9b), and Aristaios (AR 2.506-10).

Scholia to the *Odyssey* say it was his mother Alkimede who sent Jason to Cheiron, as Aison had died when Jason was a child (Σ *Od.* 12.69) as discussed above). More uniquely, the scholia to the *Theogony* say that Pelias sent Jason to Cheiron and that he intended to hand the throne over to the young hero once he returned (Σ *Th.* 993). But the scholia go on to say that the prophecy concerning the one-sandaled man and the need of Pelias to be wary of him intervened. As mentioned, the same scholia had said that Aison died while Jason was only a boy but it shows that, at least in one version, Pelias started out with good intentions for the child.

Pindar goes further and, apart from saying that Cheiron raised Jason, says that the centaur also gave the child his name (*Py.*

---

[44] Trans. West, *Hesiod* (1988), p.32-3. I will refer to this passage from the *Theogony* frequently throughout the course of this book.

[45] Trans. by Murray, revised by Wyatt, p. 555.

4.104-5).   Pindar says that Jason was pure in word and deed having completed twenty years of Cheiron's training.   Healing was a key element to the education that the centaur gave to a young hero. Indeed, the name Jason means "healer", which ties into the fact that Cheiron taught the heroes the art of medicine, a skill, however, that Jason seems to use infrequently.[46] The fact that Cheiron also names Jason when he is a child would suggest that Jason was separated from his parents at a very young age and, from Pindar's account of the story, the emotional reaction of Aison to seeing his son in the market place in Iolkos would point to there having been no contact between Jason and his parents in the intervening years.

The Return to Iolkos

In *Pythian 4,*   Pindar shows clearly that Pelias should be worried by Jason's return to Iolkos. In the *Pythian* 4 Jason has returned after years of living in the mountains with Cheiron and being educated by the centaur, and he now seeks to win back the throne for his father Aison who has had the position unjustly taken from him.   Jason appears godlike in the agora (*Py.* 4. 85-90), as the people gathered there speculate as to who he might be. However Pelias recognises the sign of the single sandal immediately. Pindar says that an oracle from Delphi tells him that death will come from one of his own race and to beware anyone appearing before him wearing only one sandal (*Py.* 4. 73-6). Pherekydes' version does not say that Pelias will be killed by the man in the single sandal but just to beware his appearance (Pher. frag. 105). But Pindar takes this further as Jason appears to Pelias with a specific objective in mind, something that does not appear in Pherekydes' version.

---

[46] 'That the name Jason meant "The Healer" for Pindar seems quite likely from the consideration that Pindar's Cheiron not only taught the art of healing but also chose the name to be worn by the bearer of his teaching' (Robbins, pp. 210-1). The name is derived from ἰα␣μαι: to heal, cure.

Aison's presence in the marketplace of Iolkos is a dramatic piece of staging with father seeing son for the first time since he was a infant.[47] As we've seen, this is in contrast to evidence from the scholia to the *Odyssey* and the *Theogony* (∑ *Od.* 12.69; ∑ Th. 993) both of which say that Aison dies and Pelias becomes king. It may be that Pindar invented this aspect of the tale, having Aison alive and thus adding to the dramatic effect of Jason's return.

The circumstances under which the hero embarks on the quest to retrieve the golden fleece is important as it sets the tone for the voyage as an arduous labour or a challenge to the young ambitious hero. Pherekydes says that Pelias asks Jason how he would deal with an oracle that said one of his citizens would kill him. Jason replies that Pelias should command that person to go to Aia and seize the golden fleece (Pher. fr. 105). This of course shows that Jason was unaware of the oracle and and that there was not a challenge from the hero to overthrow the king. It also means that the fleece was a difficult challenge as presumably Jason is suggesting one of the more difficult tasks that Pelias could set for an enemy. This is similar to Pherekydes' description of Perseus when he suggests to king Polydektes that he bring the head of the gorgon Medousa. This suggestion was made to impress the king and Perseus did not expect to have to complete the task himself. Pherekydes' version of the confrontation between Jason and Pelias differs considerably from that of Pindar, where Jason has returned with the express intention of avenging his father and winning the throne, which he feels was taken unlawfully (*Py.* 4.106-15). He tells Pelias he is back to recover the throne and the king tells him that he can have the kingship on the fulfilment of a condition. He says Phrixos had appeared to him in a dream and asked him to go to Aia and bring back the hide of the ram (the ram that Phrixos had ridden to Aia). Pelias said he consulted the oracle at Castalia and it also urged him to help in this

---

[47] The reunion between father and son is reminiscent of the meeting between Odysseus and his aged father Laertes in the Odyssey: 'His father answered him with his tears falling...' (*Od.* 24.280f. trans. Hammond, p. 250).

quest. He uses the excuse of age and challenges Jason to undertake the expedition on his behalf (*Py.* 4.156-64). Pelias appears to agree to hand over the throne to Jason, presumably expecting him to fail.

The scholia to the *Odyssey* recount a similar version (Σ *Od.* 12.69). Jason claims the throne from Pelias and Pelias sends him to Kolchis as a necessity before he can take over as king. But we have to remember that the scholia to the *Odyssey* has also said that Pelias took over the role as king when Aison died and Jason was a young child. Pelias is only in a position as king so long as he needs to be guardian of the throne for Jason. This version leads us to believe that inevitably one day Jason will return and reclaim what is rightly his. Pindar's Pelias is a far more devious character who is trying to deflect the oracle that foretold his downfall and hoping that he can still hold on to power. In the *Pythian* 4, Pelias has few redeeming qualities. When Jason enters the market place as a stranger the king questions him harshly before he is aware of his identity (*Py.* 4.97-100) and his speech is in contrast to Jason's gentle words (*Py.* 4.102, 128, 137). The single sandal has thrown him and he is under pressure. He does not conduct himself in the manner we might expect from a king or leader and Jason's control and calm further serves to contrast with Pelias' bluster. Jason is eloquent and confident in the way in which he speaks. His use of words is bold and assertive and is quite different to Pelias' desperation. The characterisation of the two leads us to suspect Pelias' motives, and this version certainly is in stark contrast to Pelias as a willing guardian of the throne, awaiting the time when Jason would assume his responsibilities, as we found earlier in the scholia to the *Odyssey* (Σ *Od.* 12.69).[48]

The final part of the evidence for the return to Iolkos by Jason relates to the oracle. Both Pindar and Pherekydes agree on one point; that the oracle prophesies that Medea is to be Pelias' downfall. In Pherekydes it is said that Hera was the one who gave Pelias the idea of

---

[48] Also, scholia to *Th.* 993 says that Pelias sent Jason to Cheiron intending to hand over the throne at a later date, but that the prophecy intervened.

asking Jason to seize the fleece (Pher. fr. 105). He says that Hera wished for Pelias to send Jason to Aia so that he would bring back Medea and she in turn would kill Pelias. As for Pindar, he says that Jason took Medea from Aia willingly and he describes her as the murderer of Pelias (*Py.* 4.250). As we will see later, the murder of Pelias was a popular theme, especially in black figure vase painting of the sixth century, and it is clear that the combination of its popularity in visual art and the appearance of the tale of the Argonauts in tragedy, meant the murder of Pelias by Medea was a well established element of the myth long before the end of the fifth century. Looking back at the oracle, Medea's actions are inevitable if the oracle is to be fulfilled. Pelias is to die since he encounters the stranger with one sandal, and Medea is the one to assist in carrying this out.

However, it is also significant that evidence for Medea arriving as the fulfilment of an oracle only appears from the time of Pindar onwards, and it may be a later development of the early myth of Jason.

What connects Hera to the destruction of Pelias is unclear. The reference to Medea and the fact that she will be the king's downfall is positioned in the story (as related by Pindar) before the return of the Argo, and therefore can't be a direct consequence of Pelias' refusal to return the throne to Jason (as requested by Jason at line 154-5). However, Apollodoros relates the story of Sidero, Pelias' stepmother. When Pelias and his brother Neleus discovered their mother Tyro, they attacked Sidero for treating her badly. Sidero fled to the sanctuary of Hera where Pelias followed her and killed her on the altar. Not only did he offend the goddess with this crime, he also continued to ignore her and failed to honour her (ApB. 1.9.8). Although this evidence is from a later source, it would form an adequate reason for Hera's treatment of Pelias in the myth.

There is no definite sign in Pindar or Pherekydes that Pelias will refuse to give up the throne if the young hero returns victorious. Indeed, as discussed, Pelias may be sending Jason away to prove himself. In the *Theogony* there is no explanation of why Hera chooses to destroy Pelias, other than to advance the position of Jason. We can't discount the later variant of the myth where Pelias offended Hera in the killing of Sidero, but there is no extant evidence in our earlier sources.

Therefore if Jason is travelling to Kolchis as a pretext for his bringing Medea back to Greece to destroy Pelias, this undermines the status of Jason, making him merely the tool by which the oracle is fulfilled. It also enhances the role played by Medea in the myth. But given the evidence before the last third of the fifth century, in particular, before Euripides' *Medea* of 431 B.C., it is my belief that this is not the case. At this stage the participation of Hera points to the goddess having a role in the voyage, possibly a position that is later taken by Athena, as seen in Attic vase painting. I will come to the detail of this material later in Chapter 3. The evidence for the support of Hera for Jason is well founded. The *Odyssey* says that the Argo was successful thanks to her support:

> One seafaring ship alone has passed by those [the
> Planktai], that Argo famed of all, on her voyage from
> Aeetes and even her [the Argo] the wave would
> speedily have dashed there against the great crags,
> had not Hera sent her through because Jason was
> dear to her (*Od.* 12. 69-72).

Therefore the death of Pelias may be tied to the success of Jason. Much the same fate befell Polydektes as a result of his treatment of Perseus when he requested that Perseus complete a near impossible challenge - to capture the head of the Medousa - only to end up as a victim of his own ruse. Perseus returned from his quest and turned Polydektes to stone, as it was believed that the gaze of the face of Medousa had this effect. Perseus' journey was supported by Athena and

Hermes, and so the support for Jason by Hera may follow a similar type of patron role.

One other possibility is that Hera, as a powerful goddess, is selflessly assisting the implementation of the oracle. However this appears to be unlikely given that the oracle is not directly her responsibility and there is evidence that she does act as patron to the Argonauts, beyond simply orchestrating the destruction of Pelias.

The return of Jason to his home in Iolkos after his education by Cheiron, is an important part of the myth, as it sets out the reason for the voyage to Colchis, and Pindar's portrayal of Jason, which covers this part of the myth in such detail, is one of the clearest portrayals of our hero from early myth. Our earliest sources describe Pelias as setting an arduous challenge for Jason (Hesiod) even if we are unsure of the rightful holder of the throne, and whether it was expected that Pelias would hand it over to Jason when he came of age (scholia to the *Theogony* and scholia to the *Odyssey*), or that it was secured by force from Jason's father Aison (Pindar). Iconography contributes to this section by way of the symbol of the single sandal. The depiction of Jason at the Kalydonian Boar Hunt [Fig. 24] is the earliest example of Jason with one sandal. The second example from art, the coin showing the head of Jason and the sandal [Fig. 1], appeared sometime between Pindar and Pherekydes (c. 460 B.C.), and these four sources together show that this was a well known symbol by the fifth century B.C.

Finally the oracle and the roles for Hera and Medea also play a key role. Our earliest source, the *Odyssey*, shows the support of Hera for the Argonautic voyage, and in particular for Jason. The role of the oracle as the catalyst for the voyage appears in Pindar and Pherekydes, and may be a relatively later development, especially the inclusion of the idea of Medea coming to Greece to destroy Pelias. This is a notion that certainly would have its roots in the later rise in her role, as Medea moves away from her position as hero-helper as played in the earlier part of this myth.

It is somewhat surprising that visual evidence does not remain for the confrontation between Jason and Pelias in Iolkos. Given the dramatic return as described by Pindar, we could imagine this as the type of scene that would appeal to a vase painter. Instead, depictions in art of these characters seem to focus on the return from Kolchis, and the death of Pelias, which we will come to discuss at a later stage.

The Building and Preparation of the Argo

There is little evidence of the construction of the ship which carried the Argonauts to Kolchis. There is no surviving visual evidence for the building of the Argo until after 400 B.C. In terms of literary evidence we only have one possible reference to where the Argo was constructed, coming from a later source. Hyginus cites a lost fragment from Pindar, saying that the Argo was built near the site of the city of Demetrias (Astr. 2.37).

Regarding its name, Pherekydes says that the ship was named after Argos, son of Phrixos (Pher. fr. 106), but this is somewhat confusing as Phrixos escaped to Aia on the golden ram, so if Argos contributed to the Argo either he or his father must have returned to Greece at some point. Pherekydes' evidence does not actually state that Argos constructed the ship, although later sources believe this was the case (ApB 1.9.16; AR 2.1187-89).

The materials used in the design of the ship were said to include a sacred timber. Both Pherekydes (Pher. fr. 111) and Aischylos (fr. 20, 20a R) point to this, and say that it was Athena who offered it to the ship. Unsurprisingly it is only Attic sources that connect their patron goddess to this gift. The New York krater [Fig. 17], which I will deal with in more depth in Chapter 3, shows the bow of the Argo is carved in the shape of a head. This is interpreted as a representation of the speaking timber but a point of debate in secondary literature is its ownership, suggesting that it belongs to Athena, Hera or Zeus. Judging by the literary sources, it is likely to be Athena. Given that we know of Hera's support for Jason from an early date, owing to the reference in the *Odyssey* (12.69), she could also be a possibility. However her role seems to be as patron of the expedition in overall terms, and a direct link between the goddess and the more specific story of the timber is never made in any of our literary sources. As for Zeus, he is suggested only by virtue of his link to the sacred oak of Dodona, where the timber may have come from[49] , but a connection is still a possibility given the interpretation of the New York krater (Fig. 17; see Chapter 3).

When considering the completed vessel, there are four pieces of visual art. A metope from Delphi from the mid sixth century shows the bow of the Argo [Fig. 6]. Although in poor condition, the two fragments of the metope show two men on horses to the left of the bow, while on the deck of the ship three people appear, two holding lyres. It is likely that one of these figures holding a lyre is Orpheus and that the two horsemen are Polydeukes and Kastor. As Carpenter points out, this is the earliest extant example of the Argo in visual art, dated to c. 570 B.C. (p. 184).[50]

The second example is catalogued by Pausanias where he describes a wall painting (now lost):

---

[49] This is an early story in myth. For example, Odysseus relates a story in the Odyssey of going to Dodona to hear Zeus' will (*Od.* 14.327-30).

[50] Susan Woodford discusses the issue of motifs and whether they are transferrable between characters in myth. Her point about the lyre is that it is used as an identifier for Orpheus but can also be used 'by any number of other mythological and non-mythological figures' (2003; p. 68). However in the case of Fig. 6, we know that this is Orpheus due to the context of the scene, namely appearance of the Argo. Pindar names Orpheus as a member of the crew (Py. 4.178) and so a character with a lyre in Argonautic scenes is correctly identified as Orpheus.

Here Polygnotus has painted the marriage of the daughters of Leucippus, which is a part of the gods' history, but Micon [depicts] those who sailed with Jason to the Colchians, and he has concentrated his attention upon Acastus and his horses (Paus. 1.18.1).

We can't be sure that the Argo was in this scene, but it is likely that the artist may have shown the crew of the ship with the possible inclusion of the Argo itself. However the fact that the Argo is the subject of wall painting as well as other forms of art, shows that it was a subject that interested early artists. The ship itself, given the speaking timber, and the fact that it voyaged to unknown lands, seems to have been an interesting subject matter for visual artists.

Two further artefacts are important, as they show the patronage of two goddesses. The first is an Attic red-figure volute krater by the Talos Painter [Fig. 8] which shows Athena with Kastor and Polydeukes and Jason facing Hera on the right side of the scene. Jason is wears a petasos and patterned chiton and leans on two spears held in his right hand. . Athena stands with her right arm out stretched towards the Dioskouri, and above her is the figure of the winged Nike. The vase is dated to the end of the fifth century and all characters can be identified as they are named. Being an Attic piece it is again unsurprising to see Athena. Hera's presence makes this the only extant visual representation of this goddess in her patronage for Jason and the Argonauts. From literary evidence we have seen her portrayal in the *Odyssey* and this shows that she forms part of the earliest tradition of the myth (*Od.* 12.69-72). We have also seen that Pherekydes links the fate of Pelias to Hera's involvement, sending Jason away so that he will bring back Medea to kill the king (Pher. fr. 105). Athena's involvement, on the other hand, is confined to the fifth century B.C. onwards and although we have a greater number of surviving pieces of evidence showing her participation, these are Attic artefacts and so more likely to have Athena represented on them to begin with.

The last of the four extant pieces showing the Argo, emphasises this point. It is an Attic red-figure calyx-krater from 460 B.C. showing Athena who stands to the left of the scene and is surrounded by Argonauts [Fig. 7], each of whom is either standing or reclining. Jason reclines holding two spears and is placed towards the lower front of the scene with Herakles appearing to the right of the goddess. It is an odd scene in one respect as it does not show any particular narrative from the story, instead showing the Argonauts at rest in a myth which normally has a constantly moving narrative. The image does not reveal a specific location for its setting. Normally the inclusion of another character would indicate the stage in the story, such as the presence of Phineus showing that the scene is set in Thrace and on the way to Kolchis. The absence of Medea may show that this is the outward voyage to Kolchis but her appearance with the Argonauts on vases tends to be from a later date than 460 B.C. anyway, and so her absence may not help in interpreting the scene being depicted here.

Overall, few specific examples connected to the preparations for the voyage to Kolchis survive in our evidence - either visual or literary.[51] What is significant is the patronage of Hera and Athena, both appearing to play roles, and in later stages of the myth, we will see Aphrodite and possibly Zeus also taking part, when the Argonauts have reached their destination. One point is clear, and that is that there is no one single patron to the voyage.

---

[51] A later fourth century scarab shows Jason standing at the bow of the Argo [Fig. 2]. This is the earliest example of Jason depicted next to the Argo in art. Richter suggests that this dates to the fifth century B.C. (see LIMC 'Argonautai' 3) However, a second Etruscan scarab dated to the fourth century [LIMC 'Argonautai' 4*] shows Jason in a similar position at the bow of the Argo and these images seem to reflect a more relaxed portrayal and a later fourth century style.

Lemnos

The encounter between the Argonauts and the women on the island of Lemnos draws attention to the epic qualities of the voyage. The story of Jason and the Lemnian queen Hypsipyle, rather like Odysseus meeting with Kirke, is almost a self-contained tale. It is a story which a poet could have recited separately, given an audience's familiarity with the broad myth, the tale can act as an independent and self sufficient story. The same is also true of other parts of the Argonautic expedition, such as the encounter with Phineus.

The island of Lemnos was said to only be inhabited by women as the men of the island had been killed.   The arrival of the Argonauts on Lemnos and the encounter with queen Hypsipyle has particular significance for Jason, as sources from early myth point to him fathering a child during this affair.

The *Iliad* tells us that Euneos was the name of this son and given that this evidence dates back to the eighth century B.C., there can be no doubt that this episode was considered important, even in our earliest extant evidence.   Jason is linked to two women in myth and although most of the focus centres on Medea, his son from this relationship with Hypsipyle appears three times in the *Iliad*

> And ships bringing wine were at hand from Lemnos,
> many of them, sent by Jason's son, Euneos, who
> Hypsipyle bore to Jason, shepherd of men (Il.
> 7.467-69).[52]

Indeed, in the dating of our sources, the relationship between Jason and Hypsipyle is at least as old as the relationship between Jason and Medea, and indeed the affair with Hypsipyle may receive more attention in early sources. In Homer there is no mention of

---

[52] See also Il. 21.47 and 23.747.

Medea, and Hesiod's *Theogony* contains the first extant reference to her (*Th.* 992 ff.). The encounter between Hypsipyle and Jason is similar to Odysseus and Kirke and serves as a test for the hero in encountering a strong female figure. For Odysseus it is the challenge of Kirke's herbs and magic that is the test (*pharmakos*: *Od.* 10.394), and for Jason, it may be being able to lead his men through a situation which may pose a risk to their lives, given the history that the inhabitants of the island have with men. The existence of a son from this union, something that surprisingly doesn't happen between Odysseus and Kirke in Homer's *Odyssey*, may indicate that the hero is establishing an lineage in different locations as he travels. A son of Jason born to Hypsipyle establishes a blood line at Lemnos and in a sense establishes the hero outside his home territory. Also, although Euneos' role is minor in the Homeric epic, the significance of his appearance may again point to a widespread knowledge of the Argonautic myth.

Apart from the *Iliad*, we also have evidence for the visit to Lemnos in Pindar and from fifth century tragedy. In *Pythian* 4, Pindar says that the Argonauts came to the island of the 'race of men-slaying Lemnian women' (*Py.* 4.252), although he seems to place the visit to the island after the Argonauts had travelled to Kolchis, and more importantly for Jason, after he had met and departed with Medea. The poet seems to pass over this part of the myth, and we can understand why; given that Medea is now one of the members of the crew, it does not make sense to introduce the relationship between Hypsipyle and Jason. We can assume that Pindar chose not to follow the version of the myth that stated that Jason had a son with Hypsipyle as seen in the *Iliad*. Pindar also says that the men took part in an athletics contest and shared the women's beds (*Py.* 4.254), although there is no specific mention of Jason.

The sequencing of this episode and its description in Pindar is affected by the poet's attempt to hurry through the detail. At line 248 he decides to cut the catalogue of the journey short and condenses a large portion of detail into a few lines. But the order is different to that found in other sources. *Pythian* 4 spends more time on the confrontation between Pelias and Jason in the agora at Iolkos and the events surrounding the reason for the Argonautic voyage, rather than providing a detailed description of the steps in the voyage itself. Pindar's attempt to move quickly through the steps and the subsequent mixing of the order should not push us to conclude that Pindar was unaware of the story of Jason and Hypsipyle as set out in Homer. It remains clear that the Argo must visit Lemnos before Kolchis if there is to be an encounter and offspring from the relationship with Hypsipyle. Pindar may have chosen to exclude the affair so that he can place Lemnos after Kolchis, and not cause difficulties in explaining how Jason can be conducting a relationship with Medea and Hypsipyle on the same voyage. *Pythian* 4.251-2 says that Jason 'stole away Medea, the slayer of Pelias' and follows this with the Argonauts' visit to 'the race of man-slaying Lemnian women'. Judging from our evidence I am inclined to think that the sequence of events is not Pindar's major concern since the relationship between Jason and Medea is the focus of this section of his *Pythian* 4, and leaving Hypsipyle out of his version of the myth simplifies matters. [53]

Evidence from *Olympian* 4 confirms that Pindar was aware of the myth of the Lemnian women even if he did not choose to incorporate it into *Pythian* 4. *Ol.* 4.17-27 describes one of the crew, Erginos, and his conversation with Hypsipyle after he wins the athletics race (*Ol.* 4.17-27), thus indicating that the Argo stopped at Lemnos, and the crew had contact with Lemnian queen.

---

[53] Gantz discusses Pindar's reference to Lemnos, and says he 'treats the matter briefly but explicitly' (p. 345). However Gantz includes discussion of this scene with his discussion of the outward journey to Kolchis and doesn't note the fact that it is positioned in the return journey in Pindar's tale. Later, when dealing with the return journey, Gantz makes no reference to Pindar's Lemnian stop (p. 362 ff..).

On this occasion it is worth examining later sources to shed light on what is a fragmented tale. In Apollonios the women of Lemnos fail to pay full respect to Aphrodite and the men of Lemnos, incited by the goddess, lose interest in their wives. Instead the men turn to Thrace and direct their affections towards the women captured from there in raids (AR 1.609-26). Angered by this snub the Lemnian women murder their husbands and the Thracian women and, to prevent any prospect of punishment for their crimes, kill all other men on the island. Apollonios says that the only man to survive was Thoas, father of Hypsipyle. The queen puts him in a chest and he is floated out to sea. Apollodoros also gives this version of the myth, but adds that Aphrodite made the women omit a noxious odour and it this caused their husbands to reject them and choose the Thracian captives (ApB. 1.9.17).

The athletics context which Pindar refers to in *Olympian* 4 is also dealt with in scholia to *Pythian* 4. We are offered two explanations as to why an athletics games is held on the island (Σ *Py.* 4.4.450a). The first is that the games are to honour the dead men of the island. For this to be the case we would have to assume that the Argonauts had received some assurances for their safety from the women, or that the truth behind the deaths of the men has been concealed from them. The second reason given in the scholia is that the games were in honour of Thoas, Hypsipyle's father. However, this would imply either that Thoas was simply killed along with the other male islanders, or possibly that Hypsipyle feigned his death and smuggled him out to sea without the knowledge of the other women. The scholia make no mention of the latter and it seems likely that the idea that Thoas was saved was only introduced by, or not long before Euripides. Herodotus says that the Lemnian women did in fact kill all the men on the island including Thoas;

> ...when the women of Lemnos murdered their husbands (and Thoas too) - is the origin of the Greek custom of referring to any specially horrible crime as a 'Lemnian deed' (*Hist.* 6.138).

In later evidence Apollodoros says that Hypsipyle saved Thoas but that the women of the island discovered this at a later stage. They then killed the king and sold Hypsipyle into slavery, where she served as a servant to Lykourgos, son of Pheres. Apollodoros may have followed Euripides' *Hypsipyle* where Thoas appears years later, to the surprise of Hypsipyle (fr. 64).

A number of further references to events on Lemnos remain in the plays of Aischylos and Sophokles. An early reference from tragedy comes from Aischylos' *Choephoroi* where it tantalisingly mentions the Lemnian horror (*Cho.* 631-6). We know that Aischylos also produced two plays on the subject, *Hypsipyle* and *Lemniai*, and from this we learn that the women would not allow the Argo to tie up at the island unless the crew agreed to share the women's beds (p. 352 R citing ∑ AR 1.769). It is unclear whether or not the Argonauts knew of the events that had occurred on the island and, if so, how they sought to ensure it was not repeated and their own lives put in danger.

The only useful piece of evidence that remains from Sophokles comes from his *Lemniai*, and it mentions a battle between the Argonauts and the Lemnian women (p. 337 R), again citing ∑ AR 1.769. This would indicate that such assurances, if received, were not honoured. In Euripides, although there is mention in a fragment from an earlier play of a second child between Hypsipyle and Jason called Thoas,[54] there is no reference to any children of Jason and Hypsipyle in his *Medea* in 431 B.C. This makes sense in the context of the *Medea*, as the focus of the play is on the children of Jason and Medea. However it does show that Euripides was aware of another version of this myth.

Therefore in this part of the journey to the island of Lemnos, we can deduce that by the end of the fifth century the Argo was said to have stopped at the island, and the men embarked on affairs with the

---

[54] In later literature: the child is called Nebrophonos in Apollodoros (ApB1.9.17) or Deipylos in Hyginus (*Fab.* 15).

Lemnian women. The men of the island had been killed, probably including the king Thoas, and at some point the Argonauts take part in an athletics contest while staying there and sharing the women's beds. The biggest gaps are in the earliest part of the tale, relating to why the women were spurned in the first place and, (if we follow Apollonios and Apollodoros' versions), what caused the anger of Aphrodite. Also it is unclear what agreements were reached between the Argonauts and the women in order for the men to agree to stay at the island, and what caused the eventual break up of this arrangement, resulting in the battle.

For Jason, it establishes that his son, Euneos, is the earliest evidence for children of the hero, and his relationship with Hypsipyle is certainly as old as the story of his involvement with Medea. It also points to two separate strands of the myth, as neither Pindar nor Euripides attempt to include the tale of Jason and Hypsipyle alongside the full tale of Medea. They do not go well into a single narrative, unless kept strictly separate, and so one version is generally chosen above the other. As mentioned above, Aischylos refers to the story at Lemnos in the *Choephoroi* at lines 631-8 and may have completed a trilogy based on the Lemnian myth. Sophokles' *Lemnian Women* shows that he used Hypsipyle in one version, and his *Aigeus*, *Kolchides* and *Rhizotomoi* show he included Medea in a second strand. Euripides also used both tales in separate plays. His *Medea* obviously deals with Medea's part in the tale, and excludes any mention of Hypsipyle. However, his *Hypsipyle* takes the other point of view, although as the play is lost we cannot say for certain that he omitted any reference to Medea on this occasion. These authors are all aware of the existence of the two women, and their relationships with Jason, but draw on each at different times in different works. For the hero, the encounter with a local female leader is similar to the encounter between Odysseus and Kirke, or Theseus' relationship with the Amazon queen. However, there is no extant visual evidence for the episode at Lemnos. We know of its early date due to its mention in the *Iliad*, but it possibly did not hold the same interest for artists as other parts of the voyage. For example, the confrontation with the serpent in

Kolchis may be a scene which captured the interests of a vase painter, whereas the visit to Lemnos does not hold any single representation which would stand out as inspiring to a vase painter or sculptor. If the Argo stopped and the crew stayed at the island, such a stopover does not conjure up an intriguing visual representation.

2

King Phineus and the Journey to Kolchis

Between Lemnos and King Phineus

On occasions when literary evidence regarding Jason is somewhat fragmentary, iconography can help us to fill in the gaps, providing information about other encounters the hero had in the course of his journey to Kolchis. It is important to study these smaller tales, since, even though direct involvement by Jason may be small, they do show that his myth and the voyage of the Argo were well-known and depicted in early art and literature. Picking up on some of these other stories connected to the voyage may also lead us to believe that there were more substantial, and now lost, sources which covered Jason and the voyage. For the encounter with Amykos or Phineus to work, for example, they must exist within an overall framework. If we have early evidence for these tales, and they connect to part of a larger tale, it seems to point to the fact that there was an overall narrative that contained them.

As we turn to the evidence concerning events after the visit to the island of Lemnos, we see that there are two significant episodes before the arrival of the Argo with king Phineus and the Harpuiai. The first of these concerns the role of Herakles and his departure from the voyage, while the second deals with the meeting between Kastor and Polydeukes and the boxer Amykos.

However, it is worth mentioning at this point one further encounter at this point and that is the story of the Argo at Dindymon. In Apollonios' *Argonautika* the Argonauts arrive at the island of Dindymon where they receive hospitality from the local leader, king Kyzikos. They depart from the island amicably but the wind turns against them and the Argo is blown back onto the shore of Dindymon at night. There is a confused battle between the two sides (AR 1.1015-58), with King

Kyzikos being killed in the conflict. Once all involved become aware of the situation the full horror of killing their host is realised. This episode however, does not appear in literary or visual evidence before 400 B.C., and it is important to separate this type of later tale from our early evidence. The only mention of this event before Apollonios comes from Herodoros (Herodoros fr. 7), and so the episode appears to play no part in the earlier versions of the myth.

So we now move to the two main episodes occurring between the departure from Lemnos and the encounter with King Phineus, and look first at the involvement of Herakles in the voyage. Scholia to Apollonios give the following Hesiodic reference;

> Hesiod in the Marriage of Ceyx says that he landed
> to look for water and was left behind in Magnesia
> near the palace called Aphetae, because of his
> desertion there (∑ AR 1.1289; Hes. fr. 263 MW).

Herodotus also follows this version of events;

> There is a place in this bay where it is said that
> Heracles at the start of the voyage of the Argo to
> fetch the golden fleece from Aea (Colchis), was put
> ashore by Jason and his companions to get water,
> and was left behind. (*Hist.* 7.193).

A third source, Pherekydes, agrees with this version and the location at which Herakles leaves, but rather than going to fetch water, he says that Herakles was set down here due to his weight. He was apparently too heavy for the ship and had to be left behind while the Argo continued towards Aia (Pher. fr. 111).

Pindar, however, makes no mention of the loss of the hero - however it might have occurred - and this may simply point to the fact that Herakles plays only a very minor role in the *Fourth Pythian*. Herodoros goes one step further, since he says that Herakles was in the service of Omphale and therefore didn't in fact embark on the trip at all (Herodoros fr. 41). This at least offers a reason for the hero's absence instead of simply omitting him from the ship's crew.

Aside from Herodoros, later sources seem more favourably disposed to Herakles' involvement in the quest, and they enhance his role, with Apollonios going so far as to say he turned down the actual leadership of the expedition (AR 1.341-7). Other sources simply say that he travelled with the ship for the whole of the journey.[55]   In the evidence up to the mid-fifth century Jason is the driving force behind the voyage, especially in his challenge to Pelias and his winning of the fleece in Kolchis. It would certainly detract from this if such a well known hero as Herakles was to assume a secondary support role, and so for clarity and focus our sources choose to either minimise his role in the expedition or exclude his participation altogether.   As far as the myth of Jason is concerned, the absence or presence of Herakles does not affect the outcome of the voyage. His inclusion is surely a concession to the fact that all of the greatest Greek heroes had to be included in the crew. An author or early artist may have felt obliged to include Herakles simply because he was such a well known figure in myth.   However, having added him to the Argo it is perfectly acceptable to have him leave at an early point, as he plays no particular role, and centre stage belongs to Jason.

The involvement of Herakles is not recorded in extant visual art of the period up to the end of the fifth century. However, a volute krater from c. 350-340 B.C., actually shows Herakles killing the snake in Kolchis [Fig. 98], which is a fairly damning piece of evidence as to the role of Jason in his own myth, although from much later sources.   In early myth, Jason is the only figure credited with killing the serpent guarding the fleece. Even the participation of Medea in this scene, which begins to emerge at the end of the fifth century, is absent from earlier

---

[55] Demaratos 2F2, Dionysios of Mitylene 32F6.

tellings of the story. Only Athena is present in vase painting as Jason confronts the serpent (as discussed in Chapter 3). The earliest signal that this role is being removed from Jason is from Euripides' *Medea*, where Medea says that it was she who killed the serpent (Eur. *Med.* 480-3). This is certainly a sign of the trend in later sources, but is completely absent in early myth.

The second and final episode that I wish to look at before we move to the encounter with Phineus is the meeting of the Dioskouri, Kastor and Polydeukes, with King Amykos. Although, as with the story of the king of Dindymon, most of the sources come from a date after 400 B.C., on this occasion there is evidence that points to the tale being known before this date. Amykos was said to have challenged Kastor and Polydeukes to a boxing match. Despite Amykos' bravado, the Dioskouri manage to defeat him.

The story of Amykos does not appear in any substantial form before the *Hymn to Dioskouroi* by Theokritos in the third century B.C. and in Apollonios' *Argonautika*. But we know that in the early part of the fifth century Epicharmos wrote a comedy on the subject where Polydeukes bound Amykos and Kastor warned him not to insult his brother (fr. 6,7 Kassel-Austin).[56]   If we place this with Theokritos' evidence we learn that Kastor and Polydeukes came across Amykos near a spring and that Amykos would not allow them to drink the water until they agreed to box against him. The terms set are that the winner can do anything to the loser; Polydeukes wins and tells Amykos never to insult or disrespect a stranger again (Theokritos 22.131-4).[57]

---

[56] Epicharmos wrote comedy during the first quarter of the fifth century B.C. and was from Sicily.

[57] Apollonios and Apollodoros both include the story and say that Amykos is killed in the fight. Apollonios says that Polydeukes strikes the king above his ear and Amykos fell to the ground (2.94-7). Apollodoros says Amykos challenged the best man of the crew to a boxing match and it was Polydeukes who fought and killed the king (1.9.20).

However, we must treat these later sources with a degree of caution and try to see what can be found in early myth. On this occasion early art may offer a new ingredient into the story. An example, dated to 440-30 B.C., is a fragment of an Attic red-figure volute krater showing the upper torso and head of Amykos, with his hands wrapped and ready to box [Fig. 4]. This, according to Beazley and others, is Amykos at the funeral games of Pelias.[58]   This raises the question of why Amykos appears here as it seems out of place with what we know about the myth. As Beazley suggests,[59] the artist may have mixed up Polydeukes versus Amykos with Polydeukes versus an opponent at the funeral games.

A Lucanian hydria dated to 420-400 B.C. shows Amykos bound to a rock [Fig. 5]. Some later sources say that Amykos was bound by the Dioskouri to a tree but on this vase he appears to be bound to a rock as the brothers stand with jugs ready to collect water from the spring emerging to the right of Amykos. This hydria is the earliest extant artistic evidence for the binding of Amykos by the Dioskouri and shows, like the Epicharmos fragments, that the aggressive figure of Amykos was an element which was known in the fifth century.

Therefore the extant evidence for the episode with Amykos before 400 B.C. points to the binding of the king and the boxing match with Kastor and Polydeukes. The extraction of a promise not to insult or harm another stranger may be a later addition. The tale also appears to stand alone as there is no direct and necessary connection to the rest of the Argonautic story. Amykos does not appear to help the Argo in its expedition and Jason does not appear to play any significant role in the tale. It acts as a satellite myth to the main Argonautic story.

---

[58] Beazley also notes that Amykos is named on this fragment.

[59] Beazley, *AJA* 1960 (64) p.223.

Phineus

The next significant event of the voyage to Kolchis concerns the Argonauts' encounter with the blind king Phineus in Thrace. This is also an episode that offers us some rich iconographical evidence.

On their stop in Thrace, the Argonauts arrive to find Phineus being persecuted by the Harpuiai, winged creatures who torment the old man by stealing his food. Living alone, the king is a prisoner until relief is offered by the Argonauts and in particular by the two Boreadai. The Boreadai were the sons of Boreas and Oreithuia (Akousilaos fr. 30), and they were two winged heroes. Boreas was a god of wind (*Th.* 378-82), and his sons' particular strength was their ability to fly.

In many of the versions of this myth, Jason may be playing a supporting role. This is perhaps appropriate since, as the leader of the Argonauts, Jason's active participation is called for at crucial junctures such as the winning of the fleece, whereas the encounter with Phineus is more of an ancillary plot. Poets may also choose different heroes to take on different roles during the voyage since it may be necessary to include various members of the crew in the action, and show their particular skills at relevant stages. The final stage of the events in Thrace when the Boreadai pursue the Harpuiai seems to be one such example, and given that the Boreadai have the ability to fly, they are probably the only suitable candidates among the Argonauts to carry out this task. However, as we will see, Jason's role may be important, and although he is not involved in the actual pursuit of the Harpuiai, he does become involved in other parts of the story.

We know from Pherekydes that Phineus was the king of the Thracians in Asia as far as the Bosphorus (fr. 27). However, we do not know from extant evidence what his status is around the arrival of the Argonauts. It is possible that Phineus is in a similar position to king Oidipous with regard to his exile. According to Sophokles' *Oedipus*

Tyrannos, Oidipous chose (though he was not immediately allowed) to go into exile following the uncovering of his grim past, the death of Iokaste, and his own blinding, and the throne of Thebes was therefore handed over to Kreon.   It is likely that the story of Phineus indicated some hand over of the Thracian throne in a similar manner.

Phineus' predicament and the episode with the Argonauts contains three primary aspects: Phineus' crime, his choice of punishments, and his penance itself.   We will remember that it was Phrixos who brought the golden fleece to Aia.   Phrixos and his sister, Helle, rode the flying ram from Greece to Kolchis, although Helle fell off into what was then called Helle's sea - the Hellespont. It would seem that at some point on their journey, Phrixos encountered Phineus and asked him for directions as to the route to Kolchis. The earliest reference to Phineus' intervention in the journey of Phrixos, comes from the *Megalai Ehoiai:*

> Hesiod...says that Phineus was blinded because he
> told Phrixos the way. (Hes. fr. 254 MW).

Apollodoros says that in one version of the myth Poseidon punished Phineus for showing Phrixos' sons the way from Kolchis to Greece (1.9.21), and as Gantz suggests, Poseidon would have been displeased at someone travelling too freely across the sea.[60]   Another late source, Istros, says Phineus helped Phrixos' son and Aietes cursed Phineus as did Helios (Aietes' father) and it was this that caused his blindness (Istros fr. 67).

According to the *Ehoiai,* Phineus had the opportunity to select his punishment from two options, and   he chooses a long life instead of retaining his sight and presumably dying early;

> ...He preferred long life to sight (Hes. fr. 157 MW).

---

[60] Gantz, p. 350.

It is unclear who offers him the choice on these terms or if they were part of a wider fate for Phineus.   In the *Etymologicum Genuinum* Phineus again has to make a decision between blindness and a short healthy life.[61]

In the early versions there is no suggestion of any malice on the part of Phineus that would lead to such a punishment, and he is rather the victim of an unfortunate mistake, simply assisting a stranger and therefore being cursed by the stranger's enemy (*Megalai Ehoiai*). His punishment could therefore appear rather harsh.   Unlike Teiresias who sided with Zeus in a dispute with Hera (Hes. fr. 276 MW), Phineus' offence against an immortal is unwitting, yet he suffers the same fate as a consequence.   Indeed his story has similarities to the choice facing Achilleus in the *Iliad*.   In his speech at Book 9 (*Il.* 9.410-16) he tells Odysseus that he has two possible fates awaiting him.   One is to stay at Troy, but to die there, and have his name live on for ever.   The second option is to sail for home and to live out a long life as an ordinary citizen. Achilleus stays to fight, and by doing so seals his future, confirming that he will die in battle at Troy.   The choice for Phineus was far more stark; it may be imminent death, or the loss of his sight.

There are also stories that connect Phineus to an actual crime rather than an insult offered to a deity, whether he was a willing participant or not, and therefore his punishment is a result of his actions. From tragedy we have three Sophoklean plays and three separate accounts for the fates of Phineus' children.   One of the plays has Phineus blind his own children (children by Kleopatra, daughter of Boreas) on the advice of his second wife Idaia (fr. 704 R).   The second *Phineus* play has the king kill the children, and he is blinded after this event (fr. 705 R).   The third play, *Tympanistai,* states that the children were blinded and imprisoned by their stepmother Eidothea (Phineus' second wife).   This matches the evidence from Sophokles' *Antigone,*

---

[61] Soph. Fr. 705R; Wendel, C. (1935) *Scholia in Ap. Rhod. vetera* 140.

where the chorus refer to the blinding of the sons with a shuttle by their stepmother (*Ant.* 968-976). Scholia to this piece suggest her name is either Eidothea, sister of Kadmos (also mentioned in Sophokles' *Tympanistai*), or Idaia, daughter of Dardanos (Σ AA 981).

Aside from the scattered extant references, there is no clear explanation as to why blindness is selected as the punishment for Phineus. It may simply be that blindness is a favoured way for a god to punish a mortal, as seen in the case of Teiresias. Phineus may have offended Poseidon to such an extent that blindness (or death) is appropriate. Therefore there seems to be two versions of the myth. The first and earliest example assumes that Phineus is blinded for showing Phrixos the way. We may be able to infer that at the time at which Phineus gives Phrixos the controversial directions he is king of Thrace and not an exile. The second version of the myth is the one found in tragedy where Phineus may have been punished for crimes committed against his own family.

Phineus appears to have been blinded before he goes into exile, and then moves to the location in Thrace where he meets the Argonauts. Therefore we can assume that he offered guidance to Phrixos prior to the time of his exile. The reason I point to this is that Phineus may guide the Argonauts in a second act of giving directions, but done now at a time when the king has little to lose. The first time he presumes to offer guidance it leads to his blindness. If there is a second time, then it occurs during his exile, while he is blind, and may be in return for a favourable act received from Jason and the Argonauts.

We move now to the Harpuiai, whose contribution to Phineus' misfortune is recorded in both literature and iconography. The earliest extant representations of the Harpuiai come from Homer and Hesiod. The *Iliad* twice names one Harpuia, called Podarge (*Il.* 16.150; 19.400), and the *Odyssey* mentions them stealing, but in this case they are known for stealing away people.[62] (*Od.* 1.241; 14.371; 20.77-8). They are referred to in the *Ehoiai* when Hesiod implies they were not killed by the Boreadai (Hes. 156 MW), and in the *Theogony*, Hesiod names two Harpuiai and gives their parentage.

> Thaumas married a daughter of the deep-flowing Oceanus, Elektra, and she bore swift Iris and the lovely-haired Harpuiai, Aello and Ocypeta, who race with the gusts of the winds and with the birds on swift wings, for they hurl on high[63] (*Th.* 265-9).

Later in Aischylos' *Eumenides* (50-1)[64] it is implied that the winged creatures steal food from Phineus and cause him to go hungry. A fragment from Aischylos' *Phineus* goes further, stating:

> and many a deceitful meal with greedy jaws did they snatch away amid the first delight of appetite (fr. 143).[65]

In Asklepiades' account, Phineus has chosen blindness over death as a punishment for his treatment of his sons. But this choice also means that Phineus has opted not to be able to see the light of the sun and in doing so offends Helios the sun-god. This immortal's revenge is to send the Harpuiai to destroy his food and this is the first account where they are sent to Phineus in the form of a punishment and not simply as scavengers for food (Asklepiades fr. 31).

Later, both Apollonios and Apollodoros add to Phineus' plight by saying that the Harpuiai first snatch some of the food and then leave a loathsome stench on the rest (AR 2 187-93; ApB 1.9.21).

---

[62] Their name derives from αρπάζω- to snatch or seize.

[63] 'Aello' means storm swift and 'Ocypeta' means swift of flight.

[64] 'The creatures tearing the feast away from Phineus' (*Eum.* 50-1).

[65] Trans by Herbert Weir Smyth, p. 469. A further fragment from Sophokles refers to the Harpuiai laying waste to their surroundings ((714 TrGF): 'χερσὶν ἁρπάγοις'.

As for the location of Phineus and the Harpuiai, Hesiod seems to imply that the Harpuiai belonged to the land of Glaktophagoi ('milk-feeders'), apparently a people of Skythia (Hes. fr. 151 MW).

We now reach the section of the story where the Argonauts arrive and, for whatever reason, assist Phineus by chasing or capturing the Harpuiai. Whereas we know conclusively that the Boreadai chase the Harpuiai away from Phineus, as shown in detail in visual representations (see below), the end fate of the Harpuiai is less clear. It appears that Aischylos (fr. 260 R), Telestes (812 PMG), and Ibykos (292 PMG), all indicate that they died or were killed. An incomplete fragment from Philodemus' *Piety* says that 'Aeschylus...and Ibycus and Telestes (represent) the Harpuiai (as being killed by the sons of Boreas?).'[66] However the text is difficult to reconstruct, and what is being said here may be unclear.

There is, however, early evidence to suggest that the Harpuiai remain alive and are pursued as they flee or are taken away from the area where Phineus is living. A fragment from scholia to Apollonios says that Iris intervenes to turn back the Boreadai from their pursuit. However, the same scholia report that it was Hermes who prevented the Harpuiai from being killed. (fr. 156 MW);

> Apollonios indeed says it was Iris who made Zetes [one of the Boreadai] and his following turn away, but Hesiod says Hermes. Others say (the islands) were called Strophades, because they turned there and prayed Zeus to seize the Harpies. But according to Hesiod...they were not killed.[67]

---

[66] Trans. D.A. Campbell (1991), p. 259.

[67] Trans. H.G. Evelyn-White, p. 179-81.

As we can see, our later source Apollonios involves the goddess Iris. He says that she promises that the Harpuiai will not harm Phineus in the future and will leave him alone (AR 2.273-300).

A third strand suggests that instead of the Harpuiai being stopped from tormenting Phineus or killed, they are taken away to Krete. Both the *Naupaktia* and Pherekydes say they were taken to a cave under a ridge at a place called Arginos in Krete (*Nau.* fr. 3 PEG; Pher. fr. 29).

What is clear throughout all of these sources is that the arrival of the Argo brings an end to the torment of Phineus. There is also the possibility that some deal is agreed between Jason and Phineus. If the king has in the past helped Phrixos to reach Kolchis, it seems likely that Jason will request similar assistance. The Argo specifically follows the path of Phrixos' original journey, a point which Pindar makes in the *Fourth Pythian* when he says that Pelias requests Jason to follow in Phrixos' footsteps;

> Phrixos orders us to go to the halls of Aietes to bring
> back his soul and to recover the thick-fleeced hide
> of the ram by which he was once preserved from
> the sea. (*Py.* 4. 159-62).

Phrixos' story is tied to the Argonautic voyage, and the connection between Jason and Phineus may be something of a reversal of the link between Phrixos and the king. Phineus is blinded for his assistance to Phrixos, but vase painting may show that Jason heals Phineus of this affliction in return for his help. Therefore we will now move to the iconographical evidence, and see how this differs from the evidence in literature.

The Phineus Myth in Art[68]

Extant representations of Phineus and the Harpuiai dominate the visual evidence of the voyage to Kolchis. As a subject, it appears to be the ideal focus for vase-painters, especially in Archaic iconography. Winged creatures being pursued by the Boreadai (themselves winged), and the capturing of these mythological tormentors, is excellent material for an art that thrived on the depiction of the civilised versus the barbarian. It is not surprising that the depictions of Phineus and the Harpuiai have a similar chronological profile to those of Perseus and Medousa. Depictions of the Phineus tale begin in 620 B.C., and the majority of the images are dated to the last half of the sixth century and the first half of the fifth century, a time when depictions of Perseus and Medousa are also at their height in terms of frequency. The same is true of images of Herakles and Theseus, both of whom are heroes who fight with monsters and uphold the values of Greek society:

> The popularity of the hero Theseus as a subject for Attic vase-paintings approaches that of his contemporary, Herakles, at the end of the sixth century.[69]

I have divided the visual material into seven segments and will look at each in turn:

1/ Phineus alone to face the Harpuiai

In trying to define a representation of Phineus alone we must look to clues that differentiate him from say Oidipous or Teiresias, both of whom can also be portrayed as old, blind men. The first element that helps us define the Thracian Phineus is the appearance of a table which has been prepared with food. Our earliest extant depiction of Phineus alone comes from Attica and is dated to 470-450 B.C. [Fig. 54]. Phineus stands to the left of the scene appearing to be ready to eat from the

---

[68] Refer to Appendix 1 for guide to visual evidence.

[69] Carpenter, p. 160.

table. The material on the table represents the food and we know from our earliest source, Hesiod (fr. 157 MW), that the Harpuiai will arrive to steal this.

In comparison, our second example, dated to 460-440 B.C., shows a more animated Phineus as he tries to fight off a Harpuia as she approaches from the right [Fig. 55]. This is quite crudely drawn, and shows Phineus raising a club above his head and trying to strike his enemy as she stretches for the table. From our literary sources we know that there are normally two Harpuiai, but here the vase-painter has chosen to show just one, giving the scene a symmetrical feel with King versus Harpuia, and possibly again showing a different, more thoughtful, and less confrontational focus of fifth century vase painting.

This scene is unusual when we compare it to the next section in which the stealing of the food takes place. From extant evidence we know that it is more common for an artist to show the food-snatching and escape of the Harpuiai rather than their entrance and approach. On Fig. 55 the table is as yet undisturbed. We know from other sources, such as Fig. 61, the chaos that the Harpuiai cause, but in Fig. 55 this has not as yet occurred. In Fig. 55, the Harpuia has arrived from the right and Phineus raises a club in his right hand as he realises someone is approaching.

Of these two artefacts, Fig. 54 is the only surviving example that shows Phineus without any other characters. His identification is helped by the presence of the table whereas all other artefacts with Phineus involve either the Argonauts or the Harpuiai. Also, Phineus does not appear to exist in any substantive form beyond the myth of the Harpuiai and the Argonauts' visit to his home, and so showing him in isolation from these elements is unusual.

2/ The Snatching of the Food

The earliest extant example of the Harpuiai snatching Phineus' food comes on an Attic white-ground lekythos [Fig. 50]. Phineus gestures towards the Harpuiai as they flee to the right, a movement indicated by the fact that their feet are turned away from Phineus. His action helps us in our identification as it emphasises his blindness by showing his vain attempts to stop his persecutors. Both Harpuiai are holding food in their hands and depart with Phineus' meal in their possession.

One of the most beautiful depictions of this type of scene appears on an Attic hydria from 480-470 B.C. and shows Phineus with three Harpuiai [Fig. 51]. Again, Phineus gestures vainly and the Harpuiai take food from the table. The Harpuia at the centre was the first to approach as she moves from left to right in the scene, with food in both hands. The Harpuia closest to the table swoops and grabs food, while the final Harpuia approaches from the right. We can see from this scene a clear indication of Phineus' blindness as his eye has been drawn as if closed. As he waves his arms we can also see that this is turned in the wrong direction and this underlines his helplessness.

The third example is an Attic red figure bell-krater, dated to 450 B.C. [Fig. 60], which shows Phineus seated in the middle of the scene. Two Harpuiai flee with food in their hands, one to the far left, and the other to the far right. The third Harpuia stoops to snatch food from the table. Along with Fig. 51, this is the only extant vase painting showing three Harpuiai up until 400 B.C.

Our last two examples dealing with the stealing of Phineus' food return to previous portrayals. An Attic red-figure column amphora [Fig. 53] shows Phineus seated, this time on the right, with two Harpuiai fleeing to the left. Both have food in their hands and Phineus is powerless to stop them. Although the vase is damaged, Phineus appears to have his right arm outstretched; we can see the drapery fall under his upper right arm indicating that it is extended out towards the Harpuiai. As we have seen before, Phineus is depicted as blind with his eyes closed, drawn as a straight line.

The second example comes from two remaining fragments of an Attic red-figure bell-krater [Fig. 58] which, although small, appear to show the theme that we have seen so far on the other four examples. The first fragment has the remains of a Harpuia fleeing to the left and Phineus leaning on a staff. All that remains of the depiction of Phineus is a finger of his hand resting on the stick, but considering his blindness and therefore the appearance of a staff on many of the extant examples, this does seem to confirm his identity. Phineus usually rests on the staff or raises it in an attempt to scare away the Harpuiai.

The number of Harpuiai depicted change over time, but in the case of vase painting this generally reflects the use of space on a vase and what an artist is trying to depict. The *Iliad* twice names one Harpuia (*Il.* 16.150; 19.400), and the *Odyssey* also mentions them (more than one as the reference is plural: *Od.* 1.241; 14.371; 20.77-8). In the *Theogony*, Hesiod names two Harpuiai and gives their parentage. (*Th.* 265-9).

The earliest visual art also shows two of the creatures is a vase by the Nettos Painter dated to 620 B.C. [Fig. 39- discussion below] shows two Harpuiai fleeing. In fact the majority of the extant visual evidence shows two figures.

They are named in the *Theogony* and the *Iliad* but have no extensive story connected to them. Indeed the depiction of three female figures in mythology appears to be more common. The Gorgons [an early example being Fig. 102], the Graiai [Figs. 103, 104, 105 & 106], the nymphs [Figs. 107, 108, 109 & 110], are all three in number in the myth of Perseus. On the other hand, male groups seem to normally be pairs, such as the Boreadai (see below), and the Dioskouri [Fig. 5].

3/ Phineus & the Arrival of the Boreadai/Argonauts

To understand this portion of the tale it is necessary to look at evidence for an agreement between the Argonauts and Phineus. It is possible that the crew assisted the king because they had seen his suffering, but given the connections to Phrixos and the evidence that Phineus had helped him on his way to Kolchis (at least in one version of the myth), it is likely that the Argonauts would ask for similar help, and would offer to assist Phineus in return for his guidance.

Returning to vase painting, an Attic red-figure stamnos [Fig. 56] and an Attic red-figure pelike [Fig. 59], show Phineus seated on his throne and in discussion with the two Boreadai. In Fig. 56 Phineus is seated at the centre with his back to one of the Boreadai, while facing and talking to the Boread on the right. Fig. 59 alters Phineus' position slightly, as the king is seated with a frontal view, while he turns his head to the right to talk to one of the men. On both vases his guests rest on their spears and both characters are winged, confirming their identification as the Boreadai. In Fig. 59 Phineus' own identity is assured, not only by his relation to the characters in the scene, but because of his eye, which is again drawn using one line indicating blindness. In these scenes there is no sign of the Harpuiai and there is no table with food. These scenes are about the meeting and discussion between the king and the men which is a prelude to any confrontation.

Thirdly, an Attic red-figure column krater [Fig. 57] by the Leningrad painter, also dated to the mid-fifth century. The king, his eye again painted with a straight line indicating blindness, is seated at the centre, and he gestures with his right hand towards a Boread. It looks as if he is explaining the situation to his guests, and they appear to be planning for the return of the Harpuiai. However the figure to the left of the scene raises his spear above his shoulder in his right hand, and stands behind Phineus' throne. He is also in a position ready to attack. Could this be Jason? It seems likely as other than the Boreadai, no other Argonautic character appears in these scenes of Phineus and the preparation for the return of the Harpuiai. As we will see later, Jason appears in some scenes with Phineus, and so his depiction here seems likely. We can definitely rule out the figure as another Boread as he doesn't have wings.

The fourth and final extant piece of evidence in this section is an Apulian red-figure krater fragment [Fig. 62] which shows one of the Boreadai standing behind the king with his spear raised to shoulder height. This is a difficult fragment to place as the full vase may have shown a number of possible scenes. I believe that it shows the Boreadai talking to Phineus about what will happen when the Harpuiai arrive. The Boread stands with his right arm raised, holding a spear, and this is the same type of pose that we saw in Fig. 57. None of our extant visual evidence shows a Boread standing behind Phineus' throne in this position if the Harpuiai are present. In all scenes where the Harpuiai and Boreadai are shown together, the Boreadai are either in pursuit, or in the act of capturing the Harpuiai. Also, Phineus appears to be seated peacefully, as his right arm and shoulder are at rest and not raised in his familiar gesture used to ward off the creatures. Therefore I believe this vase showed the scene of a discussion between the Boreadai and Phineus in advance of the Harpuiai' arrival.

4/ The Harpuiai Flee, alone

As we turn to the arrival of the Harpuiai on the scene and their pursuit by the Boreadai, there is something of a gap in the story when we look at our extant iconography. We have seen how Phineus was plagued by the Harpuiai, how he discusses the dilemma with the newly arrived Argonauts and the preparations for the next attack, but the entrance of the Harpuiai and their initial reaction to the Boreadai is not depicted. Instead we move directly to their flight and pursuit.

Evidence for the Harpuiai fleeing, without the depiction of the pursuing Boreadai, survives in only one example. It is our earliest visual depiction of the Harpuiai [Fig. 39] and shows the two creatures (named) fleeing from left to right. As there are no visual representations of the Harpuiai outside the myth of Phineus, this depiction of the Harpuiai appears to refer to the myth in some way, even if the other characters are not present.

It seems likely that this scene does show the Harpuiai fleeing the Boreadai. They are shown in a typical Archaic style. This type of running pose, where the Harpuiai appear to be moving from left to right, can be seen as the creatures in flight. Their wings flow behind them, indicating they are airborne, but more importantly, there are other examples of characters in Archaic art who are in this position and being depicted in flight. Among such examples are depictions of the Gorgons who pursue Perseus as he flees with Medousa's head. An example of this occurs on Fig. 102, where we see Medousa's sisters pursuing Perseus in this running style, with one knee bent forward, almost as if the character is kneeling on the ground. However, this generally indicates the figure moving at speed, and in the case of the Nessos amphora showing the Gorgons pursue Perseus we are shown this by the artist as fish are drawn beneath the Gorgon sisters, indicating their pursuit of Perseus across the sea.[70]

5/ The Pursuit of the Harpuiai by the Boreadai

Given the nature of Archaic vase-painting and its interest in creatures, it comes as no surprise that these next two sections containing the pursuit and capture of the Harpuiai by the Boreadai form the largest number of extant examples for the Phineus myth in art.

The first two examples are references to lost artefacts. A description from Pausanias [fig. 40] tells of the chest of Kypselos and a relief from a votive offering. Pausanias says:

---

[70] Boardman (1974), fig. 5.2.

> Phineus the Thracian is there, and the sons of the
> north-east wind are chasing the Harpies away from
> him (Paus. 5.17.11).[71]

Also from Pausanias is the description of the throne of Apollo at Amyklai [Fig. 47] dated to 550-500 B.C., where Pausanias says

> Kalais and Zetes [the Boreadai] are driving off the Harpuiai
> from Phineus' (Paus. 3.18.15).

An Attic black-figure amphora [Fig. 46] shows one Harpuia fleeing one Boread. It is not an attempt to suggest that there was only one Harpuia or Boread, but allows the artist to use the space to focus on one of each of the figures. The artist focuses on the figures and not the narrative of the myth. Both characters have full wings, appear to be running at full pace, and the two figures are remarkably similar in size and style, with the main differentiation coming in the skin colour and the clothing worn.

With Fig. 48 we return to a more familiar setting. This is a black-figure cup showing Phineus reclining on a couch and two Boreadai chasing the two Harpuiai with swords drawn. In a similar style to Fig. 46, the Boreadai and Harpuiai both have full wings and the differences lie in skin tone and hand gestures. The Harpuiai are depicted as fleeing out to sea.

Two further examples are less clear. One is a fragment of a black-figure vase showing one Boread and two Harpuiai [Fig. 49]. There is nothing here to prevent us assuming that this follows the tradition and shows a normal scene of the pursuit. The other is a white-ground lekythos [Fig. 52], and although it shows two fleeing Harpuiai, the pursuer appears to be a man rather than a winged Boread. Given the quality of the painting on this particular vase we should not read too

---

[71] Trans. by Levi, p. 250.

much into this, but what is worth noting is the possible depiction of the sea beneath their feet.   Kahil[72] suggests this as the artist has drawn ripples at the base of the scene indicating that the artist is showing the Boreadai chasing the Harpuiai out to sea, as already seen in Fig. 48.

Fig. 61 is one of only three extant vases showing three Harpuiai up until the end of the fifth century B.C. This Attic red-figure hydria shows a scene of the creatures fleeing from Phineus' table. This vase has been lost, so the image we have is a drawing of the vase painting. However it is unique for a number of reasons. First it is rare to see the Harpuiai, Phineus and the Boreadai all in one scene. Second is the issue of the third Harpuia, a somewhat unusual addition to the normal two; there are two Harpuiai to the left of Phineus and one behind his throne to the right.[73]   The third point is the issue of the assistance being offered to Phineus since to the far right of the king there appears to be a Boread. However, far from ridding the king of his tormentors, the Boread is more concerned about saving the food as it falls to the ground from the third Harpuia.   The Harpuiai are certainly startled but do not appear to be under any immediate threat.

Behind the king's throne there stands another figure who is offering more resistance, but this person is not a Boread, unless the artist has chosen to conceal the wings under his cloak.   This character is dressed in a different manner to the Boread to the far right, and holds a spear in the air, threatening the two Harpuiai to the left.   There is the possibility that this figure is Jason as his dress, especially his boots, may point to a figure of high status. If this is correct, it is the only example in extant literature or art up to 400 B.C. of Jason taking part in this specific part of the story with both the Boreadai and the Harpuiai. Although there are no direct extant literary references containing Jason and Phineus

---

[72] *LIMC* "Harpyiai" 26*, p. 448.

[73] Shapiro points out the popularity of twins in archaic depictions of myth (p. 98) and this is certainly true in the myth of Jason, with the Dioscouri and Boreadai.

together, beyond references to the Argonauts stopping at Phineus' home, Jason's presence makes sense in the overall story. The leader of the Argo must have played some role in the events at Thrace and it would seem plausible that he would co-ordinate the actions of the crew. Also, if there was an agreement between the Argonauts and Phineus that if they got rid of the Harpuiai he would help them on the direction of their voyage, Jason's presence would be essential. Therefore if there is another Argonaut appearing in scenes of the Boreadai and the Harpuiai assisting Phineus, Jason would be the most likely candidate.

Our last example in this section dealing with the Boreadai pursuing the Harpuiai is a Lukanian red-figure volute krater by the Amykos Painter [Fig. 63] which returns us to the more familiar scene of two Boreadai chasing two Harpuiai. However, the scene also contains Phineus and adds a number of the Argonauts. Food is scattered around the ground at Phineus' feet and the two Boreadai stand at different levels each facing an opposing Harpuia. As with the previous example, a man stands behind Phineus, this time watching the action between Boreadai and Harpuiai and gesturing towards them. Again this could be Jason. This raises the question of a lack of identifiable symbols for Jason in iconography. For most of the identifications of the leader of the Argo we must rely on the context of the scenes. On this occasion taking a leadership role alongside the king may be enough to identify him. Certainly this section raises the probability that Jason appeared and took an active part in the Phineus myth. It is a logical step to assume that if an agreement is made between the Argonauts and Phineus, Jason was instrumental in this discussion.

6/ The Capturing or Killing of the Harpuiai

As we saw from the literary survey at the start of the chapter, there are two possible outcomes for the Harpuiai, as they are either killed or captured by the Boreadai depending on different sources. As discussed above, the *Naupaktia* and Pherekydes said that they were taken to Krete and they stayed in a cave there (*Nau.* fr. 3 PEG; Pher. fr.

29).   Alternatively, the mythographer Akousilaos[74] says that Herakles killed the Harpuiai (Akousilaos fr. 31), but given the evidence that we have seen relating to Herakles' involvement in the voyage, we know he didn't have a major influence on the myth and this suggestion does not seem to fit with the rest of our evidence.

An ivory relief from Korinth dated to 570 B.C. [Fig. 42] shows the capture of the Harpuiai by the Boreadai. The Boreadai seem to be holding the Harpuiai, but this piece is in poor condition and it is difficult to be definitive about what is being depicted.   However, there is nothing here to suggest that this piece is any different to our other examples.

Three cups show a very similar scene of the pursuit and all date to between 570 and 540 B.C. [Figs. 43, 44, 45].   All come from Lakonia and show two Boreadai and two Harpuiai. The first is the most complete example and shows the Boreadai just as they catch the Harpuiai, with their hands outstretched, gripping the winged creatures by their throats. In this portrayal the Boreadai have winged feet whereas the Harpuiai have full wings grown from their backs, which are spread as they try to escape to the right of the scene. Showing the Boreadai in a more human form, and less like mythological creatures offers a contrast in the image showing heroic mortals pursuing wild beasts. The Boreadai do appear to be mortal, however, as in Apollonios they are killed by Herakles, when the hero takes revenge on them for persuading the Argonauts to leave him behind at Kios (AR 1.1298-1308). Apollodoros also says that the Boreadai met their end, but this time they die chasing the Harpuiai (ApB 3.15.2).   There is no conclusive evidence in early myth.

Fig. 45 is virtually identical to Figs. 43 and 44, as it shows the Boreadai with winged feet and outstretched arms as they grip the

---

[74] Akousilaos was said to have lived before the Persian Wars and came from Argos.

throats of their enemies.   In both examples, the Boreadai have their swords drawn and seem intent on taking the lives of the Harpuiai.

An Attic red-figure oinochoe from 410 B.C. [Fig. 64] shows the Boreadai attacking the Harpuiai. One of the Harpuiai lies at the feet of Phineus as the Boreadai capture the second.   The Harpuia beside Phineus is painted with an open eye and so it indicates that she is still alive, although she is depicted with blood running from the right side of her body and so she may be shown in her final moments.   The positioning of the second Harpuia shows that she is being restrained by her captors, and their stance may suggest that they are about to kill her. If this is the case, this is the most definite extant representation of the killing of a Harpuia that we have found to date. We have already seen evidence that points to their deaths in Ibykos (292 PMG), Aischylos (fr. 260 R), and Telestes (812 PMG), but none conclusively say that they were killed by the Boreadai.

Driving the Harpuiai away may   be an alternative to their capture or death, and the references from Pausanias may be pointing to this [Figs. 40 & 47].   The different versions of this myth are not conclusive on the final outcome for the Harpuiai. However Phineus is freed from the torment that he has suffered. and there is no evidence, visual or literary, to suggest that the Harpuiai return after the departure of the Argo and its crew.

7/ Other Aspects of the Tale

So far we have seen in detail the extant literary and visual evidence for the myth of Phineus, and the evidence for Jason shows that he may have been involved in the plan to rid the king of the Harpuiai. However, one final intriguing fragment does enlighten our understanding of the role of Jason in the Phineus myth, and indeed it puts him at the centre of the tale. Fragments of a black-figure Korinthian column krater [Fig. 41] show Jason, named on the fragment so his identification is beyond question, standing behind the seated Phineus with his hands placed across his eyes. The question is, is this Jason healing the blind king? Given that we know of Jason's upbringing with Cheiron and the nature of Cheiron's teaching in healing, this seems plausible. Jason's name is derived from the Greek for "healer" and we know from Pindar that:

> deep-devising Cheiron raised Jason in his rocky dwelling and then Asklepios, whom he taught the gentle-handed province of medicines... (*Nem.* 3.53-55).

Mackie builds a strong case for Jason's powers of healing and the evidence for the healing of Phineus in the myth. He points to the skills of healing which Cheiron passed on to his other pupils such as Askelpios and Achilleus (*Il.* 4.217-19 & 11.828-32) and believes that healing was an essential part of the centaur's education for the heroes.[75] Although there is no early reference in literature to Jason's skills as a healer, Mackie points to Pindar, who 'consciously plays upon the notion of Jason as a healer'[76] Mackie believes that Jason's journey is meant as a quest, the outcome of which is the healing of the city of Iolkos. While I agree with Mackie's idea that Jason heals, for instance he is said to speak with soothing words in the market place when confronting Pelias (*Py.* 4.101-2 & 136-8), the result of the voyage is not confirmed as a healing one. Pindar does not relate to us that this actually happens at the end of the journey. He points to Medea as the killer of Pelias, and this may be offer a purification of the city, but Pindar does not give us the final part of the story. However even if the details are not related by Pindar Mackie's idea is correct and ho draws comparisons with the Iliadic destroyer and healer figure, such as Achilleus in his killing of Hektor combined with his healing of Priam's grief.[77] Jason, in bringing Medea back to Greece as the killer of Pelias, may perform a similar role as the

---

[75] Mackie, p. 2.

[76] Ibid., p. 5.

[77] Ibid., p. 6

kill is killed but the city is purified. However, this rests on one variation of the myth, Pindar's version, as in Pherekydes Pelias appears to be the righful ruler.

Mackie is in no doubt that this fragment, Fig. 21, shows the healing of the king, and that Jason forms part of a trio of healers, alongside Cheiron and Asklepios, who all demonstrate the skills to bring about the return of sight.[78]   Mackie's analysis is correct as the connections between Jason and Cheiron are some of the earliest literary references we have and this alongside Jason's name seem to be strong links to this power of healing.

The Symplegades

One further major episode remains on the journey to Kolchis and this is the passing of the Argo into the Black Sea, through the Clashing Rocks. There are two main traditions regarding the name of this obstacle: the first is the Symplegades (Clashing Rocks) and evidence comes from the fifth century onwards. The second version existed as far back as Homer, as in the *Odyssey* Kirke describes the 'Planktai'[79] (*Od.* 12. 61):

> One seafaring ship alone passed by those, that Argo
> famed of all, on her voyage from Aeetes [king of
> Kolchis], and even her the wave would speedily
> have dashed there against the great crags, had not
> Hera sent her through because Jason was dear to
> her. (*Od.* 12.69-72).[80]

In the *Odyssey* the Planktai are envisaged as treacherous crags, with great waves around them through which the Argo passes with

---

[78] Mackie, p. 9.

[79] The word is derived from πλάζω, πλάζ□μαι, lead astray, roam.

[80] Trans. A. T. Murray, revised by G. E. Dimock.

Hera's assistance, and the *Odyssey* places them on the Argo's return journey. The story mentions 'the great wave of Amphitrite' (*Od.* 12.60).[81] In Homer, Amphitrite is a sea goddess, and at one point Odysseus says;

> that some god may even send forth upon me some
> great monster out of the sea, like those that glorious
> Amphitrite breeds in such numbers'(*Od.* 5. 421-22).

According to scholia to the *Medea*, Simonides called the rocks Synormades[82] (546 PMG).

Pindar says the Argo passes through the rocks on the way to Kolchis but he doesn't use the term 'Planktai' or 'Symplegades', simply speaking of them as moving rocks that formed a potential barrier for the Argo. (*Py.* 4.208-210). He says that the rocks stopped moving once the ship passed through, removing them as an obstacle (*Py.* 4.210-1). Pindar moves through the telling of the events of the voyage from Iolkos to the rocks with speed, and he makes no mention at this point of the events at Lemnos or of King Phineus. The entrance to the Black Sea is the first major episode on the voyage according to *Pythian 4,* and the sea is referred to as the 'Inhospitable Sea' (*Py.* 4.203). Pindar says that the Argonauts prayed...

> that they might escape the irresistible movements of
> the rocks that run together. For both were alive and
> used to roll more swiftly than the ranks of the load-
> roaring winds...(*Py.* 4.207-11).[83]

---

[81] *Od.* 23.327 also mentions the Planktai but only in a list of places that Odysseus told Penelope about once he returns home. Karl Meuli discusses the possibility of the wandering rocks being part of the return journey and a danger that threatened to prevent the Argonauts escape from Kolchis (Meuli, K. *Odysee und Argonautika*, Berlin, 1921 pp. 87-89). Braswell also discusses the evidence for this (p. 290).

[82] συνⱰρμάδας.

[83] Trans. Braswell p.49.

This is the only episode that Pindar discusses before the Argo reaches the shore at Kolchis at line 211. What he does do is give us the first explicit extant evidence for the movement of the rocks, a version of the tale which later authors follow.

Pindar says that the Argonauts made an offering to the gods before they passed through the rocks and specifically mentions offerings given to 'Poseidon, of the Sea' (*Py.* 4.204) and indicates that the Argo has the blessing of the gods. If we compare this to the evidence for Phrixos' earlier voyage to Kolchis, we know that he travelled without the blessing of Poseidon and, as we saw, the *Megalai Ehoiai* says Phineus was blinded for giving Phrixos information about how to navigate the route (Hes. fr. 254 MW). Pindar's reference to the Argo putting an end to the movement of the rocks once it has passed through (*Py.* 4. 210-11) is also unique to his own account. The Argo appears to have had many supporters in contrast to other travellers, as we have seen the way in which Odysseus is plagued by Poseidon in the Odyssey, and how Phrixos' flight to Iolkos obviously upset Poseidon (Hes. fr. 254 MW).

Later, Apollonios describes Athena's intervention to assist the Argo through the rocks. With her left hand she supposedly pushed back one of the rocks, and with her right she guided the ship through the pass (AR 2.598ff.).

We have two other literary references to the rocks from the fifth century B.C., one from Herodotus and the other from Euripides. Herodotus describes Darius' march from Susa to Chalcedon where he sailed to see the rocks which

> ...according to Greek story used to be constantly changing their position. (*Hist.* 4.85).

For the first time we are given an indication of the geographical location of the rocks, something absent from all previous evidence. Herodotus uses the term 'kyaneai' (dark blue) and said that earlier the Greeks called them 'planktai' (as used in the *Odyssey*).

In Euripides' *Medea* the rocks are called the Symplegades for the first time (*Med.* 1-2) but the word 'kyaneai' is also used. Overall then the rocks are given four possible names: planktai (*Od.* 12.69), synormades (Simonides 546 PMG), symplegades (Eur. *Med.* 1-2), and kyaneai (Her. 4.85; Eur. *Med.* 1-2).

In Apollodoros it is said that the Argonauts send a dove through the rocks, and if it passes safely this will be a sign that they are to be allowed to continue through. The dove makes it through with only its tail feathers being clipped. Apollonios also includes this version of the tale, and names the Argonaut Euphemos as the person who released the dove from the bow of the ship (AR 2.561). However, our early extant sources don't deal with this episode in detail. The *Odyssey*, however, does mention doves:

> ...the Planctae the blessed gods call these. By that
> way not even winged creatures pass, not even the
> timorous doves that bear ambrosia to father Zeus,
> but the smooth rock always snatches away one
> even of these... (*Od.* 12. 61-3).

It is likely that this tale from the *Odyssey* is taken from an early *Argonautika*, and combined with the later versions from Apollonios and Apollodoros, this may point to the episode being part of the early myth.

There is no visual evidence for this part of the myth, and this is not altogether surprising. This type of scene would be difficult to capture, and even later Greek and Roman art fails to record any such depictions. The scale of a scene of the Clashing Rocks may not be a subject which was suitable for early art, and may be a better subject for epic poetry than for vase painting or sculpture.

Others

There are only two other incidents which occur before Kolchis and remain in literary evidence up to 400 B.C. One is the meeting with a woman called Sinope, mentioned in a fragment from Eumelos (Eum. fr. 10 PEG). She is said to be the daughter of Asopos and we only find out later in Apollonios that she won the promise of perpetual virginity from Zeus (AR 2.946-54). The other is that the Argonauts are attacked by a flock of birds. According to a fragment of Euripides' *Phrixos* (fr. 838 N^2)[84] their feathers could be used as arrows. Later, Apollonios expands this tale and says the birds had wings made of iron (AR. 2.1033ff.).

Both of these are single references and are not described in any detail in our early sources. These types of encounters fill out the journey and even if we had the full text of these episodes, they may not have contained much more detail. Even Apollonios only mentions that the Argo stops at the Assyrian shore and meets Sinope, and, having described her background and her relationships to Zeus and Apollo, there is no more information about her character or the encounter with the crew (AR 2.946-54). The story moves on to its next encounter.

Karl Schefold points to the Argonautic voyage, the Kalydonian Boar Hunt and and the story of the Seven Against Thebes as examples of myths which emerge in illustrations from about 600 B.C., and says that:

> the impulse for their creation must have been a new treatment of the material in epic poetry...though some of the legends had certainly been circulating much earlier in oral form (1992, p. 183).

---

[84] A. Nauck, *Tragicorum Graecorum Fragmenta* (Leipzeig, 1889).

Despite the fact that neither of these episodes provide detailed descriptions of Jason, they point to widespread knowledge of the myth amongst early sources.

3

Jason and the Golden Fleece

This chapter will focus on the main events that occur once Jason arrives at Kolchis. These are the events that take place in and around the palace of Aietes, including the task of yoking the fire-breathing bulls set by Aietes for Jason, the forging of a bond between Medea and Jason, the confrontation between Jason and the serpent that guards the golden fleece, and the flight from Kolchis with the fleece.[85]

The appeal of scenes concerning the fleece is quite logical, with a classic confrontation between hero and serpent in an age of heroes journeying to the edges of the known world. We see similar depictions of Perseus and Medousa, Theseus and the Minotaur, or Herakles and Kerberos in the Underworld. This section of the Jason myth will also pose a number of questions, not least of which raises question of the value of iconographical evidence as against literary sources.

The Arrival at Kolchis and the Fire-breathing bulls

There are two key episodes involving Jason at Kolchis. The first is the challenge set down by Aietes, a struggle to yoke fire-breathing bulls, with the golden fleece as the reward. The second is Jason's winning of the fleece from under the serpent's protection.

The Argo's arrival at Kolchis is not recorded in any literature up to 400 B.C. Pindar's description in *Pythian 4* moves straight from the voyage of the ship to Jason's charming of Medea and does not give us any detail of Aietes' reaction when the Argonauts arrived. Instead Pindar moves directly to his telling of the episode of the fire breathing bulls (*Py.* 4.211ff.). However, in iconography, Fig. 22 is a bell krater showing the stern of the Argo with three Argonauts to the left and Aietes seated on a

---

[85] See Appendix 2.

throne to the right. Medea stands behind the king. One of the Argonauts is likely to be Jason. This vase is the only extant representation of Aietes up to 400 B.C. (see discussion of Fig. 17 below), and the only depiction of the arrival of the Argonauts at Kolchis.

The earliest extant literary evidence for the bulls comes from *Pythian* 4. Here Pindar says that Aietes yoked two fire-breathing, brazen hoofed bulls and ploughed a field, after which he challenged Jason to repeat this feat (*Py.* 4:220-42). Aietes requires a successful completion of this challenge before granting permission to Jason to pursue his real goal - the golden fleece. Aietes, as brother of Kirke, appears to possess the same herb-mixing skills as his sister and his daughter. He doesn't need to ask Medea for assistance to make a potion to protect himself from the bulls and their fiery breath, as he presumably makes his own.

Aphrodite intervenes on Jason's behalf, imparting to him skill with 'prayers and charms, so that he might take away Medea's respect for her parents...' (*Py.* 4.218-20). As a result, Medea prepares oils to protect him against the fire breathed from the mouths of the bulls. Her potion may have allowed Jason to get close enough to place the harness on the animals without being burnt.

Pindar says 'the powerful man accomplished the appointed measure of toil' (*Py.* 4.237-38); and Jason proves his skill to Aietes. This task is of equal measure to Herakles' and Bellerophontes' equivalent challenges. This is a test of his physical might and as with many of the challenges that Jason faces, it it a task which he is not expected to be able to pass through. Afterwards, Pindar says;

> Aietes cried out, although in inarticulate pain, astonished at the power he beheld. But his comrades were stretching forth their hands to the mighty man, covering him with crowns of leaves, and greeting him with words of kindness. (*Py.* 4.237-41).

The help Jason receives in this story is similar to help received by other heroes of myth. Aphrodite's assistance to Jason in luring Medea away from her loyalty to her parents,[86] offers similarities to Theseus' relationship to Ariadne and King Minos, with the local princess contributing to his success.

Medea's undoubted skill in herbs is of equal measure to Ariadne's knowledge of the labyrinth, and the way in which Theseus uses it to his advantage.   On both occasions a local princess intervenes to assist the hero to overcome obstacles.   Pherekydes relates that Ariadne had got a ball of thread from Daidalos and advises Theseus to tie it to the door and unravel the ball as he moved to the centre of the labyrinth.[87]   In the case of Odysseus, it could also be argued that Kirke fulfils this role of female assistant.   Kirke, Medea's aunt, guides Odysseus and his men on how to proceed on their journey home.   If the Odyssey does borrow from the Argonautika of the eighth century B.C. we can see how the character of Kirke may be based on the tale of Medea and the Argonauts.   In the Odyssey, Kirke transforms the men back to humans from pigs and they are described as 'younger than they were before' (Od. 10395-6).   Kirke's ability to transform them may also echo through to Medea's rejuvenation of Jason, a skill that I will focus on later in this book.

Pindar concludes his version of the story of the bulls somewhat abruptly at this point;
> But it is too far for me to travel on this highway,
> because the hour is pressing and I know a short
> path... (Py. 4.247-9).

---

[86] Gantz describes Medea as more of a 'victim' of Jason and the Argonauts as she loses her parents to follow him (p. 359).

[87] Pherekydes, fr. 148.

However, according to the scholia to Apollonios, Eumelos in the *Korinthiaka* related the sowing of dragon's teeth in the course of the ploughing;

> But now the earth born ones were springing up all over the plough land; the murderous War god's acre bristled with stout shields and two-edged spears and shining helmets (Eum. fr. 21 West; Eum. fr. 19 PEG).

We also have an account of this from Pherekydes. Kadmos, the Greek hero who had founded the city of Thebes, had killed a dragon, the son of Ares. Pherekydes says that Athena and Ares took teeth from the dragon and some of these were handed to Kadmos himself and some to king Aietes (Pher. 3F22). Later tradition agrees with Eumelos that if these teeth were sown into the earth warriors would grow out of the ground (ApB. 3.4.1). A fragment from Sophokles' *Kolchides* also mentions the warriors coming out of the ground;

> [Aietes] 'Did not the brood native to the land start up?' [Messenger] 'Indeed it did! They bristled with plumed helmets as with arms of bronze they came up out of their mother.'(fr. 341 R).[88]

Although this particular story does not appear in art, there are other examples of characters being born from the ground, and Erichthonios, the son of Hephaistos, is the most obvious example of this. A vase by the Oinanthe Painter[89] shows his birth as he is handed to Athena by Gaia. Gaia is painted from the waist up, showing that she has emerged from the earth to deliver the child. A similar scene appears on a stamnos by the Painter of Munich 2413,[90] where again the child is handed over by Gaia, thus linking the child to his birth from the ground. The variation

---

[88] Trans. Lloyd-Jones, p.189.

[89] Boardman (1988) fig. 329, dated tp 460-450 B.C.

[90] Ibid. fig. 350.1, dated to the second half of fifth century B.C.

in the Argonautic myth is that the characters emerge from the earth unassisted and their appearance is as the result of some magical phenomenon rather than through their creation by the gods, or delivery by Gaia.

Later Apollonios says that Jason and Aietes plough the field at the same time in direct competition. Pindar is the only early source to say that Aietes ploughed the field first, with Jason following. Given the speed with which Pindar moves through the myth, it makes sense that he omitted the teeth and the warriors.[91] As we have seen, he also omits the tale of Phineus and the account of the visit to the island of Lemnos on the way to Kolchis. The focus for Pindar is Jason's impressive showing in front of Aietes and his crew, and the winning of the fleece. Pindar's version, it could be argued, contains a more exciting finish to the competition. Aietes sets the mark by yoking the bulls and ploughing the field and he asks Jason to match this. The young hero succeeds to the astonishment of the crowd and the climax of the scene is the surprise of Aietes and the delight of Jason's crew.

The story of the earth-born warriors appears to be an early part of the myth. Its inclusion in the *Korinthiaka*, followed by the reference by Pherekydes and Sophokles in his *Kolchides*, all point to a well known part of the myth. It may also be assisted by the fact that this motif is more wide spread than just the Jason myth, the earth born warriors also forming part of the story of Kadmos[92] .

---

[91] In relation to the myth of Orestes in Pindar, March points to the way in which the poet 'passes over these aspects of the myth so swiftly and concisely that it is clear that this is already familiar ground for his audience.' (March, p. 92). This is certainly also true for the myth of Jason as Pindar appears to be selecting points in the myth on which he wants to focus, knowing that his audience are capable of filling in the gaps.

[92] The first literary reference to Kadmos and the earth born warriors is Pherekydes (3F22).

Although Gantz states that there is no visual evidence for the episode of Jason and the bulls, there is one possible piece that Jenifer Neils includes in her LIMC catalogue [Fig. 20]. A drachma from Larissa dated to 440 B.C. shows a youth grappling with some bulls. According to Neils a bull-wrestler on Thessalian coins is more usually identified as Thessalos,[93] but Moustaka argues that this is in fact Jason.[94] Moustaka believes that Jason, as the local Larissan hero, is more likely in the particular area.[95]

The reason that depictions of Jason and the bulls are so rare may lie in the fact that this is one of two major confrontations for Jason to face at Kolchis. Of the two, the struggle with the serpent which guards the fleece may have been a more attractive option for artists, given that it is the climax of Jason's quest. In the case of Bellerophontes and his challenges in Lykia, the hero faces three tasks. However the confrontation with the Chimaira is by far the more favoured by artists. The battles with the Amazons and the warrior Solymoi are not the subject of visual art and we can see how a vase-painter or sculptor selected the more interesting of the three as the Chimaira, with its fantastical and fearsome appearance, offered a more intriguing image. Similarly, with the Argonautic myth, the seizing of the fleece may have been a more appealing subject for the visual artist.

The Golden Fleece

The serpent guarding the golden fleece is presumably there to protect it from being stolen by unwanted visitors, such as Jason and the Argonauts. Phrixos, with his sister Helle, rode the golden ram from

---

[93] Neils, LIMC "Iason" p. 631. Thessalos was the son of Herakles and Chalkiope and his sons fought at Troy (Pher. fr. 78). Later, it was said that his son Antiphos settled in northern Greece and having taken possession of the region, he named it Thessaly (Apollodoros, *Epitome* 6.15).

[94] Moustaka, pp. 74-76.

[95] Ibid, p. 69-70.

Boeotia in Greece towards Kolchis in Aia, on the eastern edge of the Black Sea. As we saw in Chapter 2, along the way he received the advice of Phineus on the correct route, advice for which Phineus paid the price of his sight (Hes. fr. 254 MW). Helle didn't complete the journey as she fell from the ram, over the stretch of water that was to become known as the Hellespont. When Phrixos reached Kolchis he sacrificed the ram, and ' holding the fleece he walked into the halls of Aietes' (*Aegimius*: Hes. fr. 299 MW). It was presumably because of this gift that Aietes welcomed his guest so enthusiastically. Phrixos was said to have married Aietes' daughter, Iophossa (Hes. fr. 255 MW).

According to Pindar, Jason's journey arose out of a dream that Pelias had, where Phrixos appeared to Pelias and requested that the fleece be brought back to Greece (*Py*. 4.159-162). But Jason's appearance in Aietes' city is in stark contrast to the more hospitably received visit by Phrixos. Jason has come to take away the prize that was once donated by Phrixos.

Following on from Jason's encounter with fire-breathing bulls, Pindar says that Aietes told him to go ahead to where the fleece lay in the hope that he would be killed attempting to remove it from its resting place. He says;

> [Aietes] did not expect him to perform that further
> trial because it lay in a thicket and was right by the
> ferocious jaws of a serpent which exceeded in
> breadth and length a ship of fifty oars.... (*Py*.
> 4.242 45).

The image that Pindar conjures up is quite intimidating. The size of this serpent, and the threat it posed is certainly on a par with Theseus' confrontation with the Minotaur, or Perseus' task to behead Medousa. Pindar's portrayal of the serpent is on a far larger scale than we will see in iconography, and is closer to that of the image conjured up in depictions of   Perseus against the Ketos (sea-monster) [Fig. 100].[96] This vase shows Perseus holding a sickle sword, a weapon commonly shown with this hero in vase-paining.   An early example is a seventh century Korinthian vase [Fig. 99], where Perseus, supported by Andromeda, attacks by hurling objects at the Ketos. This type of scene seems closer to what Pindar had in mind for Jason in *Pythian 4*.

Pindar does not give the detail as to how Jason defeats the serpent and wins the fleece, instead simply saying that he killed it by using skills and devices (*Py*. 4.249). Pherekydes also says that Jason kills the serpent (Pher. fr. 31). No literary source suggests that he simply steals the fleece from beneath the creature and flees, in contrast to the depiction on the New York krater as discussed below. The slaying of the serpent is a significant part of the action, just as the killing of Medousa,[97] or the slaying of the Minotaur is in the myths of Perseus and Theseus. It is an element of the story which is used to demonstrate the strength of the hero and is the culmination of the expedition.[98]

The two earliest examples of this scene in art come from the late seventh century B.C., and both are from Korinth [Figs. 10 and 11]. The first is a black figure alabastron and it shows a long coiled serpent with a man held in its mouth. The creature has the man's lower torso and legs in its jaws, and his head and arms dangle free. We must be careful not to assume a direct correlation between the size and shape of this creature on the vase, and the type of serpent described in literature of the age. This serpent is different to the one described later in the fifth

---

[96] The identification of Perseus is somewhat uncertain here. The hero in the scene has also been identified as Herakles. Either way, the size of the creature seems to be similar to the type of creature described in *Pythian 4*.

[97] Medusa is the only mortal amongst the three Gorgons.

[98] Later sources differ on whether the serpent was killed: Herodoros says that Jason killed it (fr. 32). Apollodoros says that Medea drugged the serpent and assisted Jason in taking the fleece to the Argo (ApB 1.9.23). Apollonios says that Medea intends to drug the serpent and take off with the fleece (4.85).

century by Pindar, as it has a far more slender, snake-like appearance. However the effect is the same; Jason is confronted with a powerful adversary, and the creature takes the upper hand on the hero for at least part of the struggle.   It may be that Jason is almost devoured by the creature, only to win back the advantage.[99]

Our second example of Jason and the serpent is a similar depiction, this time from an aryballos fragment found at Heraion at Samos [Fig. 11]. Again Jason is emerging from the mouth of the serpent, but as Carpenter points out about Fig. 10, we have no source who can shed light on how Jason got into this position.[100] Another example from 600 B.C. shows a large serpent with a man's head in its mouth [Fig. 12]. This comes from a black figure lekythos and although it may be a representation of Jason, the position of the hero would be unusual, as assuming it is our hero, it is the only example of him with his head in the serpent's mouth, rather than the lower portion of his body. More usually Jason has a leg, two legs, or the whole of his lower body in its mouth. Vojatzi refuses to identify the man in this particular painting as Jason due to the sheer size of the serpent's neck.[101] It is normally thought that a depiction of a larger creature is a representation of Herakles' battle with

---

[99] Although from a later source, this story of the protagonist losing control and having to regain the upper hand is similar to the tale of Zeus and Typhoeus (better known as Typhon; also called Typhos). This giant battles with Zeus and, according to Apollodoros, removes the gods' sinews from his hands and feet and hides them in a cave. Zeus is only rescued when Hermes and Pan steal the sinews and place them back into Zeus without Typhoeus noticing. Although Zeus is immortal, the idea of a dramatic reversal of fortune is the same (ApB 1.6.3). Pindar also mentions this tale and describes Typhoeus as 'enemy of the gods' (*Py* 1.15-16; trans. Race).

[100] Carpenter, p. 184.

[101] Vojatzi, p. 89

Triton., as one of the classic examples of hero versus monster.[102] However, in the case of Jason, whereas it may be correct to note that iconography generally depicts to a more snake-like appearance for the monster, Pindar's account does show that the creature may have been larger and more fearsome.

Identification of Jason on these vases may be in question if we were to take them in isolation. However, they can be identified as Jason, due to the circumstances and setting of the scene, and due to the fact that the figure depicted   fits with later iconography and what we know of this myth. The sixth century changes this, as a south-Italian bronze hand mirror, dated to between 575 to 550 B.C. shows Jason grappling with the serpent, and on this occasion he is named [Fig. 13]. Jason holds the fleece in his left hand, and a sword in his right, while the serpent, with a strong snake-like appearance, has the hero's left leg in its mouth. In proportion to the rest of the scene, the serpent is a long coiled animal.   Comparing this to the other representation from the seventh century, we see Jason in a strong position, appearing to be ready to strike the serpent with his sword, and firmly holding the prize of the fleece in his left hand. There is far more of a narrative being displayed in this representation than in our previous vases, as   until now the fleece hasn't been depicted.   On this mirror, Jason appears to be in more control of the situation.   However it may also be unfair to directly compare this scene to the first example [Fig 10], as the alabastron may be more symbolic of the motif of hero versus the creature, and the detail of the story, such the fleece, may not have been thought necessary. We can see a progression in the way this story is displayed as the alabastron [Fig. 10] may be considered more of a motif representing the story of Jason and the serpent, whereas the later bronze mirror [Fig. 13] deals

---

[102] One example of this is a black figure neck amphora, dated to 530 B.C. which shows Herakles wrestling with Triton (Schefold, 1992, fig. 166). Usually in these scenes Herakles is gripping the creature by the neck and there is not a suggestion that Herakles is swallowed. In fact the hero wrestles with Triton trying to extract information from him about his further journey.

with the detail and the substance of his attempt to take the fleece from the serpent.

A similar scene is shown on an Etruscan bronze handle dated to the first quarter of the fifth century B.C. [Fig 15]. Again, Jason holds the fleece in his hand, while the snake holds the hero's left leg in its mouth. It is a very similar scene to the hand mirror [Fig. 13], with both examples showing Jason with one leg being held in the mouth of the serpent, and grasping the fleece in one hand. One uncertain representation is discussed by Meyer, who argues that a limestone metope dated to 550 B.C. shows Jason and the creature [Fig. 14]. This relief is one of a pair, which Meyer interprets as showing Jason. The first, to be discussed in Chapter 4, shows Jason or Pelias in a cauldron. The second metope, according to Meyer, is of Jason and the creature, although the condition of this metope makes identification extremely difficult.

The theme of Jason being swallowed is discussed by Mackie, who looks at the meaning held in these scenes, suggesting that Jason's descent into the body of the creature is similar to the descent of Theseus and Herakles into the underworld, or Odysseus' journey into the cave of Polyphemos.[103] He sees this as a 'process of personal and social benefit brought about by virtue of the successful accomplishment of the hero's quest.'[104] This may very well be true, as Mackie continues to develop this point by connecting it to the power of healing and the necessity for the hero to restore harmony in the upper and lower worlds.[105] From the evidence we saw surrounding Jason and Phineus, and the likely healing powers demonstrated in iconography, healing is certainly a gift of Jason's and it is true that the purpose of the voyage is to right a perceived wrong committed by Pelias in Iolkos. I would not go

---

[103] Mackie p. 12

[104] Ibid. p. 12.

[105] Ibid. p. 13ff

so far as to join Mackie in his analysis of the hero quest however. He suggests that the journey into the serpent by Jason (which he also aligns to the Jonah story)[106] , is similar to Priam's retrieval of the body of Hektor in *Iliad* 24. Whereas the symbol of descent and re-emergence may have credibility, especially in the myths of Herakles and Theseus, the Jason myth does not seem to fit. For me there is no tangible aim in entering the bowels of this creature. What would Jason be achieving if he was swallowed and then spat out again? Mackie may be suggesting that there is some sub-conscious need by the hero to complete this process, but for Theseus and Herakles the journey to the Underworld is a very real and conscious decision, with a real and tangible outcome. In the case of Herakles for example, the journey is to capture Kerberos on the orders of his cousin Eurystheus (*Il.* 8.367-8 & *Od.* 11.623-26). However, more importantly, Jason does not appear to be swallowed, at least not completely, by the serpent. His legs are held in the serpent's mouth, and possibly his head in one scene, but Jason does not necessarily descend into the serpent's belly and re-emerge, as Mackie believes when he compares Jason to Jonah[107] .

This brings us to what is probably the best known example of Jason in iconography. Dated to 480-470 B.C. we have a red figure kylix cup by the Douris painter showing Jason, the serpent, Athena and the fleece [Fig. 16]. The scene is set in an orchard where the fleece resides, and to the back left of the scene we can see the golden fleece hanging on the bough of one of the apple trees. To the right is the serpent, a scaled and wide-bodied monster, holding Jason in its mouth. It has quite ferocious razor sharp teeth, and its head shows a large number of folds of skin. Athena stands to the right and fills the centre of the scene. She wears a helmet, an aegis (with the head of Medousa on it), holds an owl in her left hand, and leans on the spear in her right hand. Appropriate to the shape of the vase and of the space available to the

---

[106] As does Neils (1994; p. 192).

[107] Mackie, p. 12.

artist, Athena leans forward and looks down towards the serpent and hero. There is no doubting her command over the scene. Her spear stands inserted into the ground as a vertical dividing point between the two halves of the painting.

Jason, named on the vase, is held by the creature in its mouth, with both his legs ingested. We can see that from below his hip is held in the serpent's mouth, and his head faces the ground with his arms outstretched, his finger tips pointing to the earth. An initial glance might lead us to conclude that he is dead. One hypothesis could be that he has been killed by the creature and it is about to drop his body onto the ground, possibly at the command of Athena. She may demand that the serpent release the hero for burial. Meyer believes this, saying that Jason is killed and Athena is conjuring the body out of its mouth.[108]

The flaw in this interpretation lies in the eyes of the hero. Looking closely at Jason, we see that his eyes are open, and that the artist is depicting the hero as still alive. Another vase by the Douris painter demonstrates this [Fig. 37]. It is an Attic red figure cup from a similar date of 480 B.C., and shows Eos with her son, Memnon, after he dies in battle at Troy.[109] Here we can clearly see that Memnon's eyes are drawn as a fine line, indicating death. Also, Memnon's fingers are stretched out and straight, as his body is shown to have lost all movement. The digits of his hand hang lifelessly, whereas on the kylix [Fig. 16], Jason's hands, especially the right hand, show his fingers are curled. Poor Jason may be exhausted from his struggle, but he is not dead.[110]

---

[108] Meyer, p. 81

[109] For reference in literature to the death of Memnon, see *Nem.* 6.50-53 (also *Ol.* 2.81-83, *Nem.* 3.63).

[110] Another use of the single line to depict the eye is found in portrayals of blindness. As we saw earlier, Phineus' blindness is depicted this way [Fig. 52] and the Graiai in the myth of Perseus are also drawn with a single line for their eye [Fig. 101].

Indeed the eyes in this vase play a vital role. Athena looks into the eyes of the serpent, and the creature looks back at the goddess. There is no doubt that she is instructing or willing the creature to act in some manner. Surely the serpent intends to swallow Jason until otherwise instructed by Athena. E. Simon believes that Jason was inspired by Athena to cut out the tongue of the serpent so that he couldn't be swallowed.[111] However, there are two questions over this argument. Firstly and most obviously, there is no weapon shown in this scene. It may be that Jason has dropped it through exhaustion, and it is out of view, as a large portion of the serpent is not within the boundaries of the scene. However, vase painting has up to now shown Jason both with and without a sword,[112] and so he may have attempted to wrestle with the serpent here, as suggested by Gantz, and not have brought a sword to this particular conflict.[113] If Jason did have a weapon, the second question is why didn't he kill the creature? Why take the time and effort to disable it, instead of killing it outright? A possibility might be if the orchard and the creature were under the protection of another god, and Jason wishes to inflict minimum damage in a sacred location. However this doesn't seem to be the case and the argument for cutting out the tongue doesn't seem correct.

However this still does not explain the scene satisfactorily. We have seen that both Pindar (*Py.* 4.249) and Pherekydes (Pher. fr. 31) say that Jason killed the serpent, and Fig. 13 clearly shows Jason with a sword. Athena's possible intervention is being made at a vital point in whatever action is being played out. For Jason, he is shown as alive, safe now that Athena appears to control the scene, and portrayed slightly differently to representations that we have seen before. He is shown with a beard on this vase as well as in our next example, the New York

---

[111] Simon, p. 119. Schefold follows the idea that Jason was swallowed, and then regurgitated by the serpent on the command of Athena (1992, p. 193).

[112] Jason with sword - Fig. 13; Jason without a sword, Figs. 10, 12 & 15.

[113] Gantz, p. 359.

krater [Fig. 17]. This may also point towards the earlier representations of this myth.   Neils points out the beard as a trait of early art.[114] Carpenter connects this vase to the alabastron from Korinth [Fig. 10] dated to the end of the seventh century B.C. He says that this shows the antiquity of the subject.[115] However Carpenter also says that no source explains why Athena assists Jason in this scene, rather than Medea. [116] This misses the point, as Athena   is playing her full immortal role, and as we have seen in the *Odyssey* (*Od.* 12.69), Jason and the Argonauts receive the support of the gods on this expedition. Athena's intervention at this point is not *instead* of Medea, as the presence of Medea in this situation would not be appropriate to begin with.   Athena is acting in a manner which is above and beyond the role of assistant to the hero as demonstrated by Medea or Ariadne to Theseus. It is also not surprising that Athena fulfils this role instead of Hera, as this is an Attic vase and is a typical portrayal of Athena assisting a hero. Figure 38 shows another vase by the Douris painter, with Athena standing at the centre, commanding the action of the scene. This depiction is very similar to her portrayal on the kylix: with her clothing, helmet, spear and aegis all corresponding to our other example. Her role in these scenes is that of immortal patron, towering over the other characters and staring intently at the action. Athena on the kylix [Fig. 16], facilitates the passage of the hero on his quest, even if we are unsure of the detail of what Jason was attempting.

Moving on to the aftermath of Jason's success against the serpent, the *Naupaktia* states that one of the Argonauts, Idmon, suggests that they flee the palace after dinner. It appears that Aietes has invited them to eat there after the yoking of the bulls, and possibly after Jason has killed the serpent (i.e. after all tasks are accomplished). According to the *Naupaktia*, Aietes planned to murder the men in their sleep. Instead

---

[114] Neils p. 636

[115] Carpenter p. 185

[116] Ibid.

they flee, and Medea follows, taking the fleece with her (*Nau.* frr. 6,7,8 PEG).

There is some ambiguity about whether the fleece was in the palace all along, since the fragment from the *Naupaktia* does not specifically state that Jason won the fleece or killed the serpent. However, given the iconography that we have seen, there can be no doubt that this was an integral part of the early myth. I believe that the absence of the story of Jason and the serpent from the already scant fragment of the *Naupaktia*, is not an indication of this source omitting this scene, one which must surely have been in the original work. Medea's knowledge of the palace, just like Ariadne's understanding of the labyrinth, is required at this point, so that the hero can complete his task. Jason as leader, leaves with his men for the Argo.

Moses Hadas suggests that the events in the palace surrounding the fleece are somewhat indicative of an altogether more 'puny' and 'helpless' hero.[117] Although he relies heavily on Apollonios, and in my judgement works back from later sources, Hadas discusses the evidence from the *Naupaktia*. Having described Apollonios' Jason as 'feckless' and 'helpless,' Hadas seems to look to earlier sources to seek evidence and back up this view. He points to the fact that Aphrodite assists the Argonauts in the *Naupaktia* by sending Aietes a desire for his wife, so strong that the king immediately leaves the feast and takes her to bed (*Nau.* frr. 6,7,8 PEG). Hadas' view is that '...when vigor or decision is required, Jason is imbecile; his success comes only from the help of women.'[118]   Even though Hadas says that Thetis' help to Achilleus did not discredit this particular hero, Jason's actions are somehow compromised because he receives the assistance of Aphrodite. This is not necessarily a fair reflection, as on many an occasion Herakles, and Achilleus, to name but two, are assisted by

---

[117] Hadas p. 166-7

[118] Ibid. p. 167

Athena.   The intervention of Aphrodite is surely no more than the intervention of Athena on behalf of Odysseus on the island of the Phaecians, when she directs Nausikaa to the shore to assist the hero (*Od.* 6.15ff.).   Hadas concludes his article saying that an 'effeminate' Jason was not the invention of the Hellenistic age, but a 'tradition' from the fifth century B.C.   There is no indication that he is aware of any more than a handful of examples from literature to back this up, and even so, his argument has no solid basis to it.   The argument for an 'effeminate' Jason as seen in the *Argonautika* of Apollonios does not have any basis in the early stories of Jason.

Returning to our visual evidence, we move to one of the most controversial vases connected to Jason.   A red figure Attic column krater [Fig. 17] dated to 470-460 B.C. and painted by the Orchard Painter shows Jason stealing the fleece from under the serpent with Athena again taking a prominent role.   On the left, the serpent is coiled around the rock, and the fleece rests just below it.

At the centre of the scene stands Athena.   She is the tallest figure, and is portrayed in a similar way to the Athena by the Douris painter [Figs. 16 & 38], with helmet, aegis, head of Medousa and resting on spear.   She forms the dividing line between the action to her left, and the escape route to her right.   On the right stands a man, with his left arm resting on a ship.   The ship can be certainly identified as the Argo due to the carved head at the stern.   Earlier when we looked at the construction of the Argo, we saw that Aischylos and Pherekydes (Aischylos frr. 20, 20a R; Pher. fr. 111) say Athena gave the Argo a speaking timber, and so the head on the New York krater appears to be used as a symbolic representation of this. Also, Athena stands looking towards the left of the scene, but her feet are pointing to the right.   She appears to be overseeing the action to the left, and encouraging movement to the right.

On the left, between the serpent and Athena, stands Jason. He has his right foot placed on the bottom of a rock, and he has grabbed the fleece with his right hand.   He is looking at the serpent as he gestures to pull the fleece from its resting place. His actions appear to be bold, but cautious. He is seizing the fleece, but staring intently at the snake, watching for movement, ready to snatch the fleece away by pulling with his right hand, and pushing away with his right foot. His left hand is trailing towards Athena at the centre of the scene, and this indicates that he is ready to move in this direction.

This confrontation is a very different one to the scenes we have had so far with Jason and the serpent. The serpent is snake-like, with a very thin shape. The challenge here is one of agility and timing, and not of strength or brute force, and Jason's approach is far more considered.

While a struggle and a submerging of Jason's leg(s) into the serpent as a next step can't be ruled out, it may be that the next move is for the snake to attack and for a scene similar to ones we saw earlier [for example Figs. 10, 11 & 13] to follow. There is a certain tension in this scene, as Jason's eyes are fixed on the creature. However the painting on this vase is of a very poor quality. The vase is of a very poor shape, with its rim being rough and almost corrugated around its circumference. The Orchard Painter's portrayal of Jason is also poor, but so is his portrayal of the other figures on the vase. Richter describes the Orchard Painter as 'not an artist of the first rank,' with a 'somewhat hasty style.'[119] She says Jason fetching the fleece 'is a rare subject in vase painting,' with 'most extant representations [being] on south-Italian and Roman sarcophagi.'[120] While she is right about her first point, that there are only two Athenian examples from the fifth century, the Douris kylix and the New York krater, her contention that the scene is rare seems to ignore the presence of the examples we have looked at so far [Figs 10 - 16]. Although the fleece is not always depicted in scenes of Jason and the

---

[119] Richter (1936), p. 117.

[120] Ibid. p. 118.

serpent, there can be little doubt that when Jason is grappling with the serpent the purpose is to seize the fleece. There is no example of Jason fighting a monster outside the part of the story of the winning of the fleece.

Returning to Jason and the New York krater, both Richter and Hadas point to Jason being portrayed as puny.[121]   But Hadas departs from Richter on the meaning behind this portrayal, and as noted before, he sees this as a trend dating from early art through to the *Argonautika* of Apollonios Rhodios.[122]   Richter chooses to see this representation of Jason as a 'rather rare product in Greek art - an individualised human being.'[123] and certainly the depiction of Jason is far more specific than in earlier examples. However the portrayal is simply a poor painting by an artist that has a tendency to paint in this sketchy and inelegant way. Richter's earlier point about the hasty style of the Orchard Painter, may actually seem to be more valid in this instance. Saying that this is then somehow used to the artist's advantage as he draws Jason in an individualistic way, seems to be less likely. I don't believe that the painting can be both a very poor representation and at the same time a highly individualised portrayal, as this gives the artist too much credit for a rather sub-standard piece. What is apparent is that the intention of the Orchard Painter was to show Jason as cautious but brave, and possibly to point to the hero in a manner that made him a smaller figure than the goddess he was standing next to.

One more recent commentator also follows the type of argument proposed by Hadas for this vase. H. A. Shapiro says that Jason relies on the female figures around him,[124] drawing the same conclusion as Hadas. Again there is little evidence to support this, or to

---

[121] Richter (1936) p. 118; Hadas p. 116.

[122] Hadas p. 166 ff.

[123] Richter (1936) p. 119.

[124] Shapiro, p. 97.

attempt to separate the type of help female goddesses give to other heroes in similar heroic roles.

Moving to the figure standing on the right hand side of the scene, Shapiro points out that the ship appears as one of the main protagonists in the myth,[125] and he goes on to say that it must be Aietes standing to the left of the stern, draped in a himation.[126]   Whereas Shapiro's point about the Argo appears valid, the suggestion that this is the king of Kolchis is made for the wrong reason. He says that it 'must be Aietes'[127] as he is portrayed as a villain and Jason is portrayed as a hero.   However the figure to the right of the scene does not in fact appear to be threatening. Looking at Athena and this man, both have their feet turned towards the Argo, and there is a sense of movement in the painting showing that Jason is about to snatch the fleece from under the serpent and flee to the right with the two other figures. Both Athena and the male figure are gesturing towards the ship, and this man does not appear to be blocking or interfering in Jason's escape route.

Richter and Beazley both say that this man is Aietes. Richter says that the 'voluminous himation favours this interpretation' but continues on to say that 'the fact that man has his hand on the ship would seem to suggest a close association with it.'[128]   For this latter reason, and due to the stance of the figure, I believe that Aietes can be ruled out. The stature of this second male figure is also significant. He is the same height as Athena, and the two are significantly larger in size to Jason. This character is more likely to be a god than a mortal, and it is

---

[125] Ibid. p. 97. He also says that all sources agree that the fleece was deep in the wood, a statement that has no basis when we look at the early literary and visual evidence. To the contrary, the scene on the Douris kylix shows the fleece hanging in an orchard and we might draw the conclusion that this orchard is part of Aietes palace in Kolchis, and not deep in the woodland.

[126] Ibid. p. 98.

[127] Ibid.

[128] Richter (1936), p. 118 n.1.

for this reason that I also doubt the other possible interpretation of this character being an Argonaut.

In 1935, a year before her guide to the vases in the MMA,[129] Richter suggested that the third person on this vase was either Aietes (as in her 1936 publication) or an Argonaut.[130] Indeed her 1935 publication points to Aietes and an Argonaut and spends much time explaining why an Argonaut is the more likely candidate.[131] The 1936 publication says Aietes, but follows this by saying that this is Beazley's suggestion, and it could be an Argonaut, as there seems to be a close association between the figure and the ship. She also says that it may be an Argonaut forming part of the chorus, and therefore pointing to a possible association between the vase and Greek drama.[132]

One compelling point from Richter here concerns this close proximity of the man and the ship. Looking closely at the stern, the figure has his left hand placed on the edge of the Argo, and on the top of the rudder. If we were to look to the literary sources for evidence of another prominent figure on the voyage who might be connected to the taking of the fleece from Kolchis, we could suggest Idmon as a possibility. The *Naupaktia* and Pherekydes name the seer Idmon as part of the crew (*Nau.* fr. 5-8 PEG: Pher. fr. 108), and as we saw earlier, in the *Naupaktia*, it was Idmon who suggested that the Argonauts flee the palace of Aietes. However if it was Idmon on this vase, this wouldn't explain why he is of such a stature compared to Jason. Indeed if it was Idmon, this would add to Hadas' argument of Jason's puniness and feeble standing.

---

[129] Richter, G.M.A. & Hall, Lindsey F., *The Metropolitan Museum of Art: Red Figure Athenian Vases* (1936) Oxford.

[130] Richter (1935), p. 182.

[131] Ibid. pp. 182-4

[132] Richter (1936), p. 118.

Instead, Cynthia King seems to be closer to the mark. Rather than Aietes or an Argonaut, she points to Zeus as a candidate for the identity of this figure. King points to the direction of both Athena and this third character, and to the height difference between this man and Jason.[133] I believe that there is little doubt that this figure is an immortal. King suggests that this may be Zeus because of his connection to the head at the stern of the ship. She says that 'the god's gesture should be interpreted as protectiveness for his own tree.'[134] If we take it that the stern is made of the speaking oak of Dodona, then this does make a compelling argument. However Apollonios is the first literary source to suggest that the speaking beam came from Zeus' sacred grove at Dodona (AR 1.524-7).[135] There is no extant evidence, literary or visual, before 400 B.C. to suggest that the beam on the Argo was linked to Zeus. The only surviving fragment from Aischylos' *Argo* is a line saying 'where is the sacred speaking timber of the Argo' (fr. 8). This doesn't mention Dodona, and yet Hammond and Moon assume that this must be the case.[136]

The voyage has a number of patrons as we have seen. Given that in early and late sources the only male god to support the voyage is Zeus, we should conclude that King's suggestion is correct. Hera, Aphrodite, and of course Athena have already appeared, and so the inclusion of Zeus would not be entirely surprising. The portrayal also fits into images of Zeus from this period,[137]

The New York krater has been closely connected with another vase which is also believed to be by the Orchard Painter. The

---

[133] King, p. 386.

[134] Ibid, pp. 386-7.

[135] Also Apollodoros ApB 1.9.16.

[136] Hammond and Moon p. 377.

[137] For example, Boardman, (1988), fig. 55.1, Boardman, (1995) fig. 46, both of which show Zeus with dark hair and a beard.

Bologna vase [Fig 18] is also dated to 470-460 B.C. and shows a similar scene. As with the New York krater, the serpent and the fleece rest on the rock to the left, Jason approaches with his right leg on the base of the rock, and takes a similar stance. On this occasion Athena is not present, nor is the Argo, but instead Dionysos stands behind (identifiable by his thyrsus), and gestures in much the same way as Athena did on the New York krater. Richter sees this as being inspired by a 'satyric take-off' in an Aischylean drama about the Argonauts.[138] Rademacher, followed by Meyer, goes one step further and believes that both vases are in fact a parody.[139]

The suggestion that the Bologna vase is a parody seems to be well founded. Richter points to a number of vases representing satyrs in the same position of well known heroes.[140] However the idea that the New York krater is also an example of a parody is suggested by Shapiro. He echoes the views of Rademacher and Meyer, and points to the serpent, saying that;

> the snake has wound itself several times around this boulder, giving it a tremendous length, but hardly the girth that Pindar would have us believe: but then Jason is strangely emaciated as well, leading some commentators to wonder if the scene was meant to be taken altogether seriously.[141]

Certainly I would agree with Richter. The snake is not, as Shapiro says, anything like the creature said to be the size of a fifty-oared ship in Pindar (*Py.* 4.242-45), but again the quality of the depiction on this vase is quite poor. The size of the snake, the thinness of Jason, the narrow stern of the ship, all seem to reflect a style of the artist in question.

---

[138] Richter p. 184.

[139] Meyer 82 no. III, Va 2 pl. 18,2: Rademacher p. 189 fig. 9.

[140] Richter p. 184.

[141] Shapiro, p. 97.

Richter called the painting hasty, and we are in danger of over-interpreting what may simply be a poor vase painting.

Our next image returns to what is a strong theme in the portrayal of Jason. It is an Etruscan sardonyx scarab dated to 470-450 B.C. [Fig. 19] and, like the south Italian bronze hand mirror possibly dated to a century earlier [Fig. 13], it shows Jason grappling with the serpent, with his lower body in its mouth. The serpent is no wider than Jason and this again points to its varied size in portrayals. Jason has his right arm raised and holds a sword in this hand. In his left hand he holds a shield, and he is wearing a helmet. This is in fact the most heavily equipped image of the early Jason. His representation is very clear: a man emerging from mouth of serpent, holding weapon and possibly fleece, and matching many of the scenes we have already seen.

In conclusion to this section on Jason and the fleece, there is one final vase from the end of the fifth century, and the differences in portrayals at this point are significant. This is an Apulian volute-krater dated to 425-400 B.C. and to the right of the scene it shows Jason confronting the serpent, with Medea standing behind him [Fig. 21]. To the left are the Argonauts, including the Boreadai. Medea's role here appears to replace the position that Athena filled in earlier examples. Medea stands at the centre of the scene supporting the hero and holds a box in her raised left hand. This is the first example of Medea helping Jason to seize the fleece, and the only extant example before 400 B.C. In literature, although she has appeared in the story before now, she has not had a role in this part of the myth. As we saw earlier, Pindar shows Medea mixing oils that Jason then uses to anoint himself before he takes part in the yoking of the bulls (*Py.* 4.220-42). The only connection between Medea and the fleece was the reference to her fleeing from the palace and taking it with her (*Nau.* fr. 6,7 & 8 PEG). Medea also now has a symbol that makes her recognisable - the box which presumably contains potions, oils and herbs. This is an important vase as it does show a marked change between the early Jason that we have been looking at until now. In the case of the Theseus story, Ariadne helps the hero by providing information and assistance before he faces his challenge, the minotaur, and she does not take an active part in killing the creature, instead encouraging the hero. This role is shown in vase painting and an example of this is a gold relief from 650 B.C. showing Ariadne encouraging Theseus as he attacks the Minotaur. Ariadne stands behind the hero and her left arm is raised, gesturing to the hero as he attacks his opponent.[142] The difference between the Ariadne scene and the volute krater with Medea and the box, is that the skill in this visual narrative may well lie inside the container and not in the hands of Jason as the hero. He is still shown striding forward, seizing the fleece in his left hand with a sword in his right. The serpent is resting on a rock to the right, but it is surely defenceless against the combination of the hero, Medea and the Argonauts, making this a far less significant confrontation than the vase painting we have seen earlier. A further indication may be the depiction of the Argonauts, as they seem relaxed and unconcerned about the events occurring to the right.[143] Despite the fact that this type of depiction is a trend in vase painting in the Classical period (look no further than Fig. 7 for an example of this), the image also displays the Argonauts feeling sure that all is happening according to plan. Jason may be immune to any powers the serpent may possess and the power in this scene seems to rest in the box, its prominence indicated by Medea raising it in the air.

Overall there are nine examples of Jason and the serpent (excluding two uncertain representations, Figs. 12 and 14). There is also a broad geographical spread of these images, as these artefacts are Attic [Fig. 16], Etruscan [Figs. 18 & 19], and Korinthian [Figs. 10 & 11]. As mentioned before, the story of Jason and the seizing of the fleece is

---

[142] Carpenter, fig. 245.

[143] Shapiro highlights the lack of interest displayed by the Argonauts: 'It is a style unfortunately characterized by exceedingly languid young men (and women), who here look rather bored with the life and death struggle of their captain' (p. 98).

one of the strongest elements in the myth and the location of these pieces may point to a widespread knowledge of the tale.

4

The Return to Greece

The Flight from Aietes' Palace

We learnt earlier from the *Naupaktia* that the Argonauts fled Kolchis bringing the fleece with them. Aietes had invited them to a banquet in the hope that they would eventually fall asleep and allow him to burn the Argo and murder the crew. Instead one of the Argonauts, Idmon, recommends that they flee, and Medea follows the crew taking the fleece from the palace as she departs (*Nau.* frr. 6, 7, 8 PEG). At this stage Medea has fallen in love with Jason and evidence suggests that there is some form of agreement or oath between the two. Iconography shows that Aphrodite secures this bond, as the Chest of Kypselos had an inscription saying that Aphrodite commanded that Jason marry Medea [Fig. 29]. Such a command from Aphrodite is not necessarily surprising. We remember that the *Naupaktia* said that Aphrodite was the goddess who distracted Aietes so that the Argonauts could escape, by inspiring him to take his wife to bed, while Pindar says she conspires to have Medea fall in love with Jason (*Py.* 4.211-9).

Although it is a later source, Herodoros' version might help us to explain how the fleece actually came to be in the palace. He says that Aietes had challenged Jason to yoke the bulls, followed by sending him to seize the fleece. Jason kills the serpent, retrieves the fleece, and the Argonauts go to the palace to eat (Herodoros fr. 52). Absyrtos, son of Aietes and brother of Medea, is introduced to the story at this point, as he is taken by the Argonautic crew, and then murdered and dismembered as the ship sails from Kolchis.

The murder of Absyrtos only appears in extant literary evidence from the mid fifth century, and Pherekydes is the first literary source to mention him. Jason suggests to Medea that she bring Absyrtos, a small child, with them as they flee, and once they see Aietes' ships pursuing, Jason and Medea kill the child, cut him into pieces, and scatter the body behind the ship (Pher. fr. 32). Presumably this is designed to force Aietes and his crew to stop and collect each part, so as to bury his son correctly.

However, this is not the only version of events. Sophokles gives us an interesting point from his *Skythai*, where he says that Absyrtos and Medea had different mothers (Fr. 546 R).[144] Sophokles and Euripides give a similar version of Absyrtos' death: that Absyrtos was a child and he was killed in the palace before the departure of Jason, Medea and the rest of the Argonauts (*Kolchides*, fr. 343 R).[145] Jason in Euripides' *Medea* says to Medea:

> You killed your own brother at the hearth and then
> stepped aboard the fair-prowed Argo (*Med.* 1334-5).

Euripides' reference doesn't state the age of Absyrtos, but there is little reason to doubt that he was a child as portrayed by Sophokles.

Pherekydes also says that he was a child (Pher. fr. 32) and that he was killed on board the ship, contrary to Euripides' (*Med.* 1334-5) and Sophokles' (*Kolchides*, fr. 343 R) assertion that the murder took place at the palace. What is also significant is that Pherekydes says it is Jason who suggested that Medea take Absyrtos with them, and that both of them killed the child (Pher. fr. 32). It is unclear from the evidence if Jason's involvement in the death of Absyrtos was an early part of the myth.

---

[144] 'For they were not born of the same union, but he was the child of a Nereid...lately...but her Eiduia, daughter of Ocean, bore some time before.' (trans. Lloyd-Jones, p. 277).

[145] Lloyd-Jones, p. 187.

The Route Home

In the most straightforward and simple manner, Sophokles' *Skythai* says that the Argonauts made their way back to Iolkos using the same route as they had used on arrival (fr. 547R). However, we don't know what route Sophokles had in mind. Our earliest extant source is Hesiod, who says that the Argo sailed to Oceanos, travelling up the river Phasis, and then turned round south to Libya (fr. 241 MW). In the *Ehoiai* it is said that they carry the Argo across terrain to the Mediterranean sea, so that they can sail back up the Aegean to Iolkos. Pindar says that it took them twelve days to travel across Africa (*Py.* 4.19-27), and Pherekydes also mentions the route up the river Phasis, and this is where he says Absyrtos is killed and his body scattered (Pher. fr. 32). Hekataios agrees with this route given by Hesiod, but adds that the Argo sailed down the Nile (Hek. fr. 18). Since the climax of the voyage is at Kolchis, stories about the return to Greece may be expected to be somewhat underplayed. One significant point is that Pindar differs from other sources in the way in which he chronicles the episode at Lemnos. As noted, he says that the Argo visits the island on the return voyage rather than on the way to Kolchis , and still combines this with a journey across Africa (*Py.* 4.252 ff.). It may be that Pindar feels obliged to mention the island as it was a well known and recognised element of the early myth but that he does not wish to confuse the journey by elaborating on any detail.

Talos:

Given that most of our sources point to the Argo travelling across land in Africa, and then sailing northwards to Greece, it is unsurprising that the ship may stop at Krete. The bronze giant Talos, living in Krete, is part of Apollonios' tale. He says the Argonauts attacked him by throwing rocks and that Medea used her powers to try to enchant him. Talos falls after stumbling, and catches his knee on a rock. This injury releases the ichor which flows out like molten lead (AR 4.1638-88).

Looking to see if this tale appears in the earlier evidence for Jason, we find that both Simonides and Sophokles mention Talos. In scholia to Plato, it is said:

> According to Simonides...the story of Talos, the bronze figure which Hephaestus crafted for Minos to establish as guardian of the island. It was alive, he says, and destroyed those who approached by burning them up (fr. 568 PMG).'[146]

Sophokles mentions the same story in his lost play *Daidalos* (frr. 160, 161 R), but in both these sources there is no direct reference to the Argonauts.

It is visual evidence which brings together Talos and the Argonauts in evidence from the fifth century. An early fifth century Etruscan column krater shows two youths with swords attacking a third man with the single figure defending himself using stones [Fig. 93]. Unfortunately this vase has not been published, and the interpretation of this scene, and especially the identification of the three figures, remains uncertain.

However, if this vase is not our earliest extant representation of the Argonauts attacking Talos, we have four other representations

---

[146] Trans. Campbell, p. 455.

from the fifth century, one Etruscan, and three Attic. The earliest of these is an Attic red figure column krater [Fig. 94]. Talos is taller than the other figures, and he falls backwards while being held by the Dioskouroi. In front of Talos there is a youth kneeling, and he is holding an implement with which he appears to be pulling at the plug on Talos' ankle. He is assisted by the small figure of Thanatos. Medea stands behind the youth, and she can be identified with certainty, as she holds a bowl in her hand, a symbol of her herb mixing, and similar to previous examples where she was shown holding a box [Fig. 21]. Both Neils[147] and Papadopoulos[148] suggest that this male figure may be Jason, an idea originally suggested by Albin Lesky.[149] Martin Robertson comments on Lesky's interpretation, and says that the 'very attractive suggestion that the hero busy with the nail in that picture, may be Jason himself, receives no confirmation, but is surely inherently probable.'[150] In Chapter 2 we saw scenes of Phineus and the Boreadai, and the appearance of Jason seemed to be the most likely identification for a figure depicted beside Phineus. No other figure receives prominence in portrayals of the voyage. This depiction must be Jason, and the appearance of Medea in a supporting role points to this.

An Etruscan bronze mirror relief from 420 B.C. shows two winged figures, possibly the Boreadai, struggling with a youth [Fig. 95]. The Boread to the left holds Talos' right leg, while Talos tries to hold him by the neck. The other Boread to the right, holds Talos' torso, and both Argonauts may be attempting to hold Talos down, so as to remove the plug from his ankle, thereby letting his life-blood out and killing him.

The final two examples come from the end of the fifth century. The first scene is from an Attic red figure volute krater [Fig. 96],

---

[147] LIMC "Iason" 55.

[148] LIMC "Talos" 6.

[149] *AA* 1973 p. 1115-19, figs 1-2.

[150] Robertson, p. 159.

showing Talos falling back and being supported by the Dioskouri (named). To the far left, Medea stands in oriental dress, with a box in her left hand, and her right arm and eyes point towards the fallen Talos. This scene appears on the opposite side of the vase we saw in Fig. 8, with Jason depicted with Athena and Hera.

The second is a fragment dated to 400 B.C,. and is another Attic red figure krater, showing a similar scene with Talos again falling back into the grasp of the Dioskouri [Fig. 97]. However this time, Robertson says that Medea sits to the lower left of the scene, holding the box and a knife. On the right hand side of the fragment stands a female figure, and below her is a small winged character. Papadopoulos and Robertson say that the female figure is more likely to be Athena than Hera.[151] However, Aphrodite seems even more likely, as the smaller figure at the bottom of the scene may be Eros. Aphrodite plays a role in the relationship of Medea and Jason, [152] and so her presence in an Argonautic scene is likely and consistent with our evidence so far.

Depictions of Talos include the Dioskouri (only once replaced by the Boreadai in Fig. 95). Papadopoulos' assertion that Medea 'is indispensable in scenes of the death of Talos' in Greek art is not entirely correct if we include Figures 93 and 95.[153] However, Medea's appearance in these scenes begins in the third quarter of the fifth century. Although the episode with Talos is not referred to in Euripides' *Medea*, it is likely that she begins to appear after the date of this tragedy. The first example of Medea appearing to help Jason to defeat the serpent, Fig. 21 (dated to 425-415 B.C.), appears after the *Medea* too, and she appears in Fig. 22 with Aietes and the Argonauts (dated to 420-410 B.C.). It is therefore possible to argue that the rise in prominence of Medea as a figure in visual art is an echo of a dramatic

---

[151] Papadopoulos, J. K., LIMC 'Talos' p. 835; Robertson, p.l 159.

[152] For example in *Py*. 4.211-9, or see Fig. 27.

[153] Papadopoulos p. 836.

trend, and that portrayals of her character in iconography are influenced by those in literary evidence.

Early Depictions of Medea

Much of the iconographical evidence concerning the figure of Medea occurs in the context of her interaction with the king Pelias and his daughters after the Argo's return to Iolkos. Visual representations of Medea up until the date at which depictions of Pelias begin are, at best, questionable. There are four suggested examples of Medea in visual art, three dating between 725 and 630 B.C., and none of which can be assured with any degree of certainty [Figs 26-28, 34]. Generally secondary literature doesn't mention these examples as they seem to be uncertain representations which have been suggested as Medea by one source or another. I have included them here as part of my look at visual art and to conclude these are not the earliest extant examples of Medea in visual art. A second specific group of lekythoi shows the head and shoulders of a female figure surrounded by snakes, and this too is sometimes referred to as a depiction of Medea [30-33]. Each of the vases in this group show virtually identical depictions, but again there is little to suggest they are Medea. They have been identified with her due to the magical associations of the serpents, but this seems highly speculative; depictions of the head of a female with snakes is not enough to convincingly claim that these are Medea. Other characters with associations with herbs and magic could be suggested, in particular Kirke.

However, the one certain example before the end of the sixth century is the chest of Kypselos [fig. 29], as discussed earlier. The depiction showed Medea enthroned between Aphrodite and Jason, and an inscription read that Aphrodite commanded their marriage. This assures a bond between Jason and Medea, as referred to in literary sources such as Sophokles' *Kolchides* (fr. 339 R). This seems to be an act by Aphrodite to assure the safety of her hero, by binding him in marriage to such a strong and useful ally as Medea could be.

However, this also fits in with evidence from Eumelos' *Korinthiaka* where Medea was called to Korinth to rule as queen, and Jason arrives with her to act as joint ruler;

> ...the Korinthians sent for Medea from Iolcus and bestowed upon her the kingdom.   Through her Jason was king in Korinth...(Paus. 2.3.10).

> Simonides also mentions this version;
> And he came to Korinth, he did not dwell in Magnesia, and sharing his hearth with his Kolchian wife ruled over...and Lechaeum.
> (PMG 545).

The Death of Pelias

The death of Pelias following Jason's successful return from the quest is a familiar part of the myth, but it is interesting to note that the actual manner of this death is not recorded first in literature, but instead appears initially on black-figure Attic vases from the last quarter of the sixth century.   The earliest extant visual example is dated to 520 B.C. whereas the earliest literary evidence is from Pindar (*Py.* 4.250).

Medea persuades the Peliades (daughters of Pelias), that they can rejuvenate their father.   She manages to do this by demonstrating her powers of rejuvenation on a ram which she boils in a cauldron until suddenly a young animal emerges.   The daughters are amazed and decide to follow Medea's instructions.   Having persuaded their father that this is the best thing for him, Pelias is killed and the daughters begin the process, but without Medea's herbs.   It is thought that this is the element that Medea deliberately leaves out and so ensures the king's death.

It is worth noting at this point that many commentators point to the ram being chopped up and placed in the cauldron; Carpenter (p. 185), Woodford (2003, p. 82) and Robinson (p. 13) all make this assumption. However there is no extant literary evidence for this specific detail; for instance in the in the Euripides' *Medea*, Medea admits to the murder of Pelias (486-7) but there is no specific mention of how he was killed. The vases we will see below show the ram in the cauldron, but it is alive and certainly in one piece. This could be owing to two main possibilities. In the first place it may be that the earliest presenters of this story in fact believed that the ram, and subsequently Pelias, were boiled whole in the pot. In the second place it may be that the artists were aware of the story of chopping the ram and Pelias into smaller, but chose to show the ram in the pot whole for artistic reasons. It would be far more difficult to convey the action of the story if the ram was chopped into pieces; showing the ram whole (and alive) gives a clearer indication of the Pelias story.[154] Also, some of the scenes show the women holding knives, and so Pelias' death before boiling is pointed to, even if it is not absolutely certain if the story of his chopping up is intended in the representations.

Moving now to the extant visual evidence, I have divided the examples to this part of the myth into five groups:[155]

1. The first is the role of Medea and her teaching of "rejuvenation" to the daughters of Pelias. This occurs seven times; six times in extant art between 520 and 475 B.C. [Figs 65, 66, 67, 68, 79 & 80] and one further example from 420-410 B.C. [Fig. 90].
2. The second group shows women (normally two and so identified as the Peliades) with a ram in a cauldron. There are five extant examples in this group and all are dated between 475 and 460 B.C. [Figs. 72, 73, 74, 75 & 82].

---

[154] Later, Apollodoros details the death of Pelias before he is placed in the pot, and describes the Peliades 'chopping up their father' (1.9.26).

[155] See Appendix 3 for a guide to visual evidence in this stage of the myth.

3. The third group shows women with a ram in the cauldron, and this time the depiction also includes Pelias. There are three examples in this group [Figs. 76, 84 & 87].

4. The fourth group shows Pelias and his daughters (no Medea) and instead of the Peliades demonstrating the rejuvenation of the ram, they are trying to persuade their father that it is his turn. All of these are dated to between 475 and 430 B.C. [Figs. 81, 86, 88 & 89].

5. The fifth and final group is that of the Peliades alone, with two examples of them preparing to begin their work [Figs. 77 & 85].

Group One: Medea and the daughters of Pelias

The first example in this group is an amphora [Fig. 65] dated to 520 B.C. by the artist of the Medea Group, and shows Pelias seated to the left of the scene. Beside him, Medea gestures towards the cauldron out of which a ram emerges. To the right, two women, the daughters of Pelias, stand observing the proceedings. This is the earliest extant example of Medea showing the daughters of Pelias how to rejuvenate their father. Only later sources give us the details where Apollodoros says that Medea chops up the animal, places it in a pot with some herbs, only for a new younger ram to jump out - rejuvenated (ApB. 1.9.27).

This vase is very similar to our next example which shows virtually the same scene [Fig. 67]. On this Attic black figure hydria, the figure of Medea is preserved and she is making the same gestures to the old man as in the last example. The main difference is the absence of one of the Peliades. We know that this is a representation of Medea and one of the daughters of Pelias, and not both of the Peliades, since the ram is already in the cauldron and so this shows Medea demonstrating her skills with herbs. The Peliades could not have demonstrated the rejuvenation of the ram to their father without Medea's presence. To do this they would have had to possess full knowledge of herb mixing, and therefore would not have ended by unwittingly killing their own father.

In this scene, Mastronarde points to the man who kneels on the right and stokes the fire beneath the cauldron. He suggests that this is Jason and thinks that he may be involved in the actual act of killing Pelias.[156]   However, I am not convinced that this figure in Fig. 67 is Jason, as the role of tending the fire could be a generic one. The man helps with the fire but performs no other significant role in the scene. If Jason did appear here he would not have any significant role - this is Medea's sphere of influence.   When we looked at depictions of Talos and saw a man playing some part in his death, I believed that this was Jason. The reason for this was that as leader of the Argo it was likely that Jason would take part in such a struggle, and as we saw him assist with Phineus, we can see that Jason is represented in various scenes throughout the voyage. Looking at Fig. 67, Carpenter points to this type of vase painting and sees these types of additional figures as part of the style of black figure vase painting. He looks at a black figure amphora showing Theseus and the Minotaur, and dated to 540 B.C. where Theseus is holding the creature by the neck with four people looking on. These appear to have no particular role in the story, but as Carpenter points out;

> While the onlookers here may be interpreted as young Athenians, similar figures   appear in contemporary scenes where they can have no possible connection with the myth depicted and are simply part of the formal design.[157]

Much in the same way, the figure in the hydria [Fig. 67] does not seem to be that of Jason, but rather part of the design. Whereas the figure plays a role in the overall composition of the scene, in so far as he appears to stoke the fire, he does not appear to play a role in the actual story being told. This scene in visual art is about Medea's teaching of

---

[156] Mastronarde, p. 48.

[157] Carpenter, fig. 247.

the Peliades and normally there would not be a case for Jason's involvement.

The third vase from before 500 B.C. showing this scene, is a black figure amphora [Figs. 66]. Both sides of this vase show very similar depictions; side A shows Medea to the left of the cauldron, apparently administering her magic as the ram emerges from the pot at the centre. To the right is one of the daughters of Pelias, gesturing in a similar manner to figures on the vases we have already seen [Figs 65 & 67]. The reason we can say that this is Medea is that she holds a short magic wand in her left hand with "six prongs at the top".[158] This depiction fits in with previous examples of Medea teaching the daughters of Pelias how to rejuvenate their father through the demonstration with the ram. However, on side B, we also see the ram at the centre in the cauldron, but Robinson[159] says the two women to the left and right of the ram are the Peliades. This poses a certain amount of difficulty as the two daughters of Pelias do not rejuvenate a ram on their own; this is the trick by which Medea persuades them to try this on their father. Medea has shown the Peliades the trick in the scene on side A, and on side B, they are depicted admiring the result. Figure 68 shows a similar scene to the ones we have seen, and these scenes of Medea and the Peliades have a strong degree of consistency. The fragment shows the cauldron, the ram and three other people.

The last two examples of this group [Figs 79 & 80] continue this trend; both have Medea on the left of the cauldron, and the two Peliades on the right. In Fig. 80 Medea holds a box in her right hand, indicating her use of herbs. The ram emerges from the pot at the centre. The teaching and duping of the Peliades is the earliest theme associated with this stage of the myth. All five of these examples fall within a period

---

[158] Robinson *AJA* 60 (1956) p. 12.

[159] 'These two figures are probably the daughters of Pelias, Antiope and Asteropeia, raising their hand in astonishment at the miracle.' Robinson, p. 13.

of fifty years and Medea's appearance in the scene is significant as, although the scene does not appear before 520 BC, when it does appear it always includes Medea, and her involvement in the death of Pelias is very clear.

Group Two: Women (Peliades) with Ram in Cauldron

The second group is a sub-group of the first, as it shows women, always two, standing either side of the cauldron, with the ram emerging. However the key difference is that in this group is that Medea is absent from the scene. Indeed, Medea does not appear again in extant vase painting evidence for the early myth. She appears six times in scenes of the story of Pelias, but only between 525 and 475 B.C. Only one other example, a relief sculpture from 410-400 B.C. depicts Medea in this story up to the end of the century.

Four lekythoi dated to between 500 and 475 B.C. [Figs 72, 73, 74 & 75] continue with the same theme of the rejuvenation of the ram, flanked by two women. Some show a woman holding a knife, and this must point to the more sinister intent of the demonstration, the death of Pelias. Whether or not the two women on these vases include Medea is unclear. In our previous examples Medea can be identified by being one of a set of three women. Given that there are normally two Peliades, the third figure is assumed to be Medea. She is also normally depicted with a command over the scene, in contrast to the signs of surprise from the Peliades. Also she can be identified by a symbol of her herb mixing (such as the six pronged wand; Fig. 66, or the holding of a box; Fig. 94).

On the lekythoi it seems likely that the presence of two women makes certain a representation of the daughters of Pelias admiring Medea's work, and her rejuvenation of the ram. Also, if we assume that the Peliades are being depicted within the boundaries of the scene, the artist may have envisaged that Medea was present but has stepped aside while the women admire her work. As we saw in Group 1, Fig. 66 shows this, as Medea appears on side A of the vase but on side

B the daughters of Pelias are alone, admiring the pot and the rejuvenated ram.

The fifth and last example from Group 2 is a red figure Attic stamnos dated to 470-460 B.C. and shows two figures in a state of animation surrounding the ram and the cauldron [Fig. 82].[160] The woman to the right is waving a knife, and has both of her arms raised, excited at seeing the ram emerge from the pot. Her colleague on the left also raises her hand, and she occupies the space usually taken by Medea when she is showing the Peliades how to complete the process. The scene also benefits in an artistic sense from the presentation of two Peliades rather than the two women plus Medea or Pelias. For the symmetry of the vase, the artist may favour two characters rather than three. However the scene is unmistakable, since depictions of the ram in the pot with the women alongside is unique in art to the story of Pelias.

Group Three: Peliades, Pelias and Ram in Cauldron

Group three has three vases [Figs 76, 84 and 87] from the fifth century B.C.   This group seems to show a series of synoptic compositions -   scenes which combine elements from all parts of the story in a single setting. Each vase shows the daughters of Pelias, the ram in the cauldron, and the king himself.   This combines the tale of Medea's rejuvenation of the ram with the final episode of the daughters attempting to rejuvenate their father, and it offers a synopsis of all these aspects.

The first of the three, a black figure lekythos dated to the first quarter of the fifth century [Fig. 76] (the earliest black figure lekythos in our evidence), shows a bearded Pelias standing to the left of the cauldron.

---

[160] One other example [Fig. 90] shows the same scene but doesn't include the ram. This is dated to the end of the fifth century.

On Fig. 84, side B shows the Peliades and the king, but on this occasion there are three daughters depicted. There could be two reasons for this. Firstly, the artist has decided that the number of figures comprised by Pelias and his daughters is not sufficient for his composition, and he may simply be filling out his scene. Or it may be that he wished to match the composition of side A, which shows two figures to the left of the cauldron, and one to the right. Side B has Pelias in the place of the ram and cauldron, quite symbolic considering what is about to occur, and there are the same number of people to the left (two) and right (one). However, what really draws our attention to this scene is Erika Simon's reference to Jason who stands to the far left on side A.[161] Simon only mentions him as a possible identification, and points to our Fig. 67, the black figure hydria with a man stoking the fire beneath the pot, as another example where Jason's name has been suggested.[162] However Mastronarde appears to take this for granted and mentions two further examples of vases which "apparently show Jason assisting in the ruse".[163] The flaw in this assumption is that, as we have seen, Jason's appearance is unlikely in Fig. 67, and the other examples he gives point to vases where an extra male figure is included, but there are no names on these vases and the context of the scene and what we know about the myth does not enhance the case.[164]

In the *Medea*, it is clear that Medea is the one who was involved in this deception as she herself accepts that she conspired to have Pelias murdered (*Med.* 486). This was also predicted in Pindar, and so the Pelias myth has a large impact on the story of Jason. He would stand to benefit from removal of Pelias from the throne, especially if the king has refused to surrender the throne on Jason's return, as he

---

[161] LIMC "Pelias" p. 275.

[162] By Simon herself, LIMC "Pelias" 11*

[163] Mastronarde, p. 48, n. 79.

[164] Mastronarde points to figs. 68 & 84 as showing a man stoking the fire, and fig. 81 as man seated and observing the scene.

had promised in Pindar's version of the myth. However without some clear identifiable symbol, a recorded role, or Jason actually being named on a vase, I believe that it is purely speculation to suggest his presence on these vases.

The last of the three from this group is an Attic red figure kylix krater by the Kleophron painter, dated to 440 B.C. [Fig. 87]. Although the scene is familiar, this time there is only one figure either side of the cauldron and ram, namely Pelias and another woman. Simon suggests a Peliad or Medea,[165] and the appearance of one of Pelias' daughters would seem more likely as she is demonstrating the benefits of what has happened to the ram. Medea is not normally depicted in these scenes and the last depiction of Medea and the ram in the fifth century is in 475 B.C. This scene is likely therefore to be Pelias and one of his daughters. We should also note that Pelias stands leaning on his staff, with his hand on his head, appearing to be more than a little worried by what he is being told.

Group Four: Peliades persuade Pelias

There are four examples in this group, all of which show one of the final stages of the story. Here the Peliades are bringing their father to the location where he is to be made young. The oldest surviving example is from 425-420 B.C. and is a red figure kylix krater showing two daughters leading their father [Fig. 81]. The daughter who has her left hand on her father's arm holds a knife in her right hand, a chilling foretaste of what is to come.

The second piece is a red figure kylix krater from the middle of the fifth century [Fig. 86]. The scenes are painted on both the outside and inside of the kylix, with the daughters leading their father to the cauldron painted on the exterior, and Pelias standing with one daughter painted on the interior. Poor Pelias stands with his head in his right hand

---

[165] LIMC "Pelias", p. 276.

leaning on his staff, similar to the depiction we saw in Fig. 87. Standing opposite him is a daughter, holding a knife and standing taller than her old father.

The last two examples are something of a combination of the first pair. An Attic red figure kylix shows three daughters of Pelias bringing their father towards the cauldron [Fig. 88], and one is "helping" the old man up and appears to be about to bring him to the pot. Another daughter stands by the cauldron with a knife in one hand and gestures towards her sister. The second example is a pyxis by the Painter of Heidelberg 209 [Fig. 89], and shows Pelias leaning forward on his staff, making his way towards the right of the scene, where the daughters gesture towards the pot. The third daughter on the far right has a ram beside her which demonstrates to Pelias the success which awaits him, and it is possibly painted as a symbol and reminder to the viewer of the full story. All four of these scenes show Pelias in his final moments which are the culmination of the actions of Medea, even though she does not appear.

Group Five: Peliades alone
Our last group contains two examples of the Peliades standing alone, this time without the presence of Medea or their father. Fig. 85 shows three women and it is clear that the use of three Peliades in the depiction is a trend of the late fifth century, all examples being dated to between 450 and 425 B.C. This vase is an Attic red figure hydria and shows a daughter with a knife, one with a phiale, and the third appears to be gesturing with enthusiasm moving towards the right of the scene. The phiale may contain the incorrect herbs given to the women by Medea.

Our final example shows three women appearing on a red figure stamnos, with one holding a knife [Fig. 77]. The three appear to be consulting on what to do next.

Rejuvenation of Jason and Aison:

Medea regularly uses her knowledge of magic and herbs to assist Jason, sometimes by causing terrible harm to his enemies (as we saw with the failed rejuvenation of Pelias), sometimes more innocently (as when she helped Jason yoke the fire-breathing bulls). However, her most beneficial action for the hero is reserved for the rejuvenation of Jason and his father Aison.

> The earliest source from literature is the *Nostoi*;
> And straightaway she made Aison a nice young lad,
> stripping away his old skin by her expertise, boiling
> various drugs in her golden cauldrons.[166]

If we are to look at Pindar, by the time the Argonauts arrive back in Greece, Aison may be an old man, and one who has suffered many trials over the years, losing his throne, and then believing he had lost his son. Aison is already an old man when Jason arrives back from Cheiron (*Py.* 4.120-3), and can only have aged with his increased tribulations since then.

Scholia to Euripides' *Medea* suggests that it was Jason who was the beneficiary of Medea's rejuvenative powers:

> Pherekydes and Simonides say that Medea boiled
> Jason and made him young again. (548 PMG)

Gantz cautions on this evidence however;

> ...although the scholiasts themselves themselves
> may have drawn on an erroneous source, they did
> clearly mean to suggest two separate beneficiaries
> of Medea's skills...we should probably accept Jason
> as one of them, though with some puzzlement.[167]

---

[166] *Greek Epic Fragments*, trans. by West, frag. 6, p. 153.

[167] Gantz, p. 367.

Part of the problem here are the names. We can see how 'Iason' could be transcribed incorrectly and recorded as 'Aison' with only two letters being misplaced. However it is again the visual evidence which may provide more information on this subject.

The perception remains today that it was Aison who is rejuvenated by Medea and that evidence of Jason's transformation is somehow an oddity in our sources. In Mastronarde's recent edition of the *Medea*, he includes in his introduction to the myth that 'Medea persuaded the daughters of Pelias by demonstrating her magical power to rejuvenate, either on Aeson or a ram...' (p. 48). He makes no mention of the evidence for the rejuvenation of Jason, and there appears to be a perception that Aison is the main focus of Medea's powers.

The best example of these is an Attic red-figure hydria by the Copenhagen Painter, dated to 470 B.C. [Fig. 83] which shows Medea and Jason standing either side of a cauldron as a ram emerges. Medea is holding a skyphos in her left hand and this indicates that she is using her knowledge of herbs to rejuvenate the animal. Jason stands to the right and he appears to be quite old in this depiction. He is shown holding a staff and his hair is painted white. We know that this is Jason as he is named on the vase and although we can't discount a mistaken labelling by the artist, there are visual representations on other artefacts which may help to confirm this identification.

There are also four extant pieces from the first quarter of the sixth century B.C. showing a youth emerging from a pot, which are also thought to show Jason's transformation [Figs. 69, 70, 71 & 78]. Figures 69, 70 and 71 show virtually identical scenes, with two women seated either side of a cauldron and a young man rising out of the cauldron. These vases are white-ground lekythoi and such scenes of rejuvenation seem entirely appropriate as lekythoi are used as vessels used in funerary rites. Although these scenes are not labelled, it seems likely that they are in fact representations of Jason. There is no other example in vase painting of a figure being rejuvenated from a pot and so identifying these with Jason or Aison is not surprising.[168]   Portrayals of a boy emerging from a pot appear around the same time as the vases showing Pelias and his daughters, 525-425 B.C. Combining the literary evidence, even if we include it with caution, and the visual representations, there is enough evidence to suggest that Medea did rejuvenate two people. Jason is named on Fig. 83 and this is entirely consistent with the stories about Jason which we have seen throughout this book. Medea does not help any person in literature or art other than Jason. Her rejuvenation of Jason or his father   is consistent with the myth as she has no major connections with other characters, and, as pointed out previously when we looked at the fleece, Medea's skills are not used to assist another hero in early myth.

Later art may help with the question of Jason's rejuvenation. Two fourth century bronze Etruscan hand-mirrors point to what are thought to be scenes of Jason's rejuvenation [Figs. 91 & 92].   Neils argues, convincingly in my view, that Fig. 91 showing Jason (named HEASUN) receiving a drink from Medea (named METVIA) is not in fact a scene of rejuvenation but is a depiction of an event at Kolchis, possibly where Jason has been injured and Medea is making him immortal by giving him a special potion in the presence of Minerva.[169] Neils correctly points to the role of Athena and the fact that the goddess normally appears at moments of combat, indicating that this depiction probably shows Jason at Kolchis rather than being rejuvenated in Iolkos.[170]   This mirror was believed to show Jason being rejuvenated by Medea, but given that the depiction differed from other rejuvenation scenes, Neils questioned if there could be two types of rejuvenation appearing in

---

[168] Neils gives a series of examples of immortality and eternal youth offered to figures in myth (1994; p. 190), and I would point to the fact that in these stories Medea's art of rejuvenation through boiling in the pot is unique.

[169] Neils (1994) p. 193.

[170] Ibid. p. 192.

Etruscan art around the same date, one of a revival for Jason after being disgorged by the serpent [Fig. 91], and one depicting the more usual scene of Jason emerging from the pot [Fig. 92].[171]   A later literary source, Lykophron, may take this further as he says that Jason was cut up in a pot, but he places this in Kolchis (Lykophron 1315). Meyer believes that this points to that fact that Jason needed rejuvenation after the arduous tasks (pp.105-9).   However this seems to be an even later development of the story or it could simply be a mixing of earlier elements of the tale. The idea of Jason's rejuvenation by chopping and boiling in a pot does not appear in evidence up until the end of the fifth century, even if there is some evidence suggesting that this appears in later sources.

What this examination of the two later Etruscan pieces tells us is that Fig. 91, commonly misinterpreted as a scene of rejuvenation, is not in fact such a scene, and instead Jason is simply being given a potion for protection against harm in Kolchis, and that while Fig. 92 may show Jason being rejuvenated, this is a new variant of the myth where he is used as a tool of persuasion for Pelias.   In Fig. 92, the suggestion is that Jason is rejuvenated as a demonstration to Pelias instead of using the ram and this would probably be a good deal more convincing as a demonstration for the king.

From Iolkos to Korinth

So far we have seen on a number of occasions that iconography offers us glimpses of parts of the Jason myth which are otherwise omitted or lost from our literary sources.   Another such example of this is the episode of the Kalydonian Boar Hunt, as, although the hunt itself is mentioned as early as in the *Iliad* (*Il.* 9.543-46) the first extant reference to Jason being included in the group of hunters is on a black figure dinos fragment by the Kyllenios Painter, dated to 570-560

---

[171] Neils (1994). p. 191.

B.C. [Fig. 24] Although not named, Jason can be identified, as he is shown as the hunter wearing only one sandal. This representation of Jason *monosandalos* appear to be symbolic. When Jason appeared in the market place in Iolkos to confront Pelias, he wore a single sandal and this may then link him to the role as an ephebe. However any reappearance of the image of the single sandal may simply be a recognisable motif for Jason and so the single sandal on the representation of the Boar hunt should not necessarily indicate a continued state as an ephebe on the part of Jason. The only other surviving visual example pointing to the story of the single sandal is the coin dated to 470 B.C. [discussed earlier - Fig. 1].

The second piece connected to the hunt is a black figure Attic kylix dated to the mid sixth century, and this time Jason is named, and is shown attacking the boar as part of the group of nine hunters [Fig. 25].

The chronology of the boar hunt in relation to the other parts of Jason's story may not be all that significant. Rather as the gathering of the heroes on the Argo does not necessarily fit in with a chronological record of their own individual myths, Jason's appearance at the hunt is because he was a well known hero and poets or artists would include his name along with other figures from myth. It is however assumed that the hunt occurred after Jason returns to Iolkos.

This leads us to the question of the aftermath of Jason's quest in Iolkos. As a slight aside, there is no evidence as to what happens to the fleece! Presumably Jason brought it back and presented it to Pelias, in much the same way as other returning heroes bring back the prize from their expeditions. According to Pindar (*Py.* 10.46-8) and Pherekydes (Pher. fr. 11), Perseus returns to King Polydektes with the head of the Gorgon, only to lift the head from the kibisis and use it on the king. Jason would presumably have been an unexpected visitor to the palace of Pelias, who must have believed he had seen the last of the hero.

There is no extant evidence for the idea that Jason took over as king of his city after the death of Pelias. In *Pythian* 4 we saw how Jason claimed the throne for his family (*Py.* 4.104-8), but in Pindar, as in all other sources, there is no suggestion that the return from Kolchis and the death of Pelias (as foretold at line 250) leads to Jason's accession.

Hesiod says that Jason and Medea arrive back to Iolkos after the voyage and Medea becomes Jason's wife, finally bearing a child who is named Medeios (*Th.* 992-1002). This shows that early myth may have had Jason reach some arrangement to stay in Iolkos. As we saw at the start, Pherekydes said Jason was a citizen of Iolkos, and so there is the possibility that one version of the myth had him return successfully to the city, and to continue to live under Pelias' rule.

The second version, from the *Naupaktia*, has Jason and Medea move to Kerkyra where their son, called Mermeros, is killed by a lion on the mainland (Fr. 9 PEG). However the third and most recognisable version is from Eumelos. Eumelos' *Korinthiaka* created a mythological history for Korinth and he weaves into his poem the myth of Jason and Medea saying that Medea was called to Korinth and she and Jason were made the rulers of the city (Paus. 2.7.10; Eum. fr. 5 PEG). Eumelos is not the only source to say that Medea and Jason move to Korinth, but his version is dominated by Medea and Korinth and so the inclusion of Jason is obvious. However, a scholion to the *Medea* says that both Eumelos and Simonides (545 PMG) state that Jason went to Korinth and so we have other references to this version.

Figures 10 and 11 which show Jason grappling with the serpent are both dated to the last quarter of the seventh century and both are from Korinth. Given that Eumelos may have produced his epic towards the end of the eighth or start of the seventh century, there may be an influence here as the two Korinthian vases may have been inspired by Eumelos' work.

In the fifth century a papyrus hypothesis to Euripides' *Peliades*[172] says that Jason leaves Iolkos for Korinth and it appears that the playwright is following this Korinthian strand of the myth. However there is also the suggestion that Jason gives the kingdom to Akastos, Pelias' son,[173] before he departs. This is certainly intriguing as it suggests that Jason has some form of authority in Iolkos in order to be able to designate its next ruler. One visual representation referred to by Pausanias says that the Chest of Kypselos, a Korinthian artefact, shows Jason wrestling at the funeral games of Pelias [Fig. 23]. Gantz believes that this may show Jason as being innocent of any connection to the death of the king and that Jason was actually on friendly terms with the old king.[174] This is not entirely true as Jason may have had a great deal of antagonism towards Pelias if after the return Pelias still refused to hand over the throne of Iolkos. However, as seen, Jason may not have had any direct role in the death of Pelias. Medea's actions, while possibly beneficial to Jason, did not involve our hero and so his marking the death of Pelias by his appearance at the funeral games is entirely correct and plausible. Indeed his absence would point to his guilt. If Jason was said to flee Iolkos in advance of the games, this would possibly point to his involvement in the king's death.

Therefore, literature gives us two further strands on the direction of the myth after the death of the king. The first has Jason, with Medea, living once again in Iolkos (if this is what the *Theogony*'s silence implies) or migrating to Kerkyra (*Naupaktia* fr. 9 West). The second connects them to Korinth and this begins with Eumelos' weaving of the

---

[172] The *Peliades* is dated to 455 B.C. and so precedes the *Medea*.

[173] As discussed by Gantz, p. 367.

[174] Gantz, p. 368.

myth of Jason into his history of Korinth. This is followed by Simonides and Euripides and certainly forms the basis for the *Medea*.

5
Korinth

Life in Korinth

The body of evidence pointing to events in Korinth appears to show that this tale was a later development in early myth. Most of our evidence comes from the late sixth century or the fifth century B.C. and deals with the end of Jason and Medea's marriage and the death of their children.

However the one exception to this is the evidence from Eumelos.

> ...as her children were born, [Medea] carried each to the sanctuary of Hera and concealed them, doing so in the belief that so they would be immortal. At last she learnt that her hopes were vain, and at the same time she was detected by Jason. When she begged for pardon he refused it, and sailed away to Iolkos. For these reasons too she departed [from Korinth], and handed over the kingdom to Sisyphus. (Paus. 2.7.10-11).

This Korinthian version becomes the focus for the story in later sources for the early myth, from the sixth century onwards. Other than Eumelos, three versions of the death of the children emerge. One is that Medea kills them accidentally; the other is that the Korinthians kill them deliberately.

The first of these comes from Parmeniskos, a grammarian of the second or first century B.C. who is said to draw on earlier sources. This is included in scholia to the Medea (Σ *Med.* 264) where he says that the Korinthians were beginning to become unhappy by being ruled by a foreign woman and so plotted against Medea. They planned to kill her seven boys and seven girls and so the children took refuge in the sanctuary of Hera Akraia. However the Korinthians didn't respect the goddess and they killed all fourteen of the children on the altar. As a consequence, a plague hits the city and some form of purification is therefore necessary. No more remains about what happened to Medea and we do not know what Jason's role was in all of this. It is unclear as to whether Jason is even still with Medea at this stage, or if he has already left, possibly to return to Iolkos.

Mastronarde provides an introduction to the subject of the deaths of the children in his introduction to the *Medea*, and he says that 'it is not possible to date the variants relative to each other except by guesswork but several seem to be earlier than [Euripides'] play.'[175]

The second story, again connecting the deaths of the children to Korinth and coming from scholia to the Medea (Σ *Med.* 264), comes from Kerophylos (fr. 9 PEG; Creo. fr. 3 EGM),[176] who says that Medea kills Kreon, the king of Korinth, with her use of herbs. She then leaves for Athens, fearing the revenge of the Korinthians, but leaves her children in the sanctuary of Hera Akraia. She believes that their father will protect them, but friends of Kreon kill them and spread a rumour that this was done by Medea before she left for Athens. Both Gantz and Mastronarde[177] point to the fact that the last part, the rumour being spread that Medea killed the children, may have been added later by someone who was familiar with Euripides' version of the myth where Medea kills the children.

---

[175] Medea, ed. by Mastronarde, p. 50.

[176] There are two possibilities as to the identity of Kreophylos. He may either have been an archaic epic poet and author of a poem called *The Capture of Oechalia* or he was a chronicler who is named in an inscription from Priene. See EGM I, p. 65

[177] Gantz, p. 369; Mastronarde, p. 51.

The last of the three stories of the deaths of the children which appear to follow Eumelos and come before Euripides is from scholia to Pindar (Σ *Ol.* 13.74g) and instead of the Korinthians it is Medea who is at fault:

> In Corinth Zeus fell in love with Medea, but Medea did not give her consent to him, seeking to avoid the anger of Hera. For this reason Hera in fact promised to make the children immortal. But they died, and the Corinthians honour them, calling them "half-foreign"[178]

This returns to the evidence from Eumelos where Medea is responsible for the children's deaths but more in an accidental manner, since they die while she believes that she is making them immortal. On both occasions Medea is relying on Hera to act to give the children immortality. It is unclear how they die and why they die. Medea may be attempting to perform a similar act to Demeter when that goddess tried to make Demophon immortal. When the goddess was disguised as a servant and working at the palace of Metaneira, she took the young Demophon and placed him in the fire with the aim of making him immortal. The transformation failed as the child's mother discovered Demeter and the goddess stopped the process (*Hymn to Demeter*, 239ff.). However with Medea, it is not in her own powers to transform the children. She is waiting for the intervention of Hera which does not materialise, and Medea possibly only realises this at the last minute when it is too late to reverse the process.

From the evidence of Eumelos and the three later examples of the deaths of the children, we see that there are two strands. One is the accidental death of the children at the hands of Medea, but there is no suggestion that she deliberately kills the children. There is no antipathy towards Jason and there is no suggestion in evidence that

---

[178] Trans. Mastronarde, p. 52.

Jason leaves Medea for another woman before the *Medea*. In Eumelos she appears to take matters into her own hands and finds that Jason is not willing to support her (Paus. 2.3.10-11). The second version of events has the Korinthians kill the children; in one version it is in response to Medea's killing of Kreon (Kreophylos), and in the other it is because the Korinthians grow tired of having a foreign queen (Parmeniskos).

Conclusion

The purpose of this work was twofold. The aim was to reassess all extant references to the story of Jason in early myth, covering a period of over five hundred years. Starting with epic poetry in the eighth century B.C. and finishing at the end of the fifth century, this was to establish the extent to which the myth of Jason and the Argonautic voyage was known in ancient society, but also to trace the development in the portrayal of Jason as a character in Greek myth. It was also important to examine all visual evidence connected to Jason's story, in order to see if there were lessons in how much iconography could tell us about the myth and the character of the hero. While other scholars have discussed some iconographical evidence dealing with Jason, a complete and chronological examination, relating to each step of the myth, such as I have provided here, has not previously been available. By setting iconographical evidence alongside the literary material, it also becomes possible to understand various strands in the early myth. We are also able to determine whether iconographical evidence differed substantially from literature, or indeed if some aspects of the myth are known to us from only one of these sources.

Literary evidence for the myth of Jason is scattered across a number of areas. These sources range from quite complete and focused portraits, such as Pindar's *Pythian* 4 or Euripides' *Medea,* to more fragmentary or scattered references in literature from as early as Homer and Hesiod right through to Pherekydes and tragedy in the fifth century. Looking closely at this material reveals that while there was originally a rich collection of literary sources for this myth, many do not survive to the modern day, leaving us to draw conclusions from internal references in some of the evidence that does survive.

However the combination of the evidence in epic poetry points to a geographically widespread knowledge of the myth. Hesiod in Boeotia, Eumelos in Korinth, Homer, and possibly the author of the

Naupaktia, in Ionia, all illustrate the extent to which the myth was known in geographical locations that were widely separated. This is not simply a local legend as we might assume if we only had evidence from Eumelos. This myth extends across the Greek world, and may well have been the type of story that would have been told in the outer reaches among travellers and sailors, especially given its strong links to sea travel and colonisation. The importance of Pindar's *Pythian* 4 also deserves particular note. His poem, approximately twice the length of all his other works, gives us the first extant detailed account of the voyage and portrays Jason as a model hero. This contains a special degree of significance for Pindar since his poem was an attempt to persuade king Arkesilas IV to allow an exile to return to his city. Presumably he wished the king to draw comparisons between his own behaviour and that of the hero of the ode, thus flattering Arkesilas into a merciful act. Pindar's choice of Jason as the hero of his work must point to Jason being well regarded as a figure of mythology. Pindar may be emphasising certain aspects of Jason's character in this portrayal, as it suits his needs. The focus of this poem is the confrontation between the hero, Jason, and Pelias, where Jason uses calm and wise words (*Py.* 4.137-9), in marked contrast to Pelias' panic and bluster (*Py.* 4.99-100). However, if this portrayal of Jason did not match general perceptions of the hero at the time when the ode was delivered, the ode's ability to persuade the king would probably have been less successful. If Pindar is trying to sway Arkesilas IV, he must choose a convincing hero with whom to make his point. Selecting Jason as his hero leads to an assumption that as a figure in mythology, Jason was seen as a model hero, with many positive attributes and qualities. This is of particular significance when we see the way in which Jason's character changes over time, prompting many secondary scholars to believe that he was always portrayed as somewhat less than heroic.

In reassessing the literary evidence for Jason, it becomes apparent how the extant sources differ with regard to the knowledge of the tale over time. It is frustrating that so much of the Jason myth is missing and yet that there is evidence of an extensive number of poets who once dealt with this subject. However, the evidence that is available points clearly to a very old tale, and to Jason as a well respected hero.

However, without vase painting and sculpture it would be far more difficult to gain a full sense of the myth. Iconography brings insights to a number of the key episodes in the early myth and without them our understanding of the overall tale would be greatly reduced. For example, the story of Phineus appears in extant art twenty six times between 625 and 400 B.C., a story for which we only have fragmentary evidence in literature. Iconography gives us the only extant reference to Jason healing the king of his blindness and this is a key part of the early depiction of the hero, emphasising his admirable qualities and his wide range of skills. While literature does tell us that Jason was educated by Cheiron (∑ *Od.* 12.69 and ∑ *Th.* 993), and we know from elsewhere and from the examples of other heroes, that this would have included instruction in the arts of medicine *(Il.* 11.828-32), it is only in visual evidence that we see Jason actually using his healing powers.

The struggle between Jason and the serpent as the hero tries to win the golden fleece is also an example of visual art providing information about an episode of the myth which is mostly absent in literature. Pindar does say that Jason slew the creature (*Py.* 4.249), but he doesn't describe the struggle, and no literary evidence comes close to identifying the way Jason is captured by the serpent and how he narrowly escapes being eaten. It is only in iconography that we see the serpent with Jason's leg in its mouth and how the hero battles to win the fleece [Figs 13, 15 & 19]. Neils, in looking at Jason on the New York krater and Douris kylix points to the fact that he was bearded. Jason is more usually beardless in the fifth century and so Neils questions if this may refer back to earlier known representations of this scene.

In many ways, the story of the fleece, and Jason's struggle with the serpent, is similar to the labours of Herakles or the early test for

Bellerophontes. Herakles' struggle with the Nemean lion, as seen on a red-figure hydria by the Kleophrades Painter, shows a scene which recalls with struggle between Jason and the serpent.[179] Herakles uses his bare hands and does not hold his sword (hanging in the background in this depiction) and this scene was a very popular one with vase painters. Jason is shown on a number of occasions facing the serpent without a weapon and grappling with it to win the fleece and this type of depiction fits in with a trend in the sixth and early fifth centuries to show these types of physical combats.

On the one hand, Jason's depiction in art may be part of an overall trend in the images of heroes. However he is also following a narrative structure which is played out by other characters. Both Jason and Bellerophontes are asked to complete a series of near impossible tests by a foreign king. Bellerophontes lived in Argos until the wife of King Proetus conspired to have Bellerophontes killed. She told her husband that Bellerophontes had attempted to rape her and so Proetus sent Bellerophontes to his father-in-law in Lykia. Here that old king set a series of tasks for Bellerophontes. Firstly he sent him against the Chimaira, a creature with the head of a lion, the body of a goat and the tail of a serpent (*Il.* 6. 156ff.). This tale is a very early story as it appears in the *Iliad* and depictions in early art of Bellerophontes's battle versus the Chimaira are quite popular.[180] It is interesting to note the similarities to Jason. Both arrive in foreign lands and are set arduous tasks. For Jason the eventual aim is the fleece and the yoking of the bulls is a prelude to the largest challenge against the serpent guarding the fleece. For Bellerophontes, he has two further challenges to face. He had to slay the mighty warrior tribe, the Solymi, followed by a battle against the Amazons. Given the early date of Bellerophontes's tale and the early existence of the *Argonautika* it is clear to see that these types of heroic

---

[179] Woodford 2003; fig. 13: Hydria dated to 500 B.C. Villa Giulia, Rome.

[180] Schmitt's article, 'Bellerophon and the Chimera in Archaic Greek Art,' shows that this tale was one of the earliest stories to be represented in Greek iconography (p. 341).

stories fit a pattern. Both heroes have a turbulent history in their home cities, are forced to leave home and travel to distant lands. Local kings set what are to be impossible tasks and both succeed and end up with the hand of the local princess in marriage. For Bellerophontes, the king in Lykia offers his daughter after he has witnessed how this young man brushes aside these three obstacles. For Jason, his relationship with Medea doesn't have the blessing of Aietes, but, as in the case of Theseus and Ariadne, it follows the same path of the local princess falling in love with a visiting hero.

Hadas, followed recently in part by Shapiro, has suggested that the assistance Jason receives from females tends to cast him as a weak, even unmanly hero.[181] However, my examination of early iconographical and literary evidence shows two things clearly: firstly that the support of a female goddess can actually serve to enhance the status of the hero, and secondly, that Medea's role in the capturing of the fleece comes late in the fifth century after the *Medea* and is not a large part of the early myth. Towards 400 B.C. Jason is shown in one vase receiving the assistance of Medea when he attacks the serpent, but this only exists in a single extant representation before the end of the fifth century, and I believe Shapiro and Hadas, as with many modern commentators, have built their view of Jason based on the much later source of Apollonios' *Argonautika*, and their approach has been to search backwards for earlier evidence that could confirm this portrayal. However, as is the intention of this work, if we adopt a properly chronological approach and also make the most of the iconographical evidence available to us, we are able to construct a very different view of the myth.

Visual evidence also fills in the gaps in many of the smaller aspects of the tale. To support the view that Jason's story was the subject of epic poetry, it is important not to see his myth as only involving a handful of stories. Pindar gives us the confrontation with Pelias (*Py.*

---

[181] Shapiro, p. 97.

4.78ff), the Clashing Rocks (*Py.* 4.208), the events at Kolchis (*Py.* 4.219ff), and the return voyage (*Py.* 4.250ff, including Lemnos). However, if we are to assume that this myth was an inspiration to Homer for the *Odyssey*, as pointed to by Huxley, Braswell, Page and others,[182] then the myth must have contained other episodes, especially those dealing with the voyage to Kolchis, in order for it to be properly considered as an epic tale. The *Odyssey* contains many examples such as the Kyklopes, Kirke, the Laestrygonians and the Phaecians, and the voyage of the Argo must also have included tales of places along the journey where the ship stopped and the crew encountered local inhabitants. The tale of Phineus is one such example, but the stories of the boxer Amykos, and the bronze giant Talos, are two further tales which have a special significance in iconography. For the story of Amykos there are no early extant literary references, and it is only due to the fifth century iconography that we have any pre-400 evidence for this myth. For the story of Talos, we have no literary evidence linking the giant to the Argonautic voyage before Apollonios Rhodios in the third century B.C. Only iconography connects this tale to earlier versions of the Argonautic voyage, and furthermore, possibly links Jason to the giant's death [Fig. 94].

The third example of how iconography fills the gaps in the myth concerns the story of Pelias. We know on this occasion that tragedy did deal with the myth, as Euripides' *Peliades* and Sophokles' *Root-cutters* probably presented the death of the king as the plot of the play. However, it is left to iconographical evidence to record the first examples of this, and indeed the depictions offer a clear indication of how the king died. Medea's direct persuasion of the daughters of Pelias to attempt to rejuvenate their father appears seven times in art, six of them before the date of Euripides' *Peliades* (455 B.C.). A further twelve examples show Pelias and his daughters prior to the act of "rejuvenation" (dated between 525-435 B.C.), and so it becomes evident that this subject was a popular theme at the end of the sixth century and

---

[182] Page (1973), p. 39.

on into the fifth century, even before it becomes a subject of tragic drama.

Overall I believe, we cannot hope to understand the Jason myth without the contribution of iconographical evidence. Given the absence of much of the original literary evidence for his story, iconography helps to fill these gaps and to correct what might otherwise be misinterpretations. I feel that one of the most important conclusions of this exercise is that it is both difficult and misleading to try to arrive at an understanding of a myth without looking at all types of evidence that are available to us. Concentration on literary evidence alone has led many scholars to an imperfect impression of the hero Jason, or of the adventures the hero took part in. Visual evidence can help us to correct these misinterpretations, but cannot itself function in isolation. I feel I have shown that when the two strands of evidence are viewed in conjunction with each other, we emerge with a clearer understanding of the myth and its hero.

This wide range of material covered in the course of my discussion, has clearly demonstrated that the myth of Jason is much more than the portrayal we find in the *Medea*. The story of Jason and his quest is a story with deep roots in Greek mythology, and Jason is a character who embodies many of the stock traits of a hero, enabling him to successfully seize the golden fleece, and overcome many of the obstacles he encountered in the course of his travels. Our understanding of the tale is at times hampered by lost literary sources, but the contribution of iconography is able to fill many of these gaps, and to present alternative strands which may have been lost from literature. The result of this examination is that we can now see a version of the Jason myth that is as close as possible to the original story that the early Greeks would have known, and which is free from the more negative connotations conjured up by Euripides and other, later, sources. Without the iconographical evidence, our understanding of this early myth of Jason would be greatly diminished. The visual representations discussed here have provided us with unique insights into a fascinating hero of early mythology, and have enabled us to present the most thorough version possible of his adventures and heroic successes.

Appendices

	625 - 600 B.C.	600 - 575 B.C.	575 - 550 B.C.	550 - 525 B.C.	525 - 500 B.C.	500 - 475 B.C.	475 - 450 B.C.	450 - 425 B.C.	425 - 400 B.C.
Phineus alone to face Harpuiai							√ [54] √ [55]		
The Snatching of the Food						√ [50] √ [51]	√ [53]	√ [58] √ [60]	
Phineus and the Arrival of the Argonauts							√ [56] √ [57]	√ [59]	√ [62]
Harpies Flee Alone	√ [39]								
Pursuit of Harpuiai by Boreadai		√ [40]-dated 600-550 B.C.	√ [46]	√ [47]-dated to 550-500 B.C. √ [48]	√ [49]	√ [52]		√ [61]	√ [63]
The capturing of the Harpuiai			√ [42] √ [43] √ [44] √ [45]						√ [64]
Other: Jason heals Phineus (?); Boreadai			√ [41]						

	625 - 600 B.C.	600 - 575 B.C.	575 - 550 B.C.	550 - 525 B.C.	525 - 500 B.C.	500 - 475 B.C.	475 - 450 B.C.	450 - 425 B.C.	425 - 400 B.C.
Jason & serpent; lower body in mouth	√ [10] √ [11]								
Jason & serpent; leg in s. mouth; J holds fleece						√ [15]			
Jason & serpent; leg in s. mouth; J holds sword							√ [19]		
J. & serpent; leg in s. mouth; J holds sword & fleece			√ [13] *						
Jason with Athena; disgorged by serpent						√ [16] *			
Jason with Athena; seizes fleece from serpent							√ [17] √ [18]		
Jason with Medea; seizes fleece from serpent									√ [21]
Other uncertain reps. of man and serpent		√ [12] √ [14]							
Jason & the Bulls								√ [20] ??	
Jason, Athena, Medea, Argonauts & Aietes									√ [22]

* indicates that Jason is named

	525 - 500 B.C.	500 - 475 B.C.	475 - 450 B.C.	450 - 425 B.C.	425 - 400 B.C.	Late source
Medea and Peliades with Ram in Cauldron	√ [66] √ [68]	√ [79] √ [80]			√ [90] (no ram)	
Medea and Peliades with Ram in Cauldron, with Pelias	√ [65] √ [67]					
Peliades (?) with Ram in Cauldron		√ [72] √ [73] √ [74] √ [75]	√ [82]			
Peliades (?) with Ram in Cauldron, with Pelias		√ [76]	√ [84] inc. Jason or 3 Peliades	√ [87]		
Peliades alone				√ [85]* √ [77]		
Peliades with Pelias			√ [81]	√ [86]* √ [88]* √ [89]*- ram not in cauldron		
Youth emerging from Cauldron		√ [69] √ [70] √ [71] √ [78]				√ [92]- 4th century
Rejuvenation of Aison						
Rejuvenation of Jason (named)			√ [83]			√ [91]- 370-360 B.C.

* indicates that the image shows 3 rather than the more usual 2 Peliades

Bibliography

Primary Sources:

Aeschylus   *The Oresteia*, translated by Robert Fagles with introduction, notes and glossary written with collaboration of W. B. Stanford (London, 1966).

_____ *Suppliant Maidens, the Persians, Prometheus, Seven Against Thebes*, translated by Herbert Weir Smyth (Cambridge MA, 1922).

_____ *Agamemnon, Libation-Bearers, Eumenides, Fragments*, translated by Herbert Weir Smyth, with an appendix by Hugh Lloyd-Jones (Cambridge MA, 1926).

Apollodoros T *he Library of Greek Mythology*, trans. by R. Hard (Oxford, 1997).

_____ *The Library: 1*, translated by J. G. Frazer (Cambridge MA, 1921).

_____ *The Library: 2*, translated by J. G. Frazer (Cambridge MA, 1921).

Apollonios Rhodios, *Jason and the Golden Fleece*, translated by Richard Hunter (Oxford, 1993).

_____ *The Argonautika: the Story of Jason and the Quest for the Golden Fleece*, translated with an introduction and glossary by Peter Green (London, 1997).

_____ *Argonautica*, translated R. C. Seaton (Cambridge MA, 1912).

Athenaeus,   *The Deipnosophists*, translation by Charles Burton Gulick (Cambridge MA, 1961).

Early Greek Lyric Poetry, translated with an introduction and commentary by David Mulroy (Ann Arbor, 1992).

Early Greek Mythography: Volume 1: Text and Introduction, by Robert L. Fowler (Oxford, 2000).

Epicorum Graecorum Fragmenta, edited by Malcolm Davies (Göttingen, 1988).

Euripides,   *Alcestis/Hippolytus/Iphigenia in Tauris*, translated with introduction by Philip Vellacott (London, 1974).

_____   *Children of Heracles, Hippolytus, Andromache, Hecuba*, edited and translated by David Kovacs (Cambridge MA, 1995).

_____   *Cyclops, Alcestis & Medea*, edited and translated by David Kovacs (Cambridge MA, 1994).

_____   *Ion, The Women of Troy, Helen and The Bacchae*, translated by Philip Vellacott (London, 1973).

_____   *Medea*, edited with introduction and commentary by Alan Elliott (Oxford, 1969).

_____   *Medea*, edited by Donald Mastronarde (Cambridge, 2002).

_____   *Medea*, edited with introduction and commentary by D. L. Page Oxford, 1938).

Euripides, *Orestes, The Children of Heracles, Andromache, The Suppliant Women, The Phoenician Women & Iphigenia in Aulis*, translated with an introduction by Philip Vellacott (London, 1972).

_____ *Suppliant Women, Electra, Heracles*, edited and translated by David Kovacs (Cambridge MA, 1998).

_____ *Trojan Women, Iphigenia among the Taurians, Ion*, edited and translated by David Kovacs (Cambridge MA, 1999).

Fragmente Griechischen Historiker, edited by Felix Jacoby et al. (Leiden, 1923-).

Greek Epic Fragments: from the seventh to the fifth centuries B.C., edited and translated by Martin L. West (Cambridge MA, 2003).

Greek Iambic Poetry, edited and translated by Douglas E. Gerbe (Cambridge MA, 1999).

Greek Lyric I: Sappho and Alcaeus, translated by David A. Campbell (Cambridge MA, 1982).

Greek Lyric II: Anacreon, Anacreontea, Chorla Lyric from Olympus to Alcman, translated by David A. Campbell (Cambridge MA, 1988).

Greek Lyric III: Stesichorus, Ibycus, Simonides, and Others, edited and translated by David A. Campbell (Cambridge MA, 1991).

Greek Lyric IV: Bacchylides, Corinna and Others, translated by David A. Campbell (Cambridge MA, 1992).

Greek Lyric V: The New School of Poetry and Anonymous Songs and Hymns, translated by David A. Campbell (Cambridge MA, 1993).

Greek Lyric Poetry, translated with introduction & notes by M. L. West (Oxford, 1993).

Herodotus,   *The Histories*, translated by Aubrey de Selincourt and revised with introduction by A. R. Burn (London, 1972).

Hesiod,   *The Homeric Hymns and Homerica,* translation by Hugh G. Evelyn-White (Cambridge MA, 1914).

Hesiod,   *Theogony and Works & Days*, translated with introduction & notes by M. L. West (Oxford, 1988).

Homer,   *The Iliad: Books 1-12*, translation by A. T. Murray, revised by W. F. Wyatt (Cambridge MA, 1999).

_____   *The Iliad: Books 13-24*, by A. T. Murray, revised by W. F. Wyatt (Cambridge MA, 1999).

_____   *The Odyssey: Books 1-12*, translation by A. T. Murray, revised by George E. Dimock (Cambridge MA, 1998).

_____   *The Odyssey: Books 13-24*, translation by A. T. Murray, revised by George E. Dimock (Cambridge MA, 1998).

Iambi et Elegi Graeci, edited by M. L. West (Oxford, 1972).

Lykophron's Alexandra: Griechisch und deutsch mit erklärenden Anmerkungen, edited and translated by Carl von Holzinger (New York, 1895).

Pausanias,   *The Description of Greece: Books I-II*, translated by W. H. S. Jones (Cambridge MA, 1918).

Pausanias,   *The Description of Greece: Books III-V*, translated by W. H. S. Jones & H. A. Ormerod (Cambridge MA, 1926).

_____   *The Description of Greece: Books VI, VII, VIII (chs. i-xxi)*, translated by W. H. S. Jones (Cambridge MA, 1933).

_____   *The Description of Greece: Books VIII.22-X*, translated by W. H. S. Jones (Cambridge MA, 1935).

_____   *The Description of Greece: Illustrations and Index*, translated by R. E. Wycherley (Cambridge MA, 1935).

_____   *Guide to Greece vols. I and II*, translated by Peter Levi (London, 1971).

Pherekydes, for Fragments see *Early Greek Mythography*, edited by R. Fowler, (Oxford, 2000).

Pindar,   *Pindar I: Olympian Odes, Pythian Odes,* edited & translated by William H. Race (Cambridge MA, 1997).

_____   *Pindar II: Nemean Odes, Isthmian Odes & Fragments,* edited & translated by William H. Race (Cambridge MA, 1997).

_____   *The Odes of Pindar including the Principal Fragments*, introduction and translation by John Sandys (Cambridge MA, 1919).

Poetae Melici Graeci, edited by D. L. Page (Oxford, 1962).

Scholia Vetera in Pindari Carmina, edited by A. B. Drachmann (Amsterdam, 1967).

Sophocles,   *Antigone, The Women of Trachis, Philoctetes, Oedipus at Colonus*, edited and translated by Hugh Lloyd-Jones (Cambridge MA, 1994).

_____   *Ajax, Electra, Oedipus Tyrannus*, edited and translated by Hugh Lloyd-Jones (Cambridge MA, 1994).

_____   *Fragments*, edited and translated by Hugh Lloyd-Jones (Cambridge MA, 1996).

Theocritus, edited with translation and commentary by A. S. F. Gow (Oxford, 1950).

Tragicorum Graecorum Fragmenta vol. 3 (Aeschylus), edited by Stefan Radt (Göttingen, 1985).

Tragicorum Graecorum Fragmenta vol. 4 (Sophocles), edited by Stefan Radt (Göttingen, 1977).

Tragicorum Graecorum Fragmenta, edited by A. Nauck (Hildesheim, 1977).

Gaius Valerius Flaccus, *The Voyage of the Argo: The Argonautica of Gaius Valerius Flaccus*, translated by David R. Slavitt (London, 1999).

Secondary Literature:

Aghion, I., Barbillion, C., Lissarrague, F., *Gods and Heroes of Classical Antiquity* (New York, 1994).

Beazley, J. D.,   *Attic Black-Figure Vase-Painters* (Oxford, 1956).

_____   *Attic Red-Figure Vase-Painters*, 2nd edn. (Oxford, 1963).

Biers, W.R.,   *The Archaeology of Greece* 2nd edn. (London, 1966).

Boardman, J.,   *Athenian Black Figure Vases* (London, 1974).

_____   *Athenian Red Figure Vases: The Archaic Period* (London, 1975).

_____   *Athenian Red Figure Vases: The Classical Period* (London, 1989).

_____   *Early Greek Vase Painting* (London, 1998).

_____   *The History of Greek Vases* (London, 2001).

_____   (ed.), *The Oxford History of Classical Art* (Oxford, 1993).

Boedeker, D.,   "Euripides' *Medea* and the Vanity of Logoi," *Classical Philology* 86, pp. 95-112 (Chicago, 1991).

Bowra, C. M.,   *Pindar* (Oxford, 1964).

Braswell, B. K., *A Commentary on the Fourth Pythian Ode of Pindar* (New York, 1988).

Braund, D.,   *Georgia in Antiquity* (Oxford, 1994).

Buxton, R.,   *Imaginary Greece: the Contexts of Mythology* (Cambridge, 1994).

Carpenter, T. H., *Art and Myth in Ancient Greece* (London, 1991).

Clauss, J. J. & Johnston, S. I. eds., *Medea: Essays on Medea in Myth, Literature, Philosophy, and Art* (Princeton, 1997).

Cook, R. M.,   *Greek Painted Pottery*, 2nd edn. (London, 1972).

Dugas, C.,   "Observations sur la Légende de Persée", *Revue des Études Grecques* 69, pp. 1-15 (Paris, 1956).

Easterling, P.E.,"The Infanticide in Euripides' *Medea*", *Yale Classical Studies* 25, pp. 177-91 (London, 1977).

Easterling, P. E., & Knox, B. M. W. (eds.), *The Cambridge History of Classical Literature: Volume 1, Greek Literature* (Cambridge, 1985).

Finley, M.,   *The World of Odysseus* (London, 1956).

Foley, H.,   "Medea's Divided Self", *Classical Antiquity* 81, pp. 61-85 (Berkeley, 1989).

Fowler, R.,   *Early Greek Mythography: Volume 1: Text and Introduction* (Oxford, 2000).

Gantz, T.,   *Early Greek Myth: Vols 1 & 2* (Baltimore, 1993).

Graf, F.,   *Greek Mythology* , trans. by Thomas Marier (London, 1993).

Graves, R.,   *Greek Myths: Illustrated Edition* (London, 1981).

Hadas, M., "The Tradition of a Feeble Jason," *Classical Philology* 31, pp. 166-8 (Chicago, 1936).

Hammond, N. G. L. & Moon, W. G., "Illustrations of Early Greek Tragedy at Athens", *AJA* 82, pp. 371-83 (Boston, 1978).

Heubeck, A. & Hoekstra, A., *A Commentary on Homer's Odyssey Vol. II: Books ix-xvi* (Oxford, 1989).

Hunter, R. L. "'Short on Heroics': Jason in the Argonautica," *Classical Quarterly* 38, pp. 436-53 (Oxford, 1988).

Huxley, G. L., *Greek Epic Poetry: from Eumelos to Panyassis* (London, 1969).

King, C., "Who is that Cloaked Man?: Observations on Early Fifth Century B.C. Pictures of the Golden Fleece," *AJA* 87, pp. 385-7 and plate 55 (Boston, 1983).

Kirk, G. S., *The Nature of Greek Myths* (London, 1974).

Kirkwood, G., *Selections from Pindar* (Chicago, 1982).

Kleijwegt, M., *Ancient Youth: the ambiguity of youth and the absence of adolescence in Greco-Roman society* (Amsterdam, 1991).

Knox, B. M. W., "The *Medea* of Euripides," *Oxford Readings in Greek Tragedy* ed. E. Segal, pp. 272-93 (Oxford, 1983).

Kovacs, D., "Zeus in Euripides' *Medea*," *American Journal of Philology* 114, pp. 45-79 (Baltimore, 1993).

Lefkowitz, M. R., *Women in Greek Myth* (Bristol, 1986).

Lexicon Iconographicum Mythologiae Classicae (Zurich, 1981-).

McDermott, E. A., *Euripides' Medea: The Incarnation of Disorder* (London, 1989).

Mackie, C. J., "The Earliest Jason: What's in a Name?," *G&R* 48, p. 1-17 (Oxford, 2001).

March, J. R., *The Creative Poet: Studies on the Treatment of Myths in Greek Poetry, BICS* Supplement No. 49 (London, 1987).

Masterpieces of the J. Paul Getty Museum Antiquities (Los Angeles, 1997).

Meyer, H., *Medeia und die Peliaden* (Rome, 1980).

Morford, M. P. O. & Lenardon, R. J., *Classical Mythology* (New York, 1971).

Moustaka, A., *Kulte und Mythen auf Thessalischen Münzen* (Würzburg, 1983).

Mulroy, D., *Early Greek Lyric Poetry* (Ann Arbor, 1992).

Murray, O., *Early Greece*: 2nd edn. (London, 1993).

Neils, J., "Reflections of Immortality: the Myth of Jason on Etruscan Mirrors," *Etruscans: Art & Society in Ancient Etruria*, edited by Richard Daniel de Puma & Jocelyn Penny Small, pp. 190-5 (Oxford, 1994).

Osborne, R., *Archaic and Classical Greek Art* (Oxford, 1998).

Page, D. L., *Folktales in Homer's Odyssey* (Cambridge MA, 1973).

Palmer, R. B., "An Apology for Jason: A Study of Euripides' *Medea*," *Classical Journal* 53, pp. 49-55 (1957).

Pedley, J. G., *Greek Art and Archaeology, 2nd ed.* (London, 1998).

Podlecki, A. J., *The Early Greek Poets and their Times* (Vancouver, 1984).

Preziosi, D. & Hitchcock L. A., *Aegean Art and Architecture* (Oxford, 1999).

Radermacher, L., *Mythos und Sage bei den Griechen* (Munich, 1938).

Richter, G. M. A. & Hall, L. F., *The Metropolitan Museum of Art: Red Figure Athenian Vases* (Oxford, 1936).

Richter, G. M. A., *A Handbook of Greek Art: a Survey of the Visual Arts of Ancient Greece* 9th edn. (Oxford, 1987).

_____ "Jason and the Golden Fleece," *AJA* 39 pp. 182-4 (Boston, 1935).

Robbins, E., "Jason and Cheiron: the Myth of Pindar's *Fourth Pythian*," *Phoenix* 29, pp. 205-13 (Toronto, 1975).

Robinson, D., "Unpublished vases in the Robinson Collection," *AJA* 60 pp. 1-19 (Boston, 1956).

Robinson, M., "The Death of Talos," *Journal of Hellenic Studies* 97, pp. 158-60 (London, 1977).

Rose, H. J., *A Handbook of Greek Mythology*, 6th edn. (London, 1958).

Rutter, N. K. & Sparkes, B. A., *Word and Image in Ancient Greece* (Edinburgh, 2000).

Schefold, K. & Jung, F., *Die Urkönige, Perseus, Bellerophon, Herakles und Theseus in der Klassischen und Hellenistischen Kunst* (Munich, 1988).

Schefold, K., *Myth and Art in Early Greek Art*, trans. Audrey Hicks, (London, 1966).

_____ *Gods and Heroes in Late Archaic Greek Art*, trans. by Alan Griffith (Cambridge, 1992).

Schlesinger, E., "On Euripides' *Medea*," *Oxford Readings in Greek Tragedy* ed. E. Segal, pp. 294-310 (Oxford, 1983).

Schmitt, M. L., "Bellerophon and the Chimera in Archaic Greek Art," *AJA* 70, pp. 341-7, pl. 1-9 (Boston, 1966).

Segal, C., *Pindar's Mythmaking: the Fourth Pythian Ode* (Princeton, 1986).

Seton-Williams, M. V., *Greek Legends and Stories* (London, 1993).

Shapiro, H. A., "'Old and New Heroes: Narrative, Composition, and Subject in Attic Black-Figure," *CA* 9, pp. 114-48, pl. 1-11 (Berkeley, 1990).

_____ *Myth Into Art: Poet and Painter in Classical Greece* (London, 1995).

Simon, E., *Die Götter der Griechen* (Munich, 1969).

Simon, E., "Die Typen der Medeadarstellung in der antiken Kunst," *Gymnasium*, pp. 203-227 (Berlin, 1954)

Snodgrass, A., *Homer and the Artists: Text and Picture in Early Greek Art* (Cambridge, 1998).

Sourvinou-Inwood, C., *Theseus as Son and Stepson: a tentative illustration of the Greek mythological mentality, BICS* Supplement No. 40 (London, 1979).

Sparkes, B. A., *Greek Pottery: an Introduction* (Manchester, 1991).

_____ *The Red and the Black: Studies in Greek Pottery* (London, 1996).

Spivey, N., *Greek Art* (London, 1997).

Stanford, W. B., & Luce, J. V., *The Quest for Ulysses* (London, 1974).

Vickers, M., *Ancient Greek Pottery* (Oxford, 1999).

Vojatzi, M., *Frühe Argonautenbilder* (Wurzburg, 1982).

Williams, D., *Greek Vases* (London, 1985).

Woodford, S., *Images of Myths in Classical Antiquity* (Cambridge, 2003).

Illustrations

Note on Illustrations

The purpose of this collection of images is to provide an easy reference for the reader. I have attempted to gather as many of the images as possible, and where I have not been able to do this, I have provided reference details instead. I have also decided to include these references in this collection for continuity, even though the image may not be available.

The descriptive details of the artefacts are not intended to be a detailed guide, but rather a few descriptive words to help identification of the piece. Detailed descriptions are included in the discussion within the book. A section directing the reader to other published references is also included for convenience.

Figure No. 001

Character	Jason
Episode	Alone
Name	
Artifact	Triobol
Item Style	
Made in	
Found	
Date	470 B.C.
Artist	
Details	Coin with head of Jason; single sandal on other side
Mus. /Lit. Ref.	
Refs.	LIMC "Iason" 1

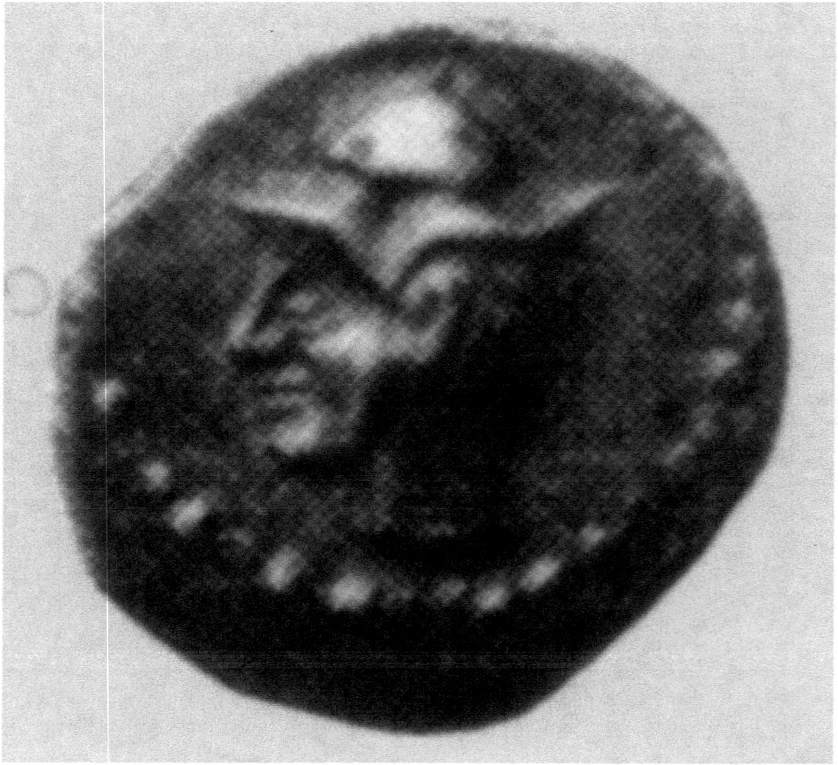

Figure No. 002

Character Jason
Episode Alone

Name
Artifact Carnelian scarab
Item Style Gem, scarab
Made in
Found
Date 350 B.C.

Artist
Details Jason (named Easun) and the Argo

Mus. /Lit. Ref. London, British Museum 669

Refs. LIMC "Argonautai" 3

LIMC "Iason" 5

LIMC "Iason" 5

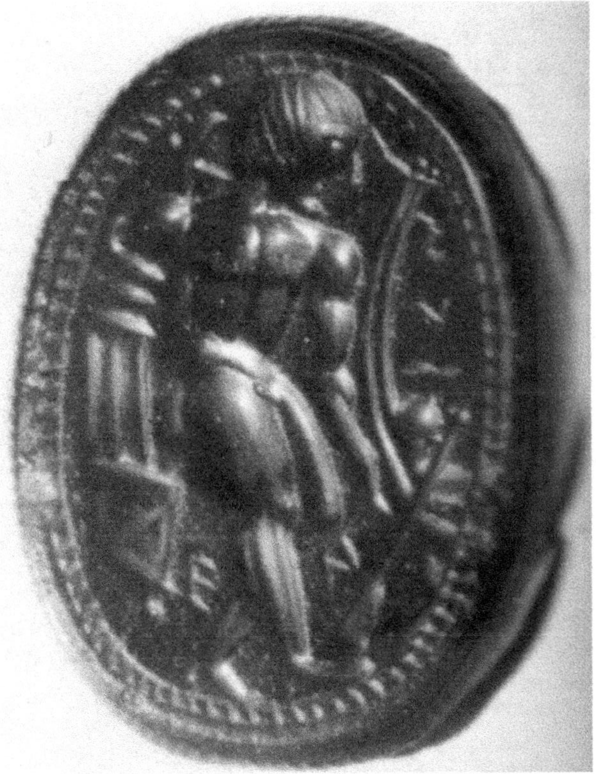

Character	Jason
Episode	Fleece & Events at Kolchis
Name	
Artifact	Painting
Item	
Style	
Made in	Athens
Found	
Date	Fifth century
Artist	Mikon
Details	Wall Painting described in Pausanias 1.18.1

Mus. /Lit. Ref.	Pausanias 1.18.1

Refs.

Character	Jason
Episode	Amykos
Name	
Artifact	Volute krater fragment
Item Style	Red-figure
Made in	Attica
Found	
Date	440–430 B.C.
Artist	Peleus Painter
Details	Amykos with bound hands ready to box.
Mus. /Lit. Ref.	Ferrara, Mus. Nat. Spina, Valle Trebba T. 404
Refs.	LIMC "Amykos" 14*
	LIMC "Atalante" 73*
	LIMC "Argonautai" 22

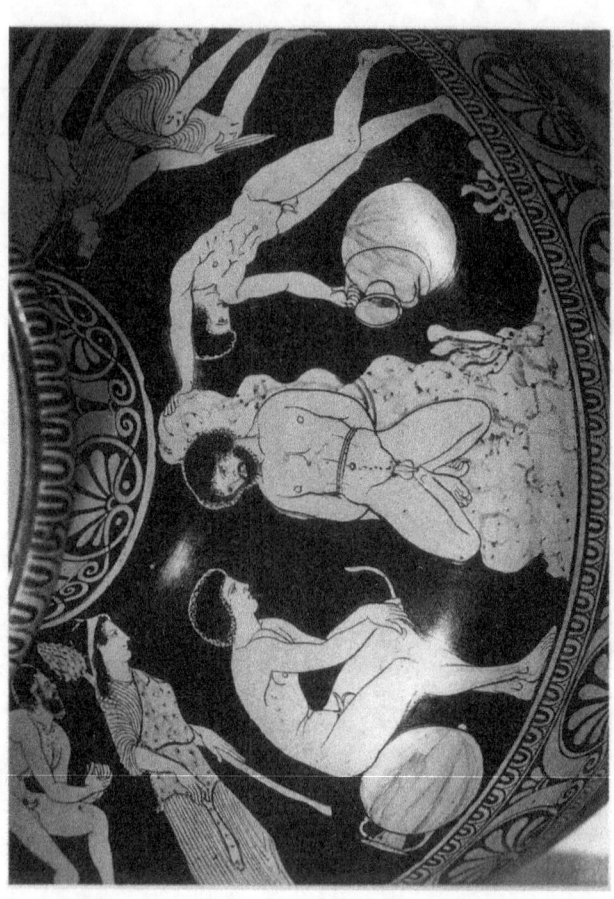

Character Jason
Episode Amykos

Name
Artifact Hydria
Item Red-figure
Style
Made in Lucanian
Found
Date 420-400 B.C.

Artist Amykos Painter
Details Amykos and the Dioskouroi. Jason (?)
stands by Argo with 2 spears

Mus. Paris, Cab. Med. 442
/Lit.
Ref.

Refs. Carpenter, T.H., fig. 274

LIMC "Boreadai" 19*

LIMC "Iason" 8

LIMC "Argonautai" 9 & "Amykos" 11*

Figure No. 005

Character Jason

Episode Argonauts

Name

Artifact Metope sculpture

Item
Style Limestone relief

Made in Delphi, Treasury
Found

Date 570 B.C.

Artist

Details Argonauts

Mus. Delphi Museum
/Lit.
Ref.

Refs. Carpenter, T.H., fig. 273

LIMC "Argonautai" 2

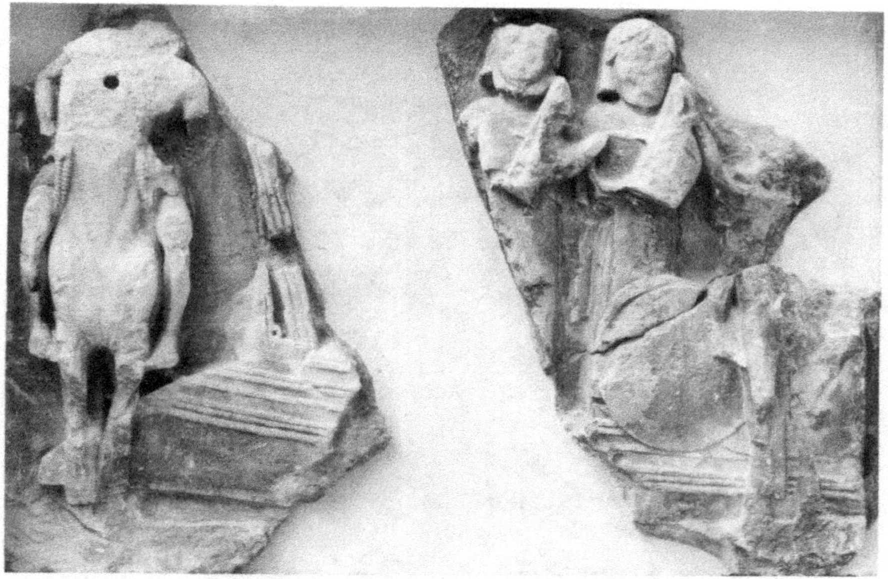

Figure No. 006

Character	Jason
Episode	Argonauts
Name	
Artifact	Calyx krater
Item Style	Red-figure
Made in	Attica
Found	Orvieto
Date	460 B.C.
Artist	Niobid Painter
Details	Possibly Athena and the Argonauts but Boardman calles it gods and heroes before Marathon (?)
	Other side is Artemis, Apollo and the children of Niobe.
Mus. /Lit. Ref.	Paris, Louvre G 431
Refs.	Graves, R. p. 194
	Boardman (1989), 4.2

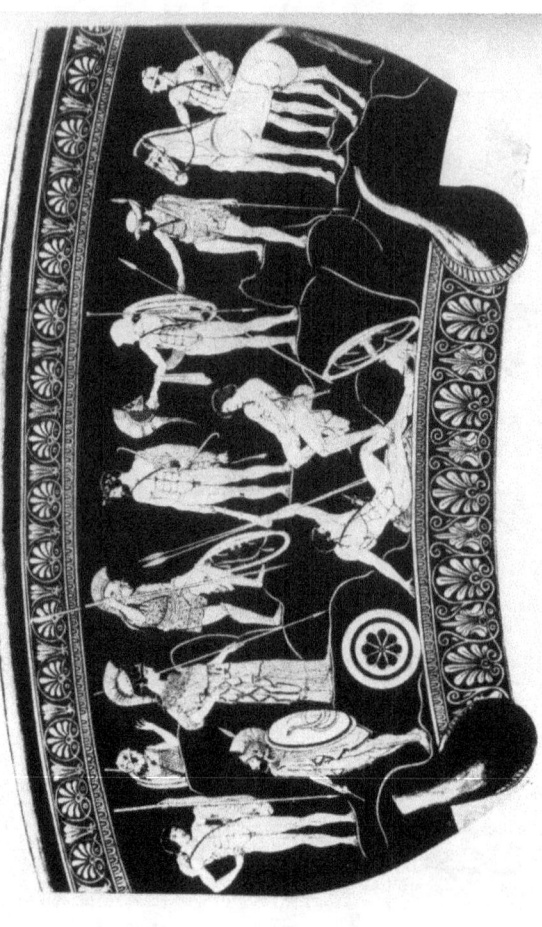

Figure No. 007

Character	Jason
Episode	Argonauts
Name	
Artifact	Volute krater
Item	Red-figure
Style	
Made in	Attica
Found	Ruvo, Italy
Date	400 B.C.
Artist	Talos Painter
Details	Dioscouri, Nike, Athena, Jason and Hera (named)
Mus. /Lit. Ref.	Ruvo, Mus. Jatta 1501
Refs.	LIMC "Iason" 56*
	LIMC "Hera" 452
	LIMC "Dioskouri" 220
	Beazley, J.D., Attic Red-Figure Vase-Painters, 2nd edition (Oxford, 1963), 1338.1

Figure No. 008

Figure No. 009

Character	Jason
Episode	Argonauts

Name	
Artifact	Sculpture
Item	Relief
Style	
Made in	
Found	
Date	

Artist	
Details	Building of the Argo

Mus. London, British Museum
/Lit.
Ref.

Refs. Seton-Williams, M.V., p. 151

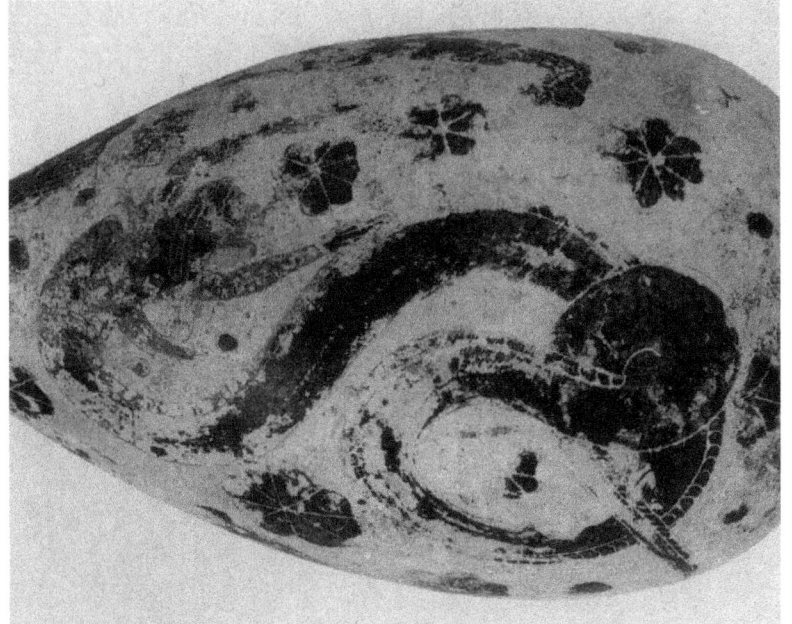

Character Jason
Episode Fleece & Events at Kolchis

Name
Artifact Alabastron
Item Black-figure
Style

Made in Korinth
Found

Date 625-600 B.C.

Artist

Details Upper body of man in mouth of long coiled serpent

Mus. Bonn, Akad. Kunstmus. 860
/Lit.
Ref.

Refs. LIMC "Iason" 30*

Character	Jason
Episode	Fleece & Events at Kolchis
Name	
Artifact	Aryballos fragment
Item Style	
Made in	Korinth
Found	Heraion, Samos
Date	625-600 B.C.
Artist	
Details	Man emerging from mouth of serpent.
Mus. /Lit. Ref.	Samos, Mus. K 3431, 3490
Refs.	LIMC "Iason" 31

Character Jason
Episode Fleece & Events at Kolchis

Name
Artifact Deianeira lekythos
Item
Style Black-figure
Made in Attica
Found
Date 600 B.C.

Artist Manner of the Gorgon Painter
Details **UNCERTAIN REPRESENTATION:**
On shoulder, large serpent with man's head in its jaws.

Mus. Staatliche Museen zu Berlin-Preußischer
/Lit. Kulturbesitz, Antikensammlung V.i 3764
Ref. (lekythos)

Refs. LIMC "Iason" 77

Character Jason

Episode Fleece & Events at Kolchis

Name

Artifact Hand-mirror

Item Style Bronze

Made in Found South Italian

Date 575-550 B.C. or possibly 4th century

Artist

Details Jason (named) grapples with serpent; fleece in left hand

Mus. /Lit. Ref. Staatliche Museen zu Berlin-Preußischer Kulturbesitz, Antikensammlung Fr. 148 (mirror)

Refs. Meyer, pl. 19 (no. 1)

LIMC "Iason" 35*

Neils, J., pp. 190-5; image- p. 192 fig.17.5

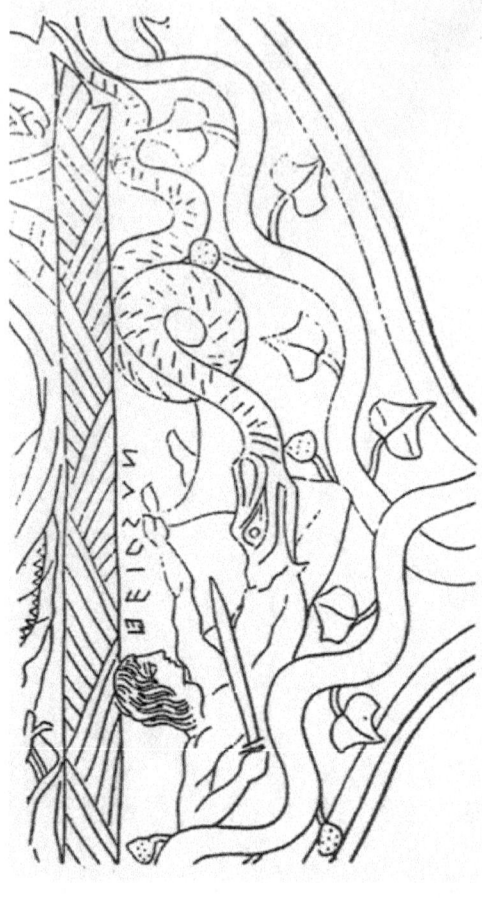

Figure No. 013

Character	Jason
Episode	Fleece & Events at Kolchis
Name	
Artifact	Metopes
Item Style	Limestone
Made in Found	Foce del Sele
Date	550 B.C.
Artist	
Details	**UNCERTAIN REPRESENTATION:** Two metopes showing rejuvenation and the dragon (Metopes no. 32 and 26 respec.).
Mus. /Lit. Ref.	Paestum, Mus. Naz.
Refs.	Meyer, pls. 22 (no. 5) LIMC "Iason" 78

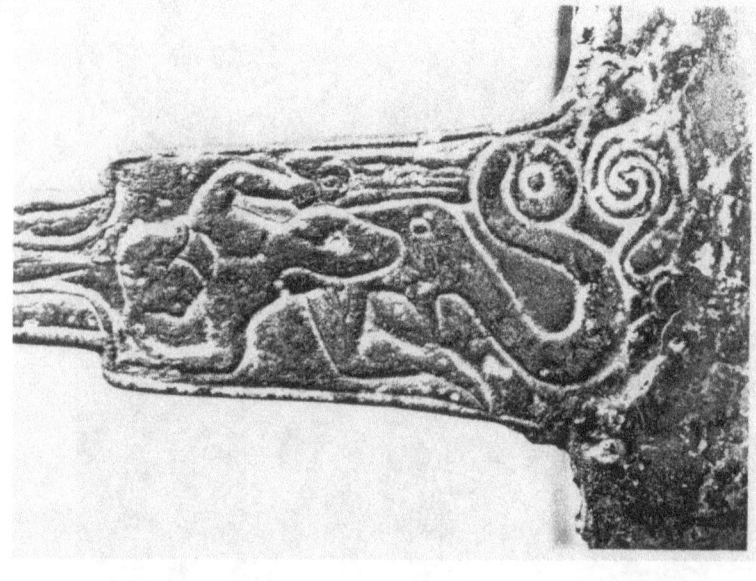

Character Jason

Episode Fleece & Events at Kolchis

Name

Artifact Bronze handle

Item Style Simpulum relief

Made in Etruscan

Found Bologna

Date 500-475 B.C.

Artist

Details Jason, holding the fleece, with leg in mouth of serpent

Mus. /Lit. Ref. Bologna, Museo Civico 190

Refs. LIMC "Iason" 34*

Meyer, pl. 19 (no. 1)

Character Jason

Episode Fleece & Events at Kolchis

Name

Artifact Kylix cup

Item Style Red-figure

Made in Attica

Found Cerveteri

Date 480-470 B.C.

Artist Douris Painter

Details Jason (named inscription- "Iason") is disgorged by the serpent with the help of Athena; fleece hangs in background. Jason's eyes are open.

Mus. /Lit. Ref. Rome, Vatican Museums 16545

Refs. LIMC "Iason" 32*

Mackie, fig. 2 (p. 11)

Meyer, pl. 18 (no. 1)

Graf, fig. 11

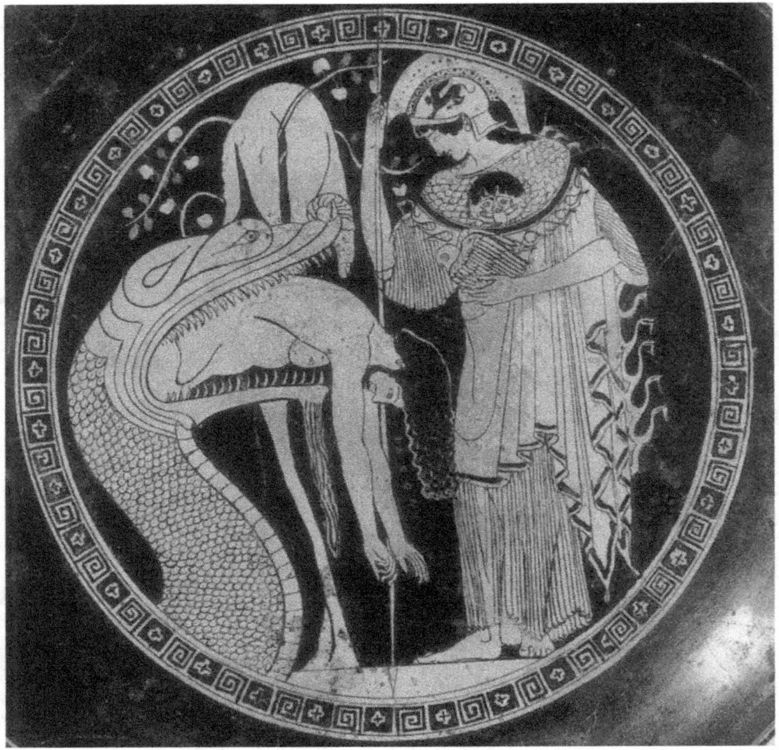

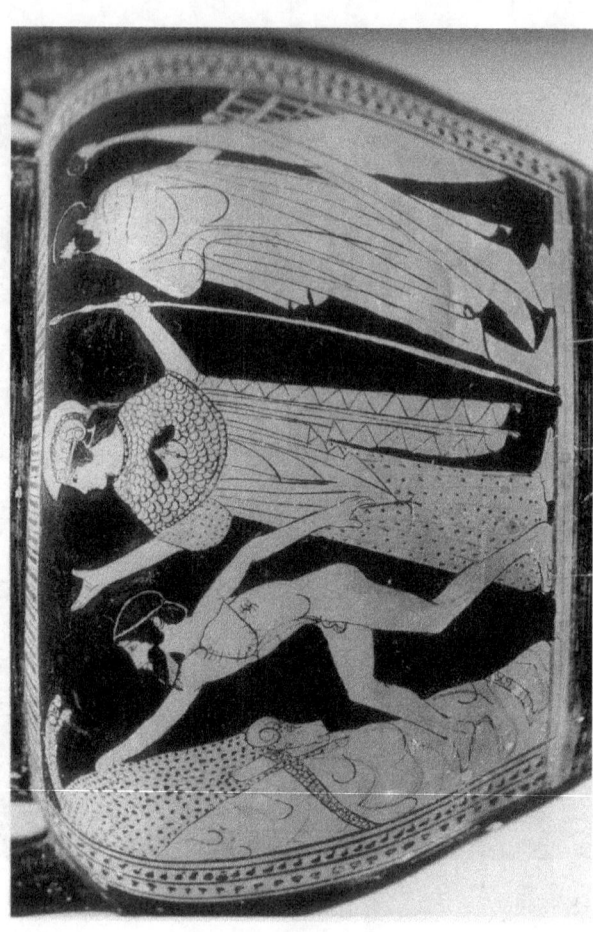

Character	Jason
Episode	Fleece & Events at Kolchis
Name	New York krater
Artifact	Column krater
Item Style	Red-figure
Made in	Attica
Found	
Date	470-460 B.C.
Artist	Orchard Painter
Details	Jason steals the fleece from under the snake; Athena observes. Argo to right of vase with unknown person (Zeus?)
Mus. /Lit. Ref.	New York, MMA 34.11.17
Refs.	Graves, R., p. 203
	LIMC "Iason" 36*
	Shapiro, fig. 65
	Carpenter, fig. 278
	Meyer, pl. 18 (no. 2)

Figure No. 017

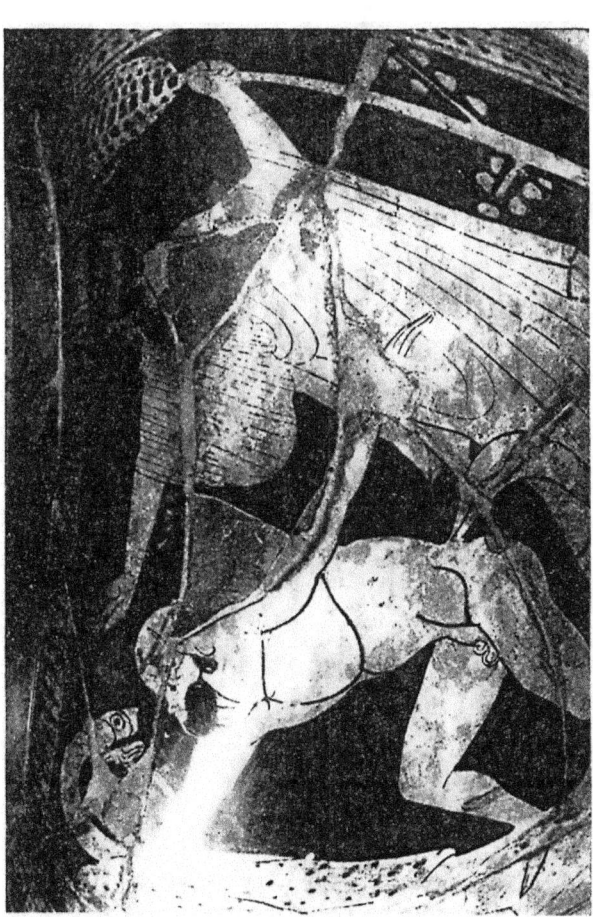

Character   Jason
Episode   Fleece & Events at Kolchis

Name   Bologna vase
Artifact   Amphora
**Item
Style**   Red-figure
**Made in
Found**   Attica
Date   470-460 B.C.

Artist
Details   Same as Orchard painter vase, but
                possibly based on satyr play from 5th
                century drama.

**Mus.
/Lit.
Ref.**   Bologna, Museo Civico

Refs.   Richter, (1935) pp. 184 fig. 4

                Meyer, pl. 25 (no. 11)

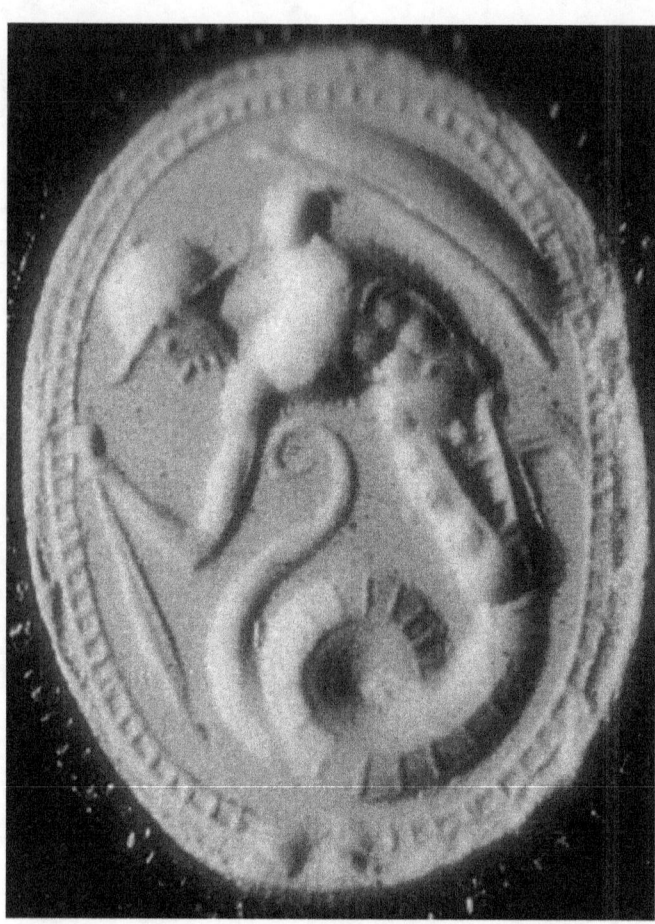

Figure No. 019

Character	Jason
Episode	Fleece & Events at Kolchis
Name	
Artifact	Sardonyx scarab
Item Style	Relief
Made in Found	Etruscan
Date	470-450 B.C.
Artist	
Details	Jason, holding sword and shield, grappling with serpent. **Note: this is an impression of the scarab.**
Mus. /Lit. Ref.	Boston, Museum of Fine Art 21.1203
Refs.	LIMC "Iason" 33*

Character Jason

Episode Fleece & Events at Kolchis

Name

Artifact Coin, drachma

**Item
Style**

**Made in
Found** Larissa, Thessaly

Date 440 B.C.

Artist

Details Youth grapples with the bulls; usually this
sort of scene is Thessalos, but Moustaka
argues for Jason (Moustaka, A. Kulte und
Mythen auf Thessalischen Munzen (1983)
69-70.74-76).

**Mus.
/Lit.
Ref.** Museum of Thessaly

Refs. LIMC "Iason" 15

Character Jason

Episode Fleece & Events at Kolchis

Name

Artifact Volute-krater

Item Style Red-figure

Made in Apulian, South Italian

Found Ruvo

Date 425-415 B.C.

Artist Sisyphos Painter

Details Lower frieze on vase: Argonauts, Medea, Boreadai. Jason takes fleece to right.

Note: this is the first extant example of Medea helping Jason to seize the fleece.

Mus. /Lit. Ref. Munich, Antikensammlungen 3268

Refs. LIMC "Iason" 37*

Shapiro, H.A., fig. 66

LIMC "Argonautai" 20

LIMC "Amykos" I 1

LIMC "Boreadai" 20

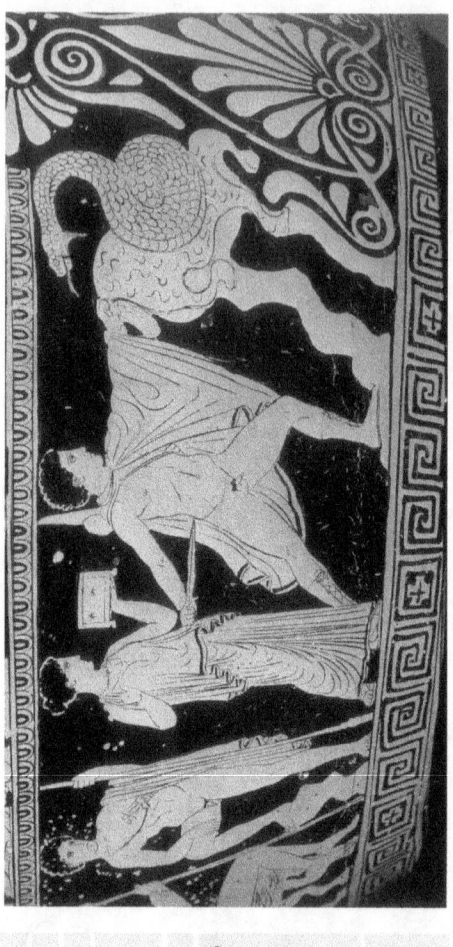

Figure No. 021

Character	Jason
Episode	Fleece & Events at Kolchis
Name	
Artifact	Bell-krater
Item Style	Red-figure
Made in	Attica
Found	Gela
Date	420-410 B.C.
Artist	Dinos Painter
Details	Stern of Argo with 3 Argonauts on left; Athena in centre; Aietes with white hair sits on throne to right. Medea stands behind him. Jason probably man with 2 spears with petasos, chlamys & sword.
Mus. /Lit. Ref.	Gela, Arch. Museum
Refs.	LIMC "Iason" 11

Character Jason

Episode Funeral Games/Boar Hunt

Name Chest of Kypselos
Artifact Relief

Item Votive offering
Style

Made in Korinth

Found Olympia

Date 600-550 B.C.

Artist

Details At funeral games for Pelias, Jason takes part in a wrestling match.

Mus. /Lit. Ref. Literature: Pausanias 5.17.9-11

Refs. LIMC "Iason" 65

LIMC "Argonautai" 24

Character Jason

Episode Funeral Games/Boar Hunt

Name

Artifact Dinos fragment

Item Black-figure
Style

Made in Attica
Found

Date 570 - 560 B.C.

Artist Kyllenios Painter

Details Jason with one sandal attacking boar from left

Mus. Switzerland, Bollingen, Blater Coll. *Para 42*
/Lit.
Ref.

Refs. LIMC "Iason" 75

LIMC "Meleagros" 9

Character Jason

Episode Funeral Games/Boar Hunt

Name

Artifact Kylix

Item Black-figure
Style

Made in Attica

Found Vulci

Date 550 - 540 B.C.

Artist Archikles and Glaukytes (signed by)

Details Jason (IAΣON), nude and bearded, is second from far left, attacking the boar with 2 spears in the company of eight other hunters and six dogs.

Mus. Munich, Antikenslg. 2243
/Lit.
Ref.

Refs. LIMC "Meleagros" 19*

LIMC "Iason" 76

Schefold (1992), fig. 238

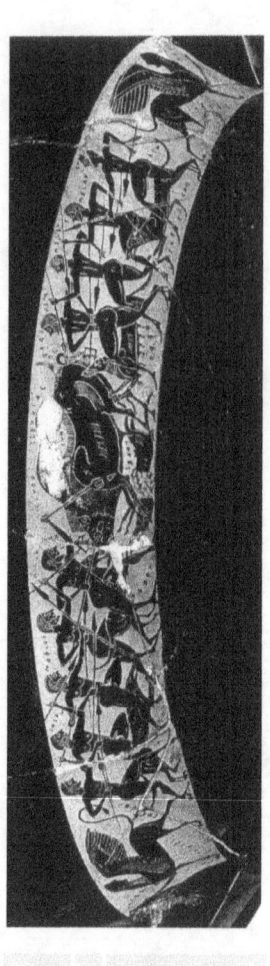

Figure No. 025

Character	Jason
Episode	Medea
Name	
Artifact	Relief pinax (?)
Item Style	Relief
Made in	
Found	Perachora
Date	725-700 B.C.
Artist	
Details	Medea, Jason Hera (?)
Mus. /Lit. Ref.	National Archaeological Museum, Athens 16482
Refs.	LIMC "Hera" 450

Character Jason

Episode Medea

Name

Artifact Amphora

Item Style Black-figure

Made in

Found Ceveteri

Date 660-640 B.C.

Artist

Details **UNCERTAIN REPRESENTATION:**
Medea

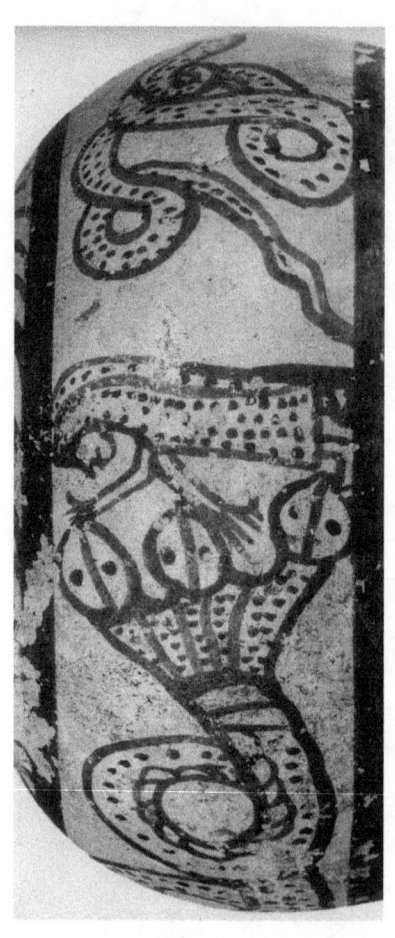

Mus. /Lit. Ref. Amsterdam Allard Pierson 10.188
Image provided by courtesy of the Allard
Pierson Museum, Amsterdam

Refs. LIMC "Medeia" 2*

Character	Jason
Episode	Medea
Name	
Artifact	Olpe
Item Style	Bucchero with relief anc engraved decoration
Made in	Etruscan
Found	Ceveteri
Date	630 B.C.
Artist	
Details	**UNCERTAIN REPRESENTATION:** Medea

Mus. /Lit. Ref. Ceveteri Nr. 110 976

Refs. LIMC "Medeia" 1*

Character Jason
Episode Medea

Name Chest of Kypselos
Artifact Relief

Item Votive offering
Style

Made in Korinth
Found Olympia
Date 600-550 B.C.

Artist
Details Medea enthroned between Jason and Aphrodite- inscription reads "Aphrodite commands: Jason marries Medea"

Mus. Literature: Pausanias 5.18.3
/Lit.
Ref.

Refs. LIMC "Iason" 10

Character	Jason
Episode	Medea
Name	
Artifact	Lekythos
Item Style	Black-figure
Made in	Attica
Found	
Date	530 B.C.
Artist	Cock Group
Details	**UNCERTAIN REPRESENTATION:** Medea
Mus. /Lit. Ref.	London, British Museum 1926.4-17.1
Refs.	LIMC "Medeia" 3*

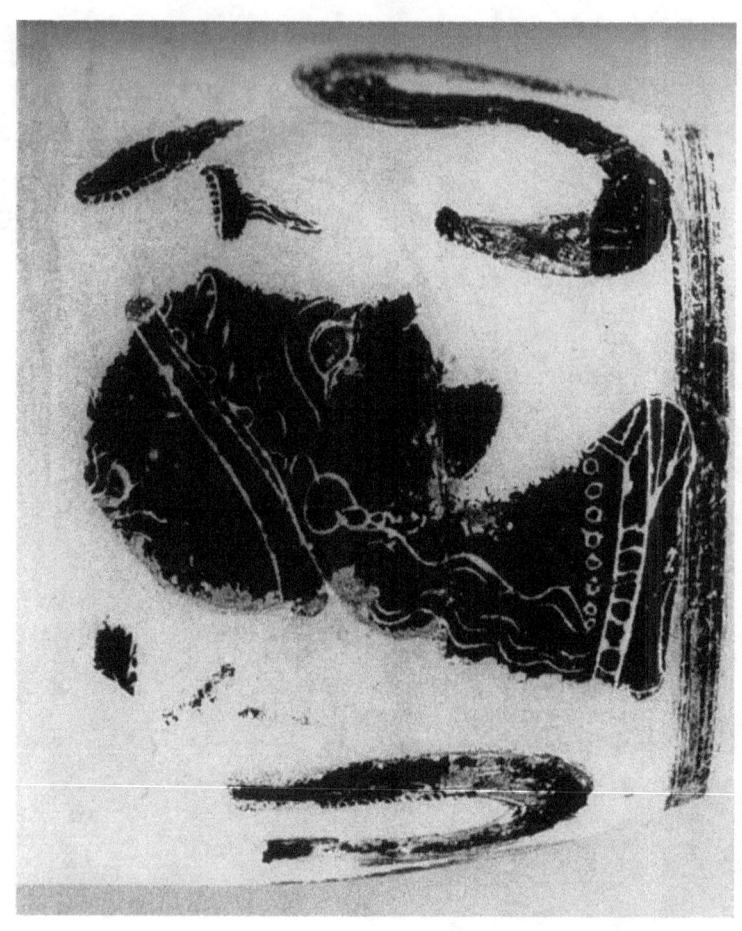

Character	Jason
Episode	Medea
Name	
Artifact	Lekythos
Item Style	Black-figure
Made in	Attica
Found	Athens
Date	530 B.C.
Artist	Cock Group
Details	**UNCERTAIN REPRESENTATION:** Medea

Mus. /Lit. Ref. L 359, Martin von Wagner Museum der Universität Würzburg. Photo: K. Oehrlein.

Refs. LIMC "Medeia" 4*

Character	Jason
Episode	Medea
Name	
Artifact	Lekythos
Item Style	Black-figure
Made in	Attica
Found	Rhitsona
Date	530 B.C.
Artist	Cock Group
Details	UNCERTAIN REPRESENTATION: Medea
Mus. /Lit. Ref.	Theben, Mus. R 31.166
Refs.	LIMC "Medeia" 5

Character	Jason
Episode	Medea
Name	
Artifact	Lekythos
Item Style	Black-figure
Made in	Attica
Found	Rhitsona
Date	530 B.C.
Artist	
Details	**UNCERTAIN REPRESENTATION:** Medea

Mus. /Lit. Ref. Theben, Mus. R 31.166A

Refs. LIMC "Medeia" 6

Character Jason
Episode Medea

Name

Artifact Terracota

Item Relief
Style

Made in Magna Graecian

Found

Date 460-440 B.C.
But LIMC Hera says 550 B.C.??

Artist

Details **UNCERTAIN REPRESENTATION:**
A pair flanked by two women- the pair
may be Jason and Medea???
Possibly, the other woman is Hera.

Mus. Antikenmuseum Basel und Sammlung
/Lit. Ludwig Inv. BS 318
Ref.

Refs. LIMC "Aphrodite" 1410*

LIMC "Iason" 79

LIMC "Hera" 451

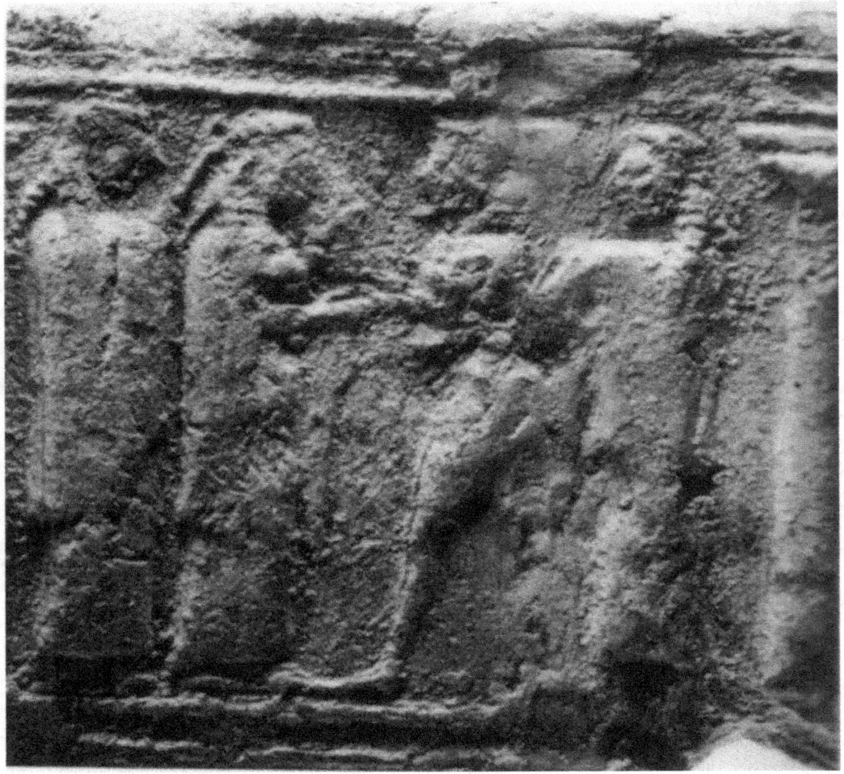

Character Jason
Episode Medea
Name
Artifact Hydria
Item Style Red-figure
Made in Early Luc.
Found Policoro (1963 tomb)
Date 415 B.C. or 400 B.C. (LIMC)

Artist
Details Medea departs in chariot led by dragons- post Euripides

Mus. /Lit. Ref. Policoro, Mus. Naz. 35296

Refs. LIMC "Iason" 70*
LIMC "Aphrodite" 1412*
LIMC "Medeia" 35*

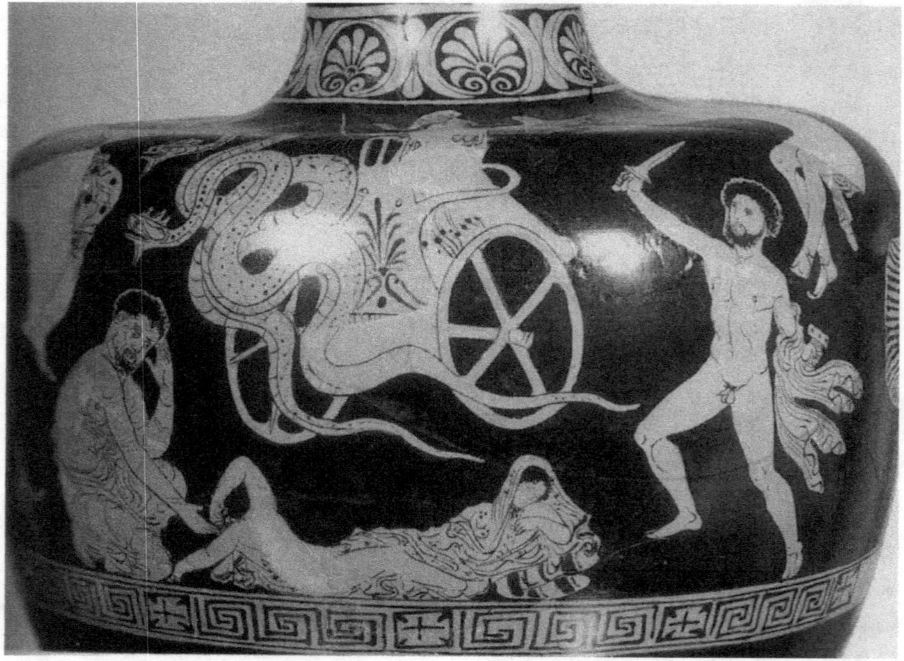

Figure No. 035

Character Jason

Episode Medea

Name

Artifact Calyx-krater

Item Style Red-figure

Made in Found Luc. South Italian

Date 400 B.C.

Artist Policoro Painter

Details Jason, half-draped, standing at lower left looks up at Medea in her snake driven chariot

Mus. /Lit. Ref. Once Fort Worth, Kimbell Art Mus., Hunt Coll.

Refs. Cartledge, P., (ed.), p. 247

LIMC "Medeia" 36*

LIMC "Iason" 71

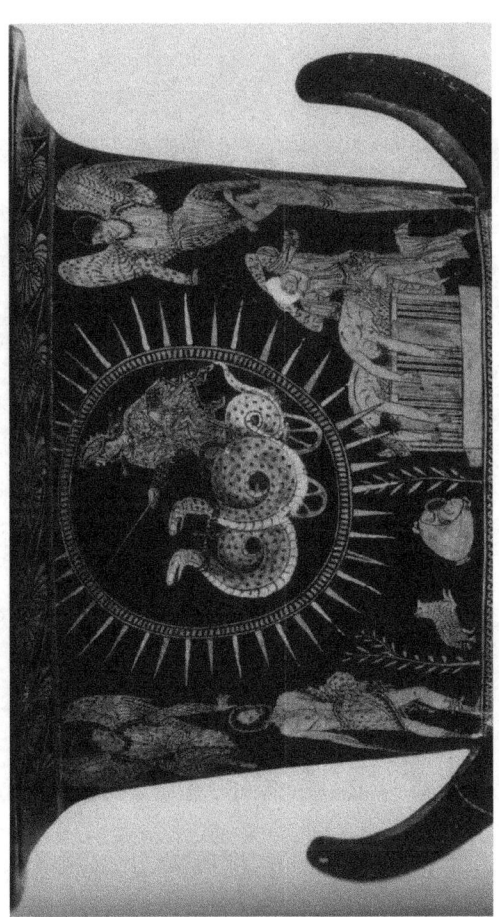

Character Athena
Episode Other

Name
Artifact Cup
Item Red-figure
Style
Made in Attica
Found Capua
Date 480 B.C.

Artist Douris Painter
Details Eos and her son Memnon; Memnon dead

Mus. Paris, Louvre G 115
/Lit.
Ref.

Refs. Boardman (1988), fig. 292

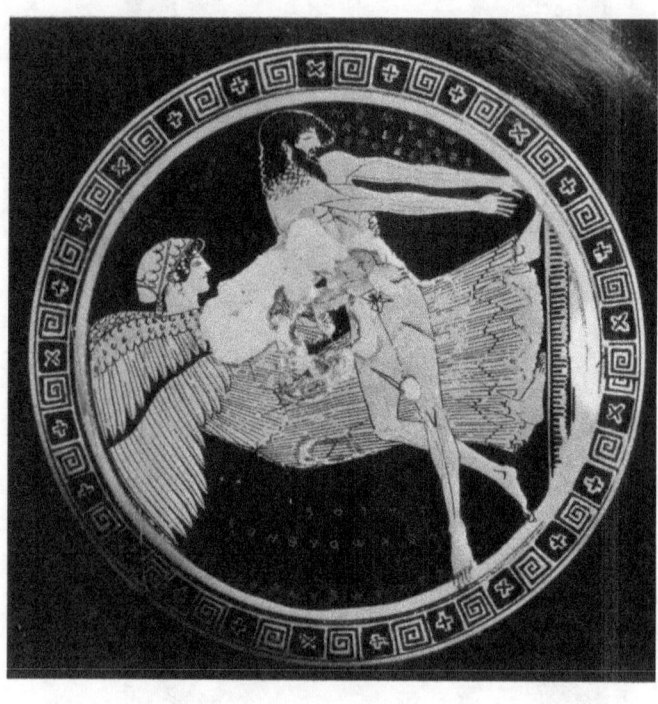

Character	Jason
Episode	Other
Name	
Artifact	
Item Style	Red-figure
Made in	Attica
Found	Ceveteri
Date	470-460 B.C.
Artist	Douris Painter
Details	Athena
Mus. /Lit. Ref.	Vienna, Kunsthistorisches Mus. 3695
Refs.	Boardman (1988), fig. 285.1

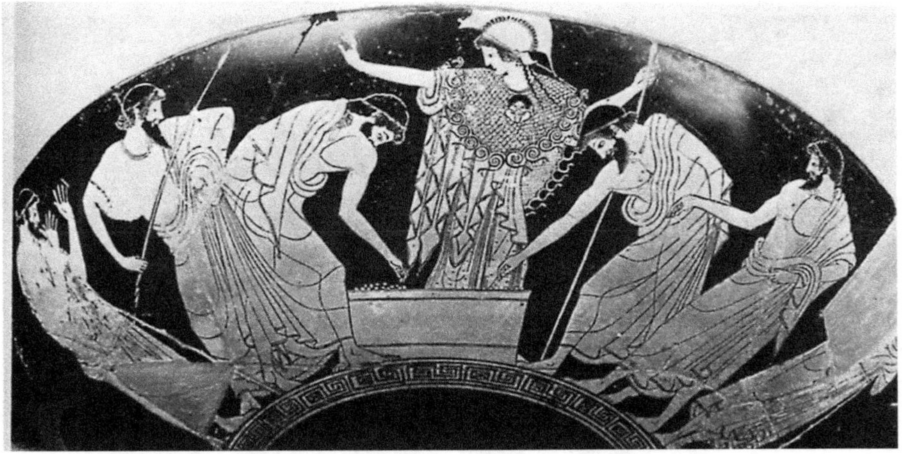

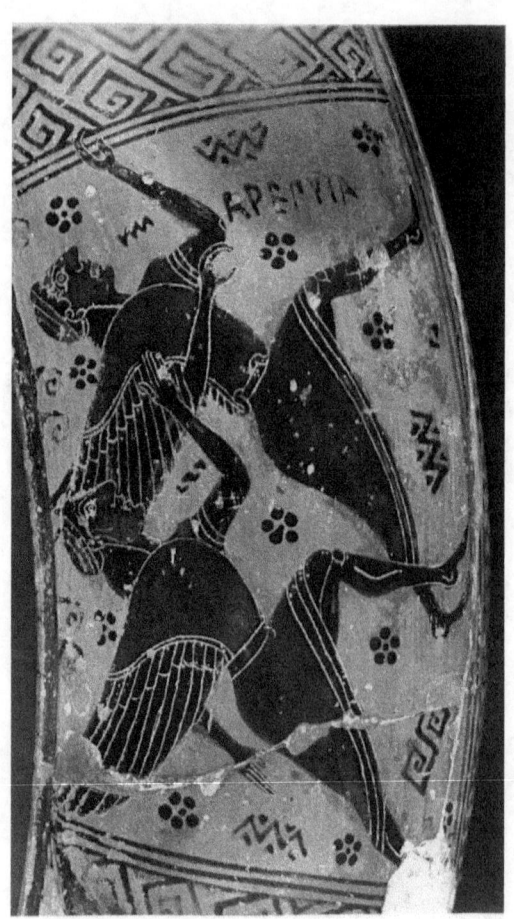

Character Jason
Episode Phineus

Name
Artifact Louterion fragment
Item Black-figure
Style
Made in Attica
Found Aegina
Date 620 B.C.

Artist Nettos Painter
Details Harpuiai (named) fleeing

Mus. /Lit. Ref. Berlin, Staatl. Mus. F 1682 (lost)

Refs. LIMC "Harpyiai" 1*

LIMC "Boreadai" 3

Beazley, J.D., Attic Black-Figure Vase-Painters (Oxford, 1956), 5.4, 679

Figure No. 039

Character Jason
Episode Phineus

Name Chest of Kypselos
Artifact Relief
Item Votive offering
Style
Made in Korinth
Found Olympia
Date 600-550 B.C.

Artist
Details They meet Phineus and the Boreads
chase the Harpuiai

"Phineus the Thracian is there, and sons
of the north-east wind are chasing the
Harpuiai away from him" (trans. Levi).

Mus. Literature: Pausanias 5.17.11
/Lit.
Ref.

Refs. LIMC "Phineus" 14

LIMC "Harpyiai" 18

LIMC "Boreadai" 12

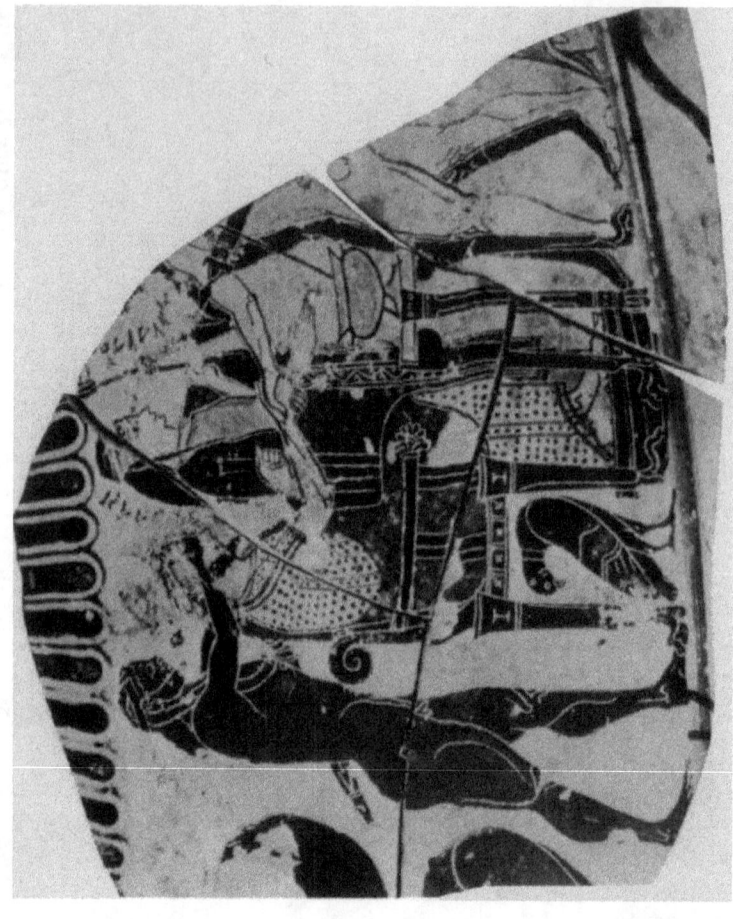

Character Jason
Episode Phineus

Name
Artifact Column-Krater fragment
Item
Style Black-figure
Made in Korinth
Found Sanctuary of Artemis in Sane, Chalkidike
Date 575-560 B.C.

Artist
Details Image 1/Frag. 1: Jason heals Phineus (?).
Names inscribed.

Image 2/Frag. 2: Harpuiai or Boreadai

Mus. Inv. 23656, Archaeological Museum
/Lit. of Thessaloniki
Ref.

Refs. Eurydice Kefalidou, "The Argonauts Krater in
the Archaeological Museum of Thessaloniki",
AJA 112 (2008) 617-624 and also in the
LIMC, suppl., s.v. "Kleite".

LIMC "Iason" 7*, "Boreadai" 4* & "Phineus"
18

Figure No. 041

Character Jason
Episode Phineus

Name
Artifact Sculpture
Item Ivory relief
Style
Made in Korinth
Found Delphi
Date 570 B.C.

Artist
Details Boreadai and Harpuiai

Mus. /Lit. Ref. Delphi, Museum, 1355 (9944)

Refs. Carpenter, T.H., fig. 275

LIMC "Boreadai" 13*

LIMC "Phineus" 15

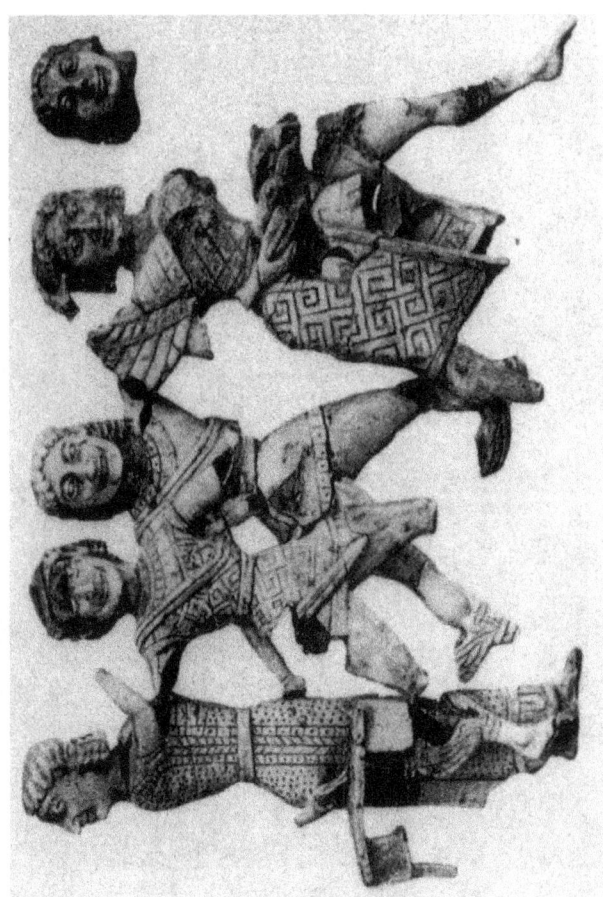

Figure No. 042

Character	Jason
Episode	Phineus
Name	
Artifact	Cup
Item Style	Black-figure
Made in	Laconia
Found	Cerveteri
Date	560-550 B.C.
Artist	
Details	Boreadai and Harpuiai

Mus. /Lit. Ref.	Rome, Villa Giulia
Refs.	Boardman (1998), fig. 417
	Schefold, K., fig. 231
	LIMC "Boreadai" 6*
	LIMC "Harpyiai" 23*

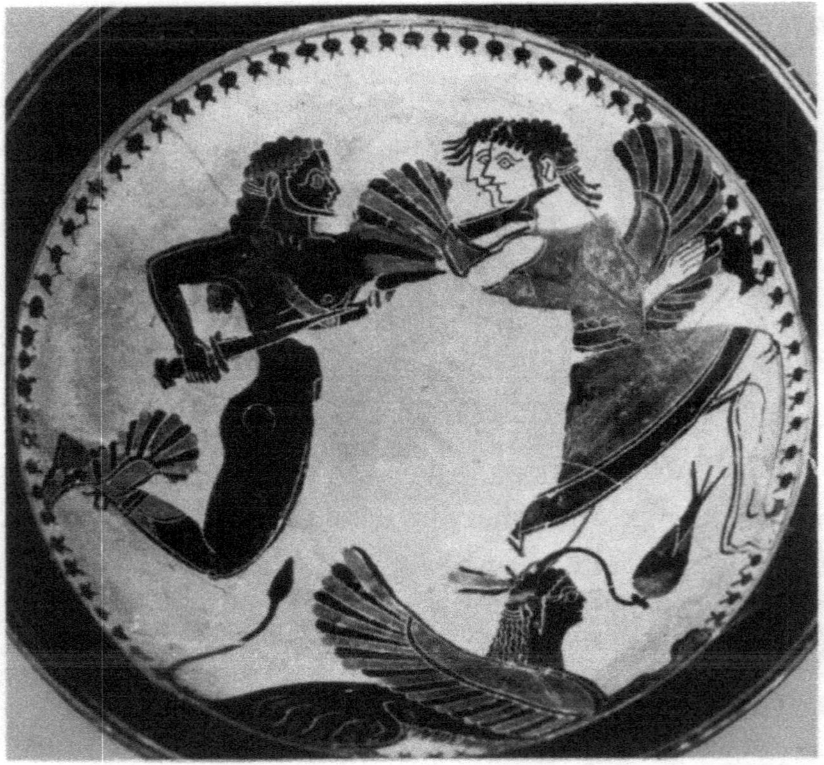

Character	Jason
Episode	Phineus
Name	
Artifact	Cup fragment
Item Style	Laconia
Made in	Laconia
Found	Samos
Date	560 B.C.; 575-570 B.C. (LIMC "Harpyiai" 22*)
Artist	
Details	Harpuiai flee
Mus. /Lit. Ref.	Samos, Vathy, Mus. K 1540 & 1206
Refs.	LIMC "Harpyiai" 22*
	LIMC "Boreadai" 5

Character	Jason
Episode	Phineus
Name	
Artifact	Cup
Item Style	Black-figure
Made in Found	Laconia
Date	550-540 B.C.
Artist	
Details	Two Harpuiai pursued by two Boreadai
Mus. /Lit. Ref.	Malibu, Getty Museum 85.AE.461
Refs.	LIMC "Harpyiai" 24*

Character Jason
Episode Phineus

Name
Artifact Amphora
Item Black-figure
Style

Made in Attica
Found Amathus, Cyprus
Date 550-530 B.C.

Artist
Details Side A: Boread
Side B: Harpy

Mus. London, British Museum 1894.11-1.161.
/Lit.
Ref.

Refs. LIMC "Boreadai" 8*

LIMC "Harpyiai" 2*

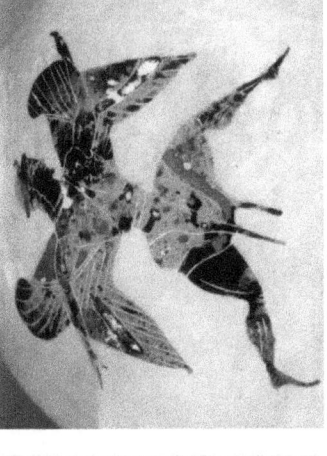

Figure No. 046

Character	Jason
Episode	Phineus
Name	Throne of Apollo at Amyklai
Artifact	Throne of Apollo at Amyklai
Item	
Style	
Made in	Amyklai
Found	
Date	550-500 B.C.
Artist	Bathykles
Details	"...and Kalais and Zetes are driving off the Harpies from Phineus" (trans. Levi)
Mus. /Lit. Ref.	Literature: Pausanias 3.18.15
Refs.	LIMC "Phineus" 16
	LIMC "Harpyiai" 20
	LIMC "Boreadai" 14

Figure No. 047

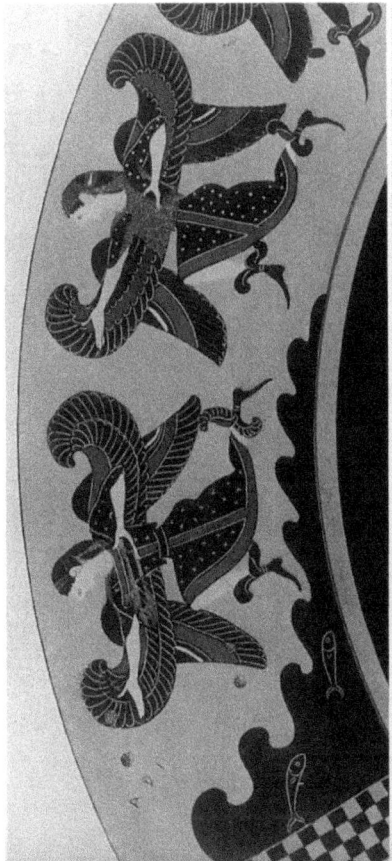
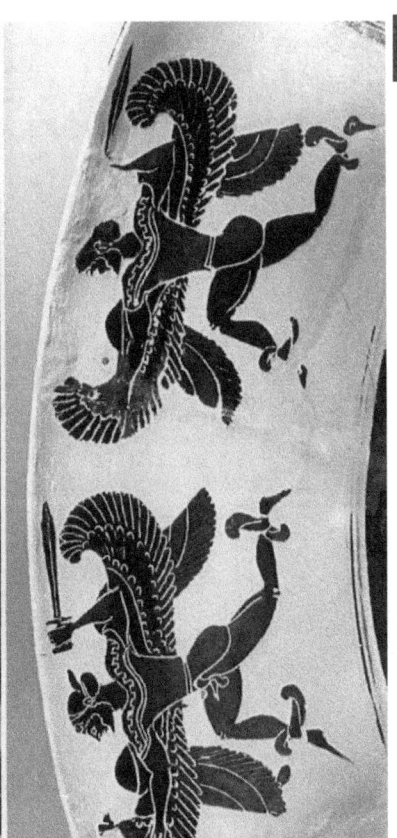

Character	Jason
Episode	Phineus
Name	Cup of Phineus
Artifact	Cup
Item Style	Black-figure
Made in	Chalchis
Found	Vulci (?)
Date	530 B.C.
Artist	Phineus Painter
Details	Phineus, Boreadai and the Harpuiai

Mus. /Lit. Ref. L 164, Martin von Wagner Museum der Universität Würzburg. Photo: K. Oehrlein.

Refs. Boardman (1998), fig. 479

LIMC "Horai" 19*

LIMC "Boreadai" 7*

LIMC "Harpyiai" 14*

Schefold, K., fig. 232

Character	Jason
Episode	Phineus
Name	
Artifact	Fragment
Item Style	Black-figure
Made in	Ionia
Found	
Date	525-500 B.C. or 1st half of 5th century B.C.
Artist	
Details	One Boread chasing two Harpuiai?
Mus. /Lit. Ref.	Ismir, Museum of Smyrna
Refs.	LIMC "Harpyiai" 25*

Figure No. 049

Character **Jason**
Episode **Phineus**

Name
Artifact **Lekythos**
Item
Style **bf White-ground**
Made in **Attica**
Found
Date **500-475 B.C.**

Artist **Sappho Painter**
Details **Phineus stretches arms out at Harpuiai**

Mus.
/Lit. **Basle, private collection**
Ref.

Refs. **LIMC "Harpyiai" 8***

LIMC "Phineus" 3

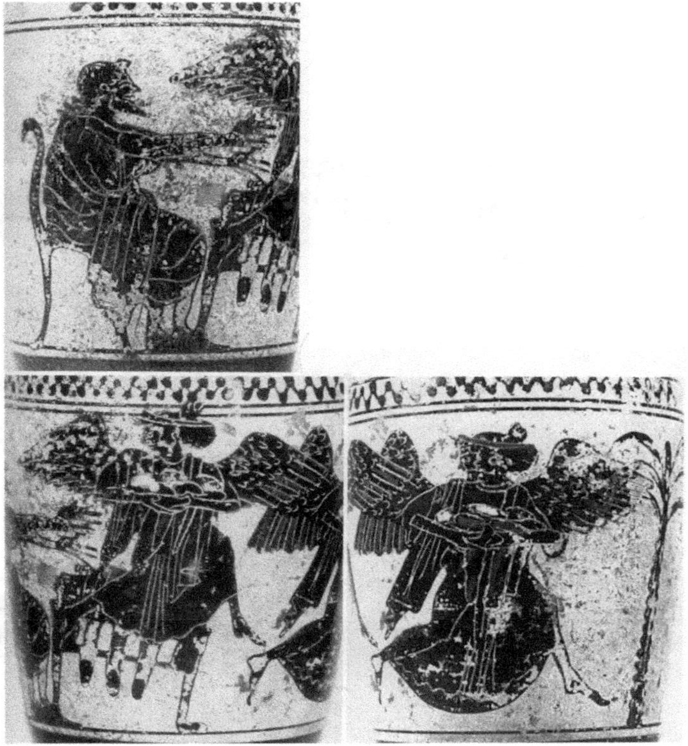

Character	Jason
Episode	Phineus
Name	
Artifact	Kalpis-hydria
Item Style	Red-figure
Made in	Attica
Found	
Date	480-470 B.C.
Artist	Kleophrades painter
Details	Phineus gestures at Harpuiai as they steal his food.

Mus. /Lit. Ref. Rome (formerly Malibu, Getty Museum 85. AE.316)

Refs. LIMC "Harpyiai" 9*

LIMC "Phineus" 4

Oakley, J.H. et al., Athenian Potters and Painters, The Conference Proceedings (Oxford, 1997), 150, FIG.11

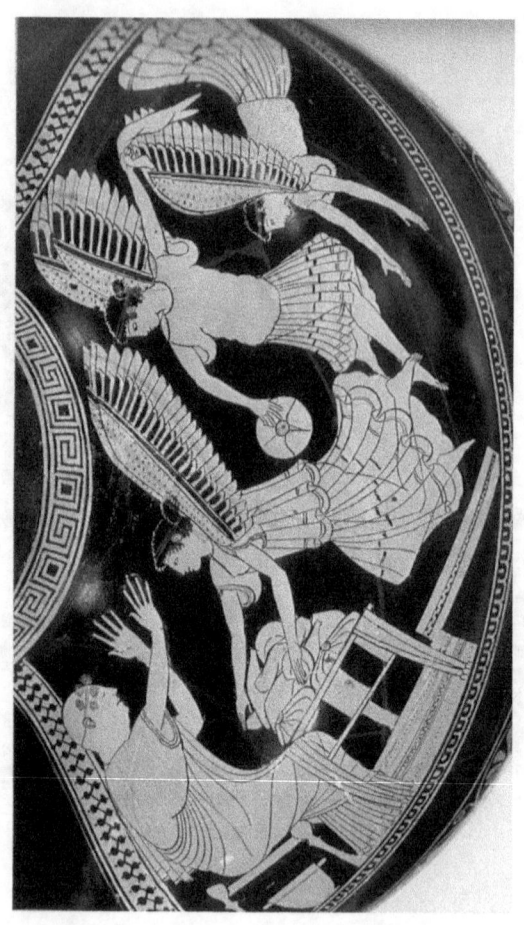

Figure No. 051

Character Jason
Episode Phineus

Name
Artifact bf Lekythos
Item White-ground
Style
Made in Attica
Found
Date 480-470 B.C.

Artist
Details Male chases two Harpuiai?

Mus. Budapest, Mus. Beaux Arts 50.161
/Lit.
Ref.

Refs. LIMC "Harpyiai" 26*

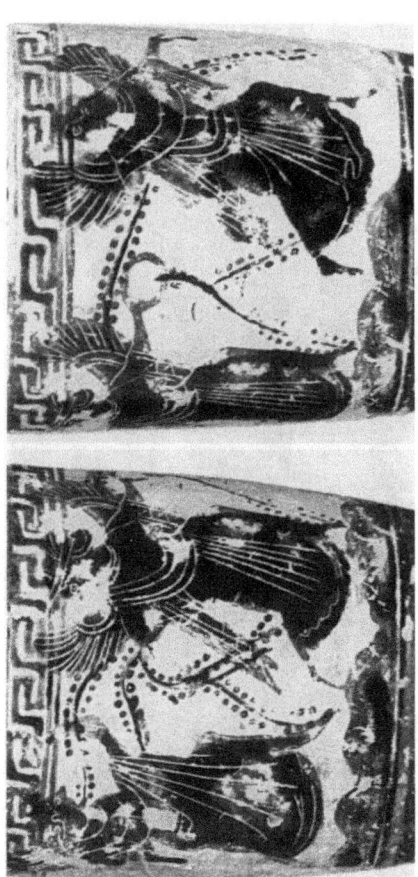

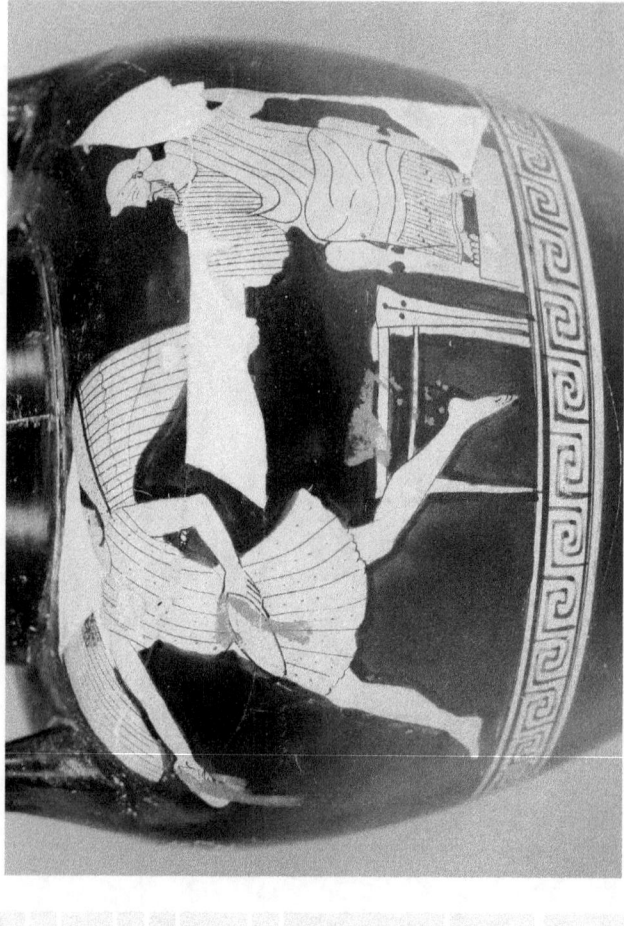

Character Jason

Episode Phineus

Name

Artifact Column-amphora

**Item
Style** Red-figure

Made in Attica

Found Camiros

Date 475-450 B.C.

Artist Nikon Painter

Details Phineus seated to the right on his chair,
has food stolen by two Harpuiai

**Mus.
/Lit.
Ref.** London, British Museum E 302

Refs. LIMC "Harpyiai" 10*

LIMC "Phineus" 5

Figure No. 053

Character	Jason
Episode	Phineus
Name	
Artifact	Amphora
Item Style	Red-figure
Made in	Attica
Found	Nola
Date	470-450 B.C.
Artist	Painter of the Yale Lekythos (?)
Details	Phineus alone with table
Mus. /Lit. Ref.	London, British Museum E 291
Refs.	LIMC "Phineus" 1*

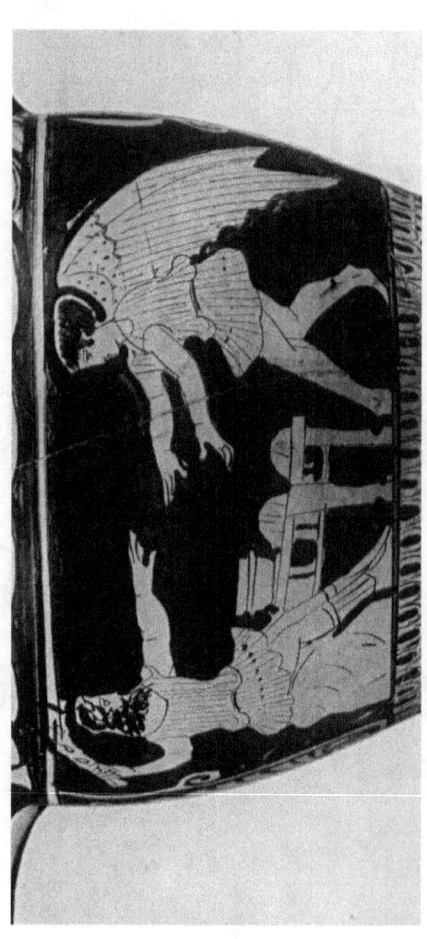

Character	Jason
Episode	Phineus
Name	
Artifact	Skyphos
Item Style	Red-figure
Made in	Boiotia
Found	Boiotia
Date	460-440 B.C.
Artist	
Details	Phineus and one Harpy; gestures towards creature
Mus. /Lit. Ref.	Berlin, Staatl. Mus. V.I.3413
Refs.	LIMC "Harpyiai" 11*
	LIMC "Phineus" 8

Figure No. 055

Character	Jason
Episode	Phineus
Name	
Artifact	Stamnos
Item Style	Red-figure
Made in	Attica
Found	Nola, Italy
Date	460 B.C.
Artist	Painter of the Yale Oinochoe
Details	Phineus seated at centre
Mus. /Lit. Ref.	Copenhagen, The National Museum of Denmark, Collection of Classical and Near Eastern Antiquities, inv.nr. Chr.VIII. 540
Refs.	LIMC "Boreadai" 16*
	LIMC "Phineus" 19
	Beazley, J.D., Attic Red-Figure Vase-Painters, 2nd edition (Oxford, 1963), 502.7

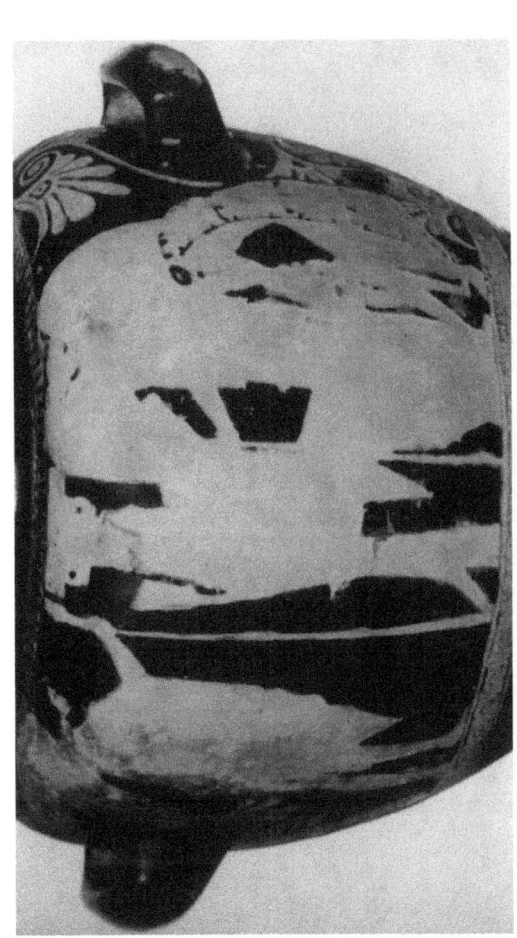

Figure No. 056

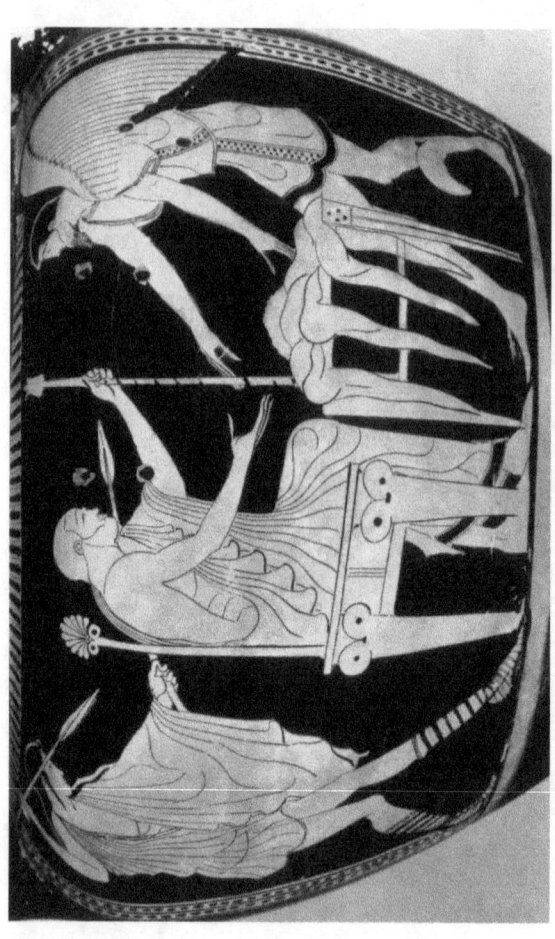

Character	Jason
Episode	Phineus
Name	
Artifact	Column krater
Item Style	Red-figure
Made in	Attica
Found	Altamura
Date	460 B.C.
Artist	Leningrad Painter
Details	Jason(?), Phineus & Boread
Mus. /Lit. Ref.	Paris, Louvre G 364 (MNC 478)
Refs.	LIMC "Boreadai" 18*
	LIMC "Phineus" 21

Character Jason

Episode Phineus

Name

Artifact Bell-krater fragments

Item Style Red-figure

Made in Attica

Found Locres

Date 450-425 B.C.

Artist Danae Painter

Details Two fragments showing
1: a Harpy plus a finger of the hand of
Phineus resting on a staff
2: the right foot of a Harpy, the base of a
column and the foot of Phineus.

Mus. /Lit. Ref. Locres, Reggio de Calabre, Mus. Naz. De
Locres

Refs. LIMC "Phineus" 7

LIMC "Harpyiai" 13

Beazley, J.D., Attic Red-Figure Vase-
Painters, 2nd edition (Oxford, 1963), 1076.2

Character Jason
Episode Phineus

Name
Artifact Pelike
Item
Style Red-figure
Made in Attica
Found
Date 450 B.C.

Artist Nausicaa Painter
Details Two-handled jar (pelike) depicting Phineus with the sons of Boreas

Mus. /Lit. Ref. Boston, Museum of Fine Art 1979.40

Refs. Carpenter, T.H., fig. 276

LIMC "Phineus" 20*

LIMC "Boreadai" 17*

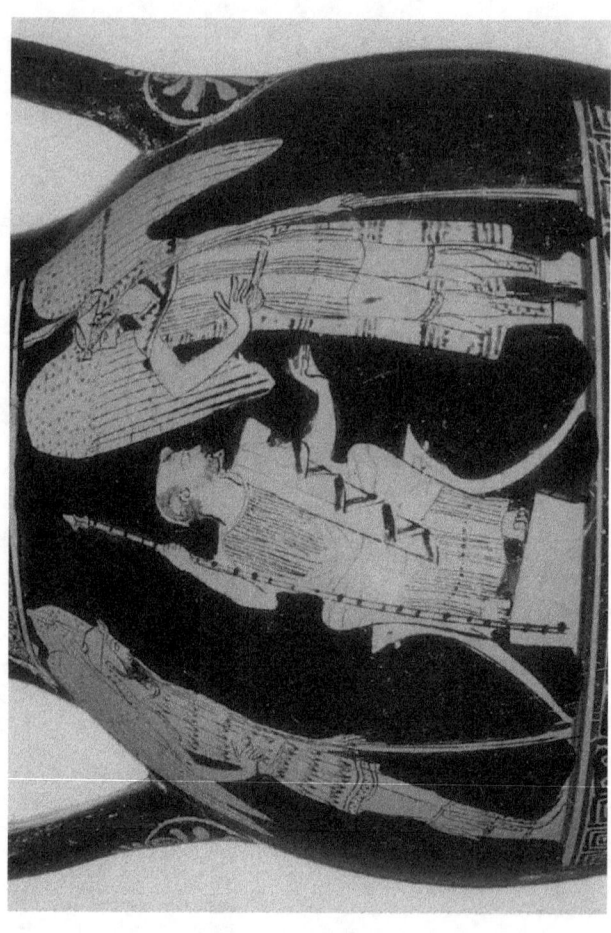

Figure No. 059

Character Jason
Episode Phineus

Name
Artifact Bell-krater
Item
Style Red-figure
Made in Attica
Found Spina, Italy
Date 450 B.C.

Artist
Details Side A: Three women; two women make libation (?)

Side B: Phineus at centre (?)

Mus. Ferrara, Mus. Nat. 20294
/Lit.
Ref.

Refs. LIMC "Phineus" 2*

LIMC "Harpyiai" 12*

LIMC "Phineus" 6

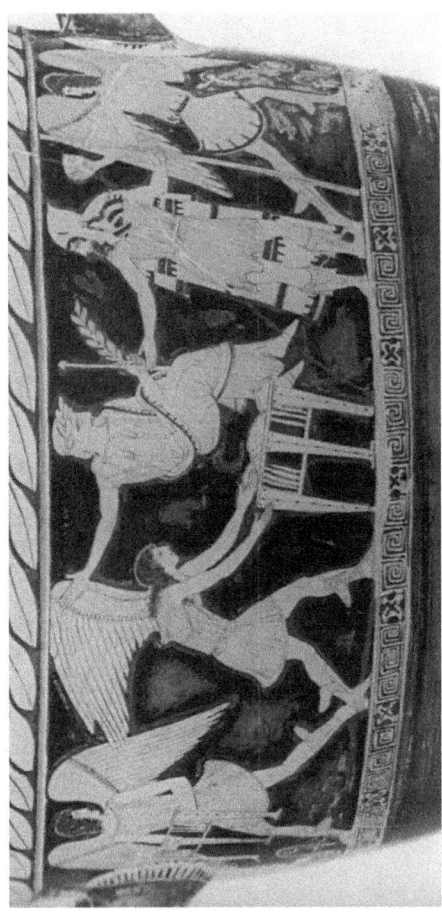

Figure No. 060

Character Jason
Episode Phineus

Name
Artifact Hydria
Item Style Red-figure
Made in Attica
Found Athens
Date 430 B.C.

Artist
Details Phineus at centre; Two harpuiai to left and two Argonauts (inc. Boreadai) to right.

Mus. /Lit. Ref. Lost

Refs. LIMC "Harpyiai" 15•

LIMC "Phineus" 10

LIMC "Boreadai" 9

Beazley, J.D., Attic Red-Figure Vase-Painters, 2nd edition (Oxford, 1963), 400

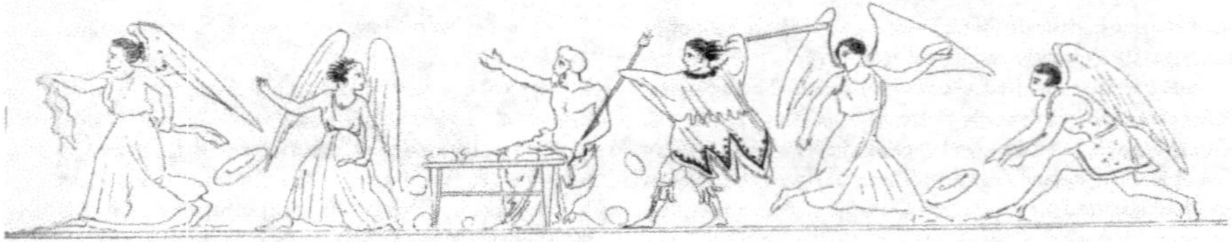

Figure No. 061

Character	Jason
Episode	Phineus
Name	
Artifact	Krater fragment
Item Style	Red-figure
Made in Found	Apulia
Date	420 B.C.
Artist	Hearst Painter
Details	Boread and Phineus; Phineus' eye is shut showing blindness.
Mus. /Lit. Ref.	Amsterdam, Allard Pierson Museum 2534 Image provided by courtesy of the Allard Pierson Museum, Amsterdam
Refs.	LIMC "Boreadai" 10*
	LIMC "Phineus" 12

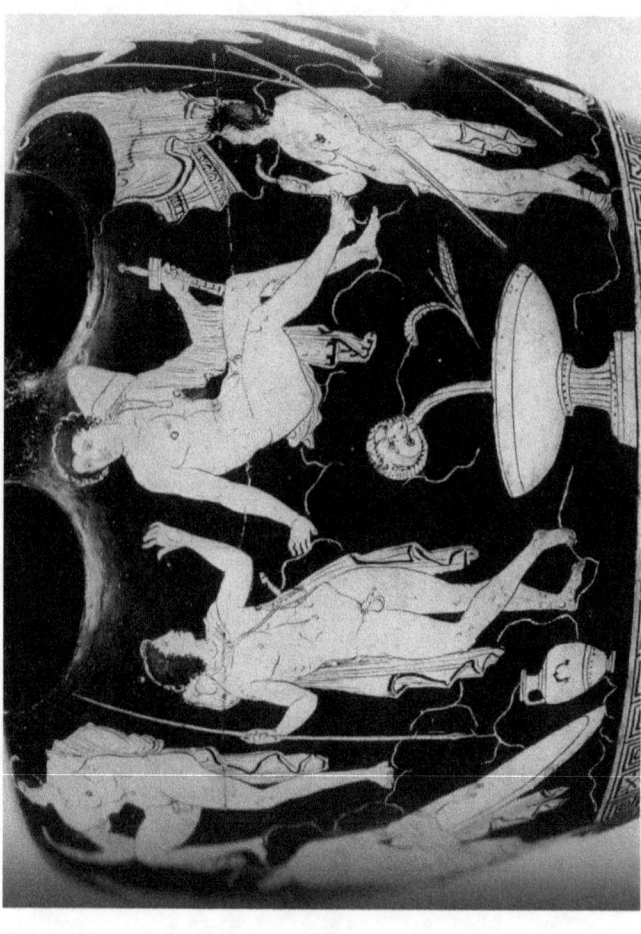

Figure No. 063

Character	Jason
Episode	Phineus
Name	
Artifact	Volute krater
Item Style	Red-figure
Made in	Lucanian
Found	Ruvo
Date	410-400 B.C.
Artist	Amykos Painter
Details	1: Argonauts
	2: Boreadai and the Harpuiai
	3: Phineus and Argonauts
Mus. /Lit. Ref.	Ruvo, Mus. Jatta J 1095
Refs.	LIMC "Argonautai" 11*
	LIMC "Harpyiai" 17*
	LIMC "Phineus I" 13*
	LIMC "Boreadai" 11*

Character	Jason
Episode	Phineus
Name	
Artifact	Oinochoe
Item Style	Red-figure
Made in	Attica
Found	Randazzo, Sicily
Date	410 B.C.
Artist	
Details	Phineus seated; Boreadai attack two Harpuiai. Iris on the top left.
Mus. /Lit. Ref.	Randazzo, Museum Vagliasindi 7637
Refs.	LIMC "Boreadai" 15*
	LIMC "Phineus" 11
	LIMC "Harpyiai" 16

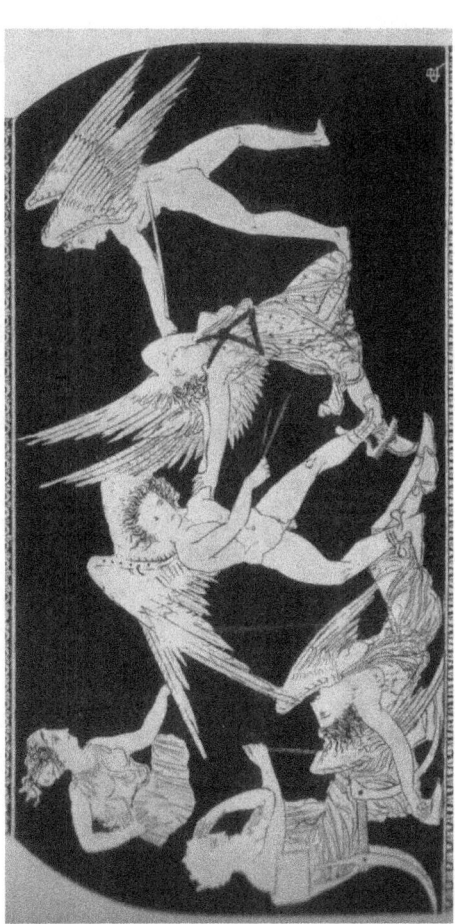

Figure No. 064

Character	Jason
Episode	Rejuvenation
Name	
Artifact	Amphora
Item Style	Black-figure
Made in	Attica
Found	Vulci, Etruria
Date	520 B.C.
Artist	Medea Group
Details	
Mus. /Lit. Ref.	London, British Museum B 221
Refs.	LIMC "Pelias" 10*
	Meyer, pl. 3 (no. 1)
	Beazley, J.D., Attic Black-Figure Vase-Painters (Oxford, 1956), 321.4

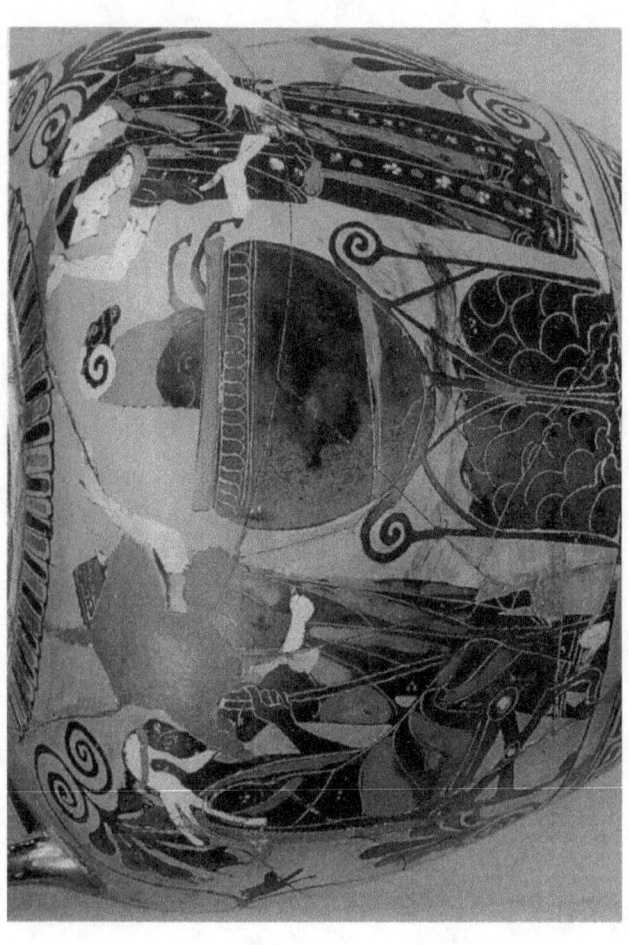

Figure No. 065

Character Jason
Episode Rejuvenation

Name
Artifact Amphora
Item
Style Black-figure

Made in Attica
Found Vulci, Etruria
Date 520-500 B.C.

Artist Leagros Group
Details A: Medea, daughter of Pelias and ram B: Peliades and Ram

Mus. Harvard Art Museum, Arthur M. Sackler
/Lit. Museum, Bequest of David M. Robinson,
Ref. 1960.315 Photo: Junius Beebe

Refs. LIMC "Peliades" 4*
SIDE A OF VASE

Robertson (1956), pl. 9 fig. 43
SIDE B OF VASE

Robertson (1956), pl. 9 fig. 42
SIDE A OF VASE

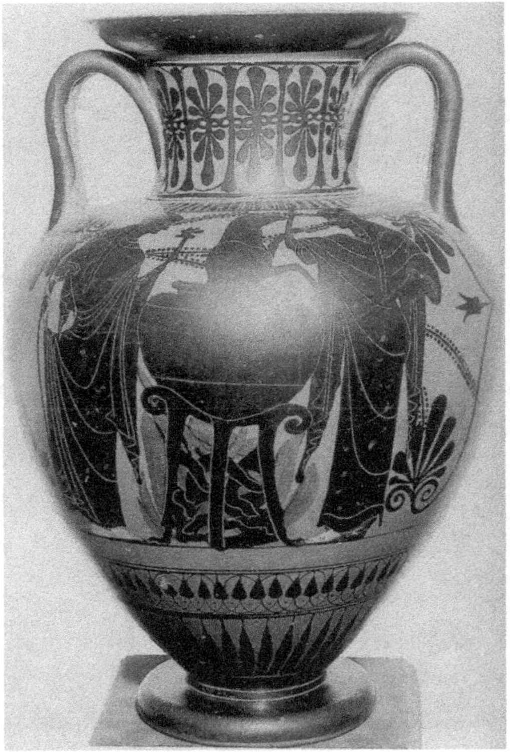

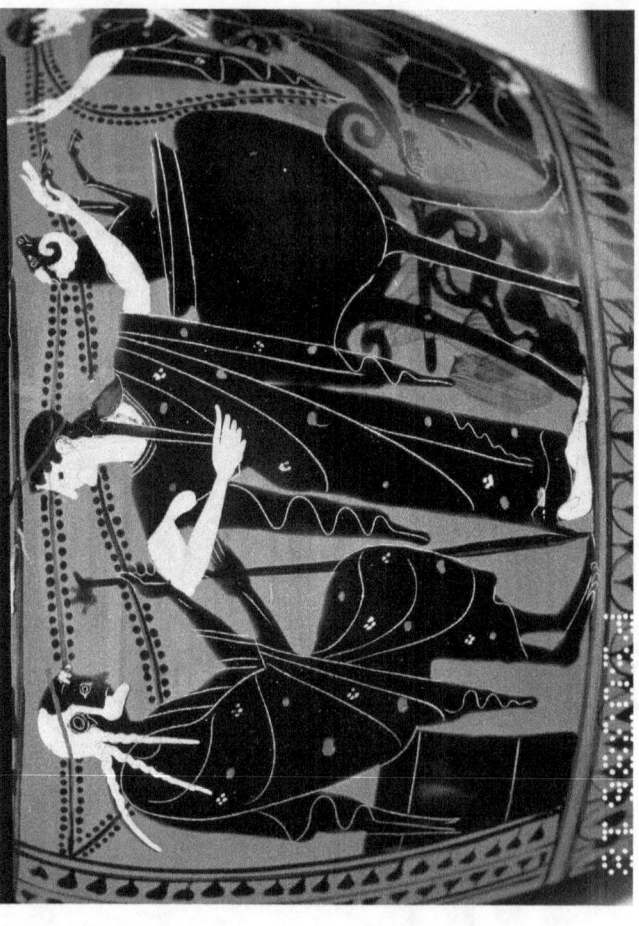

Character	Jason
Episode	Rejuvenation
Name	
Artifact	Hydria
Item Style	Black-figure
Made in	Attica
Found	Vulci
Date	510 B.C.
Artist	Leagros Group
Details	Pelias, Medea, ram and Peliades
Mus. /Lit. Ref.	London, British Museum B 328
Refs.	Carpenter, T.H., fig. 280
	LIMC "Pelias" 11*
	Meyer, pl. 1 (no. 1)
	Beazley, J.D., Attic Black-Figure Vase-Painters (Oxford, 1956), 363.42, 358

Figure No. 067

Character	Jason
Episode	Rejuvenation
Name	
Artifact	Fragment
Item Style	
Made in	Attica
Found	
Date	500-490 B.C.
Artist	
Details	

Mus./Lit. Ref. Malibu, Getty Museum 79.AE.19

Refs. Meyer, pl. 8 (no. 1)

LIMC "Peliades" 9

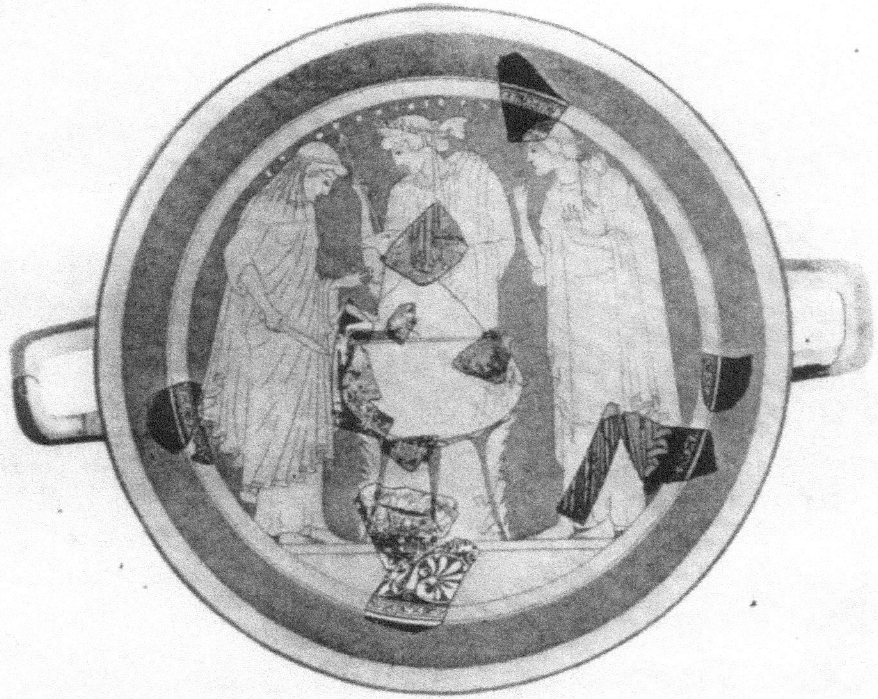

Figure No. 068

Character	Jason
Episode	Rejuvenation
Name	
Artifact	Lekythos
Item Style	White-ground
Made in	Attica
Found	Vulci
Date	500-475 B.C.
Artist	Haimon Painter
Details	Youth in pot, flanked by two draped women and two bearded men on far sides.
Mus. /Lit. Ref.	Leiden, Rijksmus, PC 32
Refs.	LIMC "Iason" 59*
	Neils, J., pp. 190-5; image- pp. 191 fig.17.3
	Meyer, pl. 16 (no. 2)

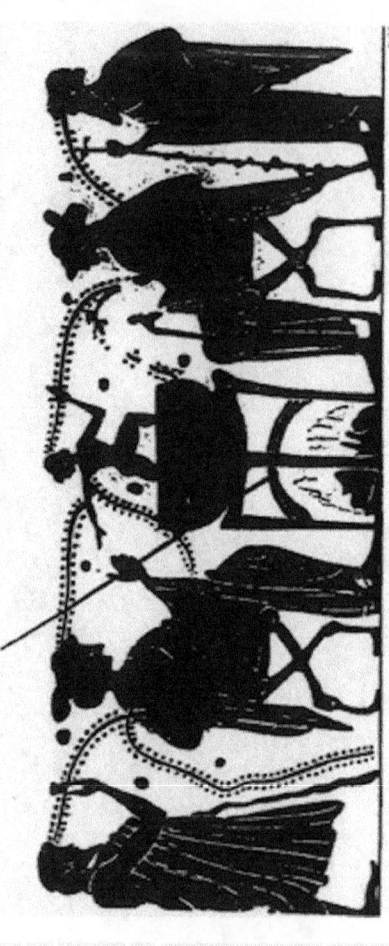

Figure No. 069

Character Jason

Episode Rejuvenation

Name

Artifact Lekythos

Item
Style White-ground

Made in Attica

Found Chiusi

Date 500-475 B.C.

Artist Haimon Painter

Details Same as Image 70:
youth in pot, flanked by two draped
women and two bearded men on far
sides.

**Mus.
/Lit.
Ref.** Chiusi, Boncicasuccini Coll.

Refs. LIMC "Pelias" 16b*

Meyer, pl. 17 (no. 1)

LIMC "Iason" 60

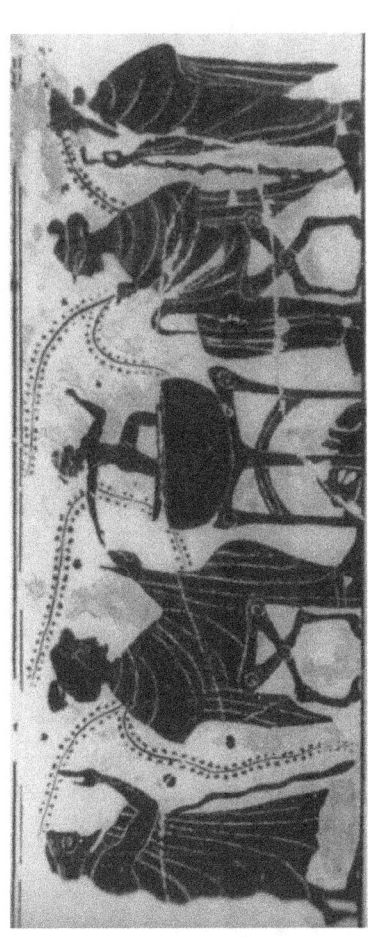

Figure No. 070

Character	Jason
Episode	Rejuvenation
Name	
Artifact	Lekythos
Item Style	White-ground
Made in	Attica
Found	
Date	500-475 B.C.
Artist	Class of Athens 581
Details	Head of a youth emerges from the cauldron over fire flanked by two women seated on diphroi
Mus. /Lit. Ref.	Ostwestfalen, D. J. Coll.
Refs.	LIMC "Iason" 61

Character	Jason
Episode	Rejuvenation
Name	
Artifact	Lekythos
Item Style	Black-figure
Made in	Attica
Found	
Date	500-475 B.C.
Artist	Beldam Painter
Details	
Mus. /Lit. Ref.	National Archaeological Museum, Athens E1566
Refs.	LIMC "Peliades" 6a*
	Meyer, pl. 4 (nos. 2 & 3)
	Boardman (1974), fig. 278.1,2
	Beazley, J.D., Attic Black-Figure Vase-Painters (Oxford, 1956), 585.57

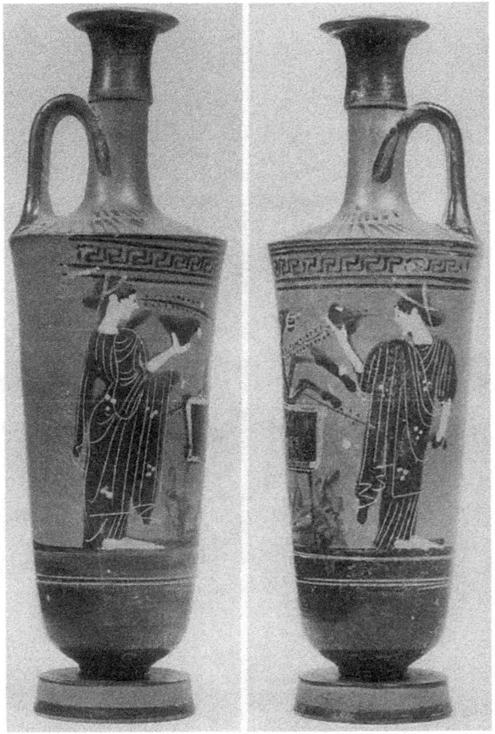

Character	Jason
Episode	Rejuvenation
Name	
Artifact	Lekythos
Item Style	Black-figure
Made in	Attica
Found	
Date	500-475 B.C.
Artist	Beldam Painter
Details	

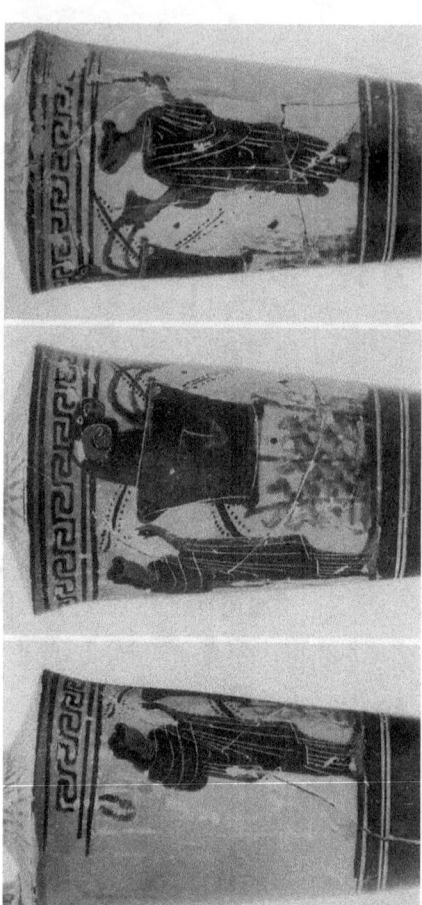

Mus. /Lit. Ref.	National Archaeological Museum, Athens 12805
Refs.	LIMC "Peliades" 6b*
	Meyer, pl. 5 (no. 1)
	Meyer, pl. 5 (no. 2)
	Meyer, pl. 5 (nos. 1-3)
	LIMC "Peliades" 6c

Figure No. 073

Character	Jason
Episode	Rejuvenation
Name	
Artifact	Lekythos
Item	Black-figure
Style	
Made in	Attica
Found	
Date	500-475 B.C.
Artist	Beldam Painter
Details	
Mus.	National Archaeological Museum, Athens
/Lit.	18633
Ref.	
Refs.	LIMC "Peliades" 6c*
	Meyer, pl. 6 (no. 1)
	Meyer, pl. 6 (no. 2)
	Meyer, pl. 6 (no. 3)

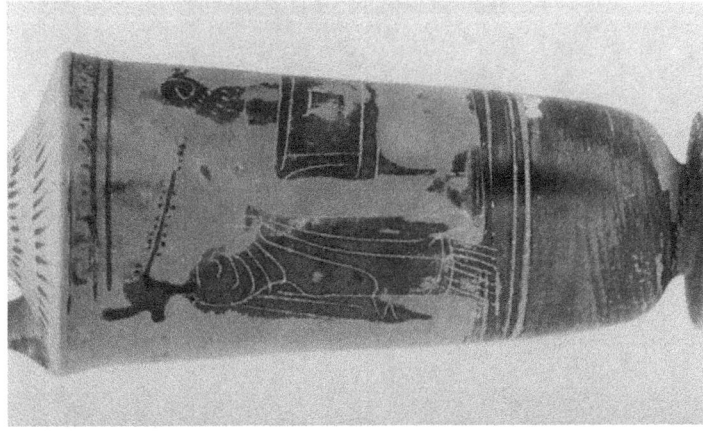

Character	Jason
Episode	Rejuvenation
Name	
Artifact	Lekythos
Item Style	Black-figure
Made in	Attica
Found	
Date	500-475 B.C. ?
Artist	Beldam Painter
Details	
Mus. /Lit. Ref.	Erlangen, Univ. I 429
Refs.	LIMC "Peliades" 6d*
	Meyer, pl. 7 (no. 1)

Figure No. 075

Figure No. 076

Character	Jason
Episode	Rejuvenation
Name	Medea and Pelias
Artifact	Terracotta Lekythos
Item Style	
Made in	
Found	
Date	500-475 B.C.
Artist	
Details	

Mus. /Lit. Ref. 26.673 Black Figure Lekythos, "Medea and Pelias", Corcoran Gallery of Art, Washington, D.C. William A. Clark Collection.

Refs. LIMC "Pelias" 16c*

Meyer, pl. 7 (nos. 2 & 3)

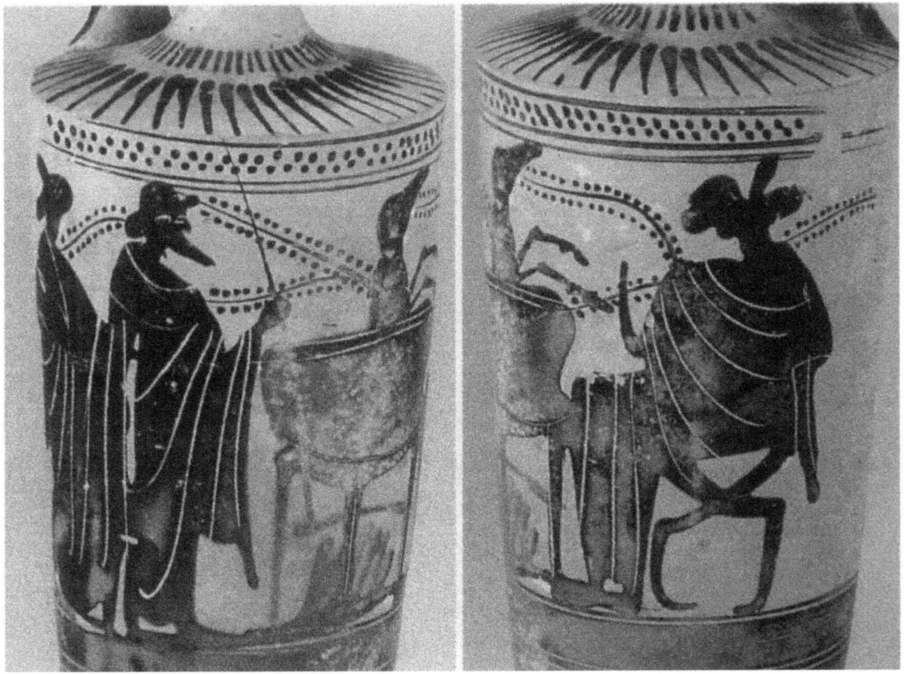

Character Jason
Episode   Rejuvenation

Name
Artifact   Stamnos
Item   Red-figure
Style
Made in   Attica
Found
Date   500-400 B.C.

Artist
Details

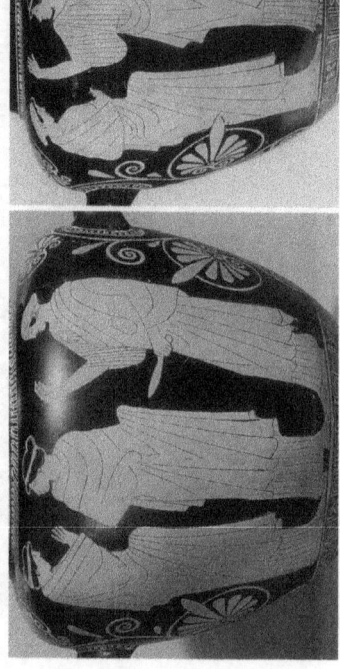

Mus.   Cambridge, Fitz. Mus. GR 2.1935
/Lit.
Ref.

Refs.   LIMC "Peliades" 13*

Character Jason

Episode Rejuvenation

Name

Artifact Lekythos

**Item
Style** White-ground

Made in Attica

Found Gela

Date 500 B.C.

Artist Sappho Painter

Details Upper body of youth in cauldron above
fire; flanked by two draped women

**Mus.
/Lit.
Ref.** Syracuse, Museum Naz. 20936

Refs. Meyer, pl. 16 (no. 1)

LIMC "Iason" 58

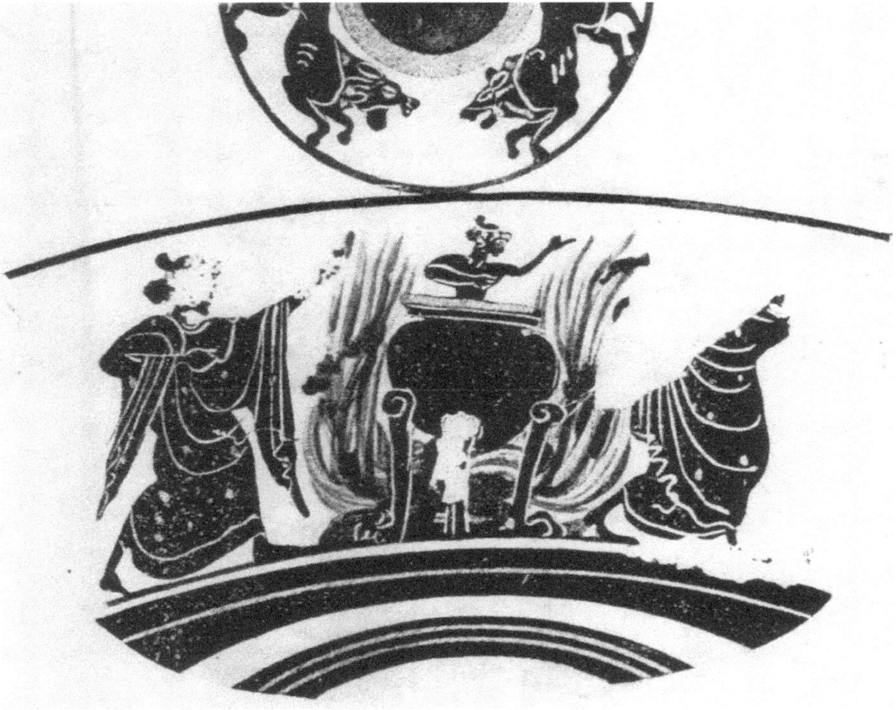

Figure No. 078

Character	Jason
Episode	Rejuvenation
Name	
Artifact	Amphora
Item Style	Black-figure
Made in	Attica
Found	
Date	500 B.C.
Artist	
Details	
Mus. /Lit. Ref.	Kurashiki (Japan), Ninagawa Mus.
Refs.	LIMC "Peliades" 8*
	Meyer, pl. 1 (no. 2)

Character Jason
Episode Rejuvenation
Name
Artifact Oinochoe
Item Black-figure white ground
Style
Made in Attica
Found
Date 480 B.C.

Artist Athena Painter
Details

Mus. Paris, Louvre F 372
/Lit.
Ref.

Refs. LIMC "Peliades" 5*

Meyer, pl. 4 (no. 1)

Beazley, J.D., Attic Black-Figure Vase-
Painters (Oxford, 1956), 531.1

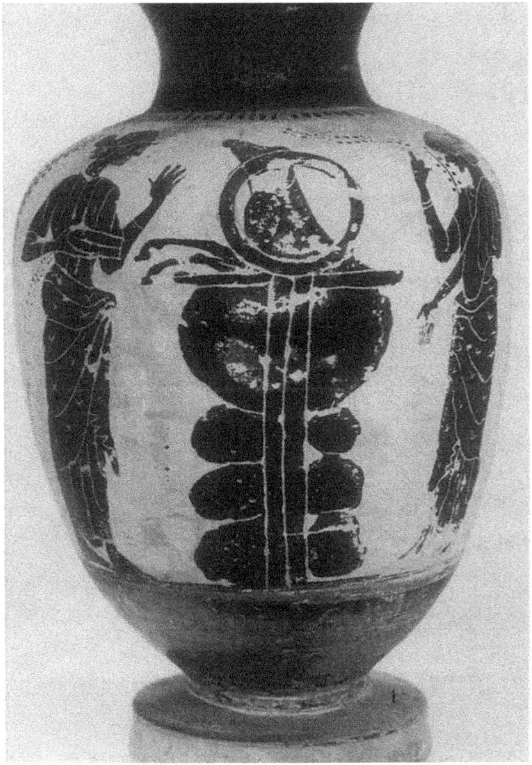

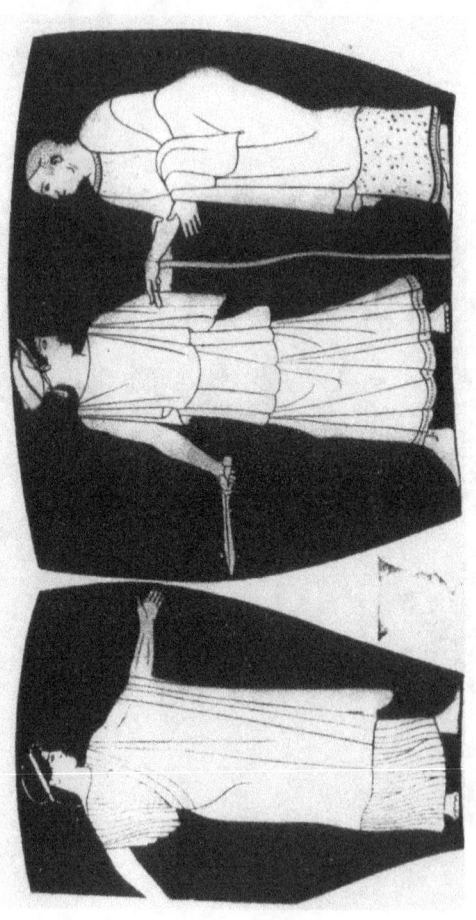

Character	Jason
Episode	Rejuvenation
Name	
Artifact	Calyx-krater
Item Style	Red-figure
Made in	
Found	Tarquinia
Date	475-450 B.C.
Artist	Pistoxenos Painter
Details	
Mus. /Lit. Ref.	Museo Nazionale Tarquiniese, Tarquinia 685
Refs.	Meyer, pl. 9 (no. 3) Beazley, J.D., Attic Red-Figure Vase-Painters, 2nd edition (Oxford, 1963), 864.16

Character	Jason
Episode	Rejuvenation
Name	
Artifact	Stamnos
Item Style	Red-figure
Made in	Attica
Found	Vulci
Date	470-460 B.C.
Artist	Hephaisteion Painter
Details	
Mus. /Lit. Ref.	Berlin, Staatl. Mus. F 2188
Refs.	LIMC "Peliades" 7*
	Meyer, J.D., pl. 10 (no. 1)
	Beazley, J.D., Attic Red-Figure Vase-Painters, 2nd edition (Oxford, 1963), 1603

Character	Jason
Episode	Rejuvenation
Name	
Artifact	Hydria
Item Style	Red-figure
Made in	Attica
Found	Vulci
Date	470 B.C.

Artist	Copenhagen Painter
Details	Medea, ram and Jason with white beard (named ΙΑΣΟΝ). Medea holds a skyphos in her left hand.

Mus. /Lit. Ref.	London, British Museum E 163

Refs.	Graves, p. 210
	Cartledge, P., (ed.), p. 183
	LIMC "Iason 62"
	Meyer, pl. 9 (no. 2)

Character	Jason
Episode	Rejuvenation
Name	
Artifact	Stamnos
Item	Red-figure
Style	
Made in	Attica
Found	Vulci, Etruria
Date	470 B.C.
Artist	Copenhagen Painter
Details	

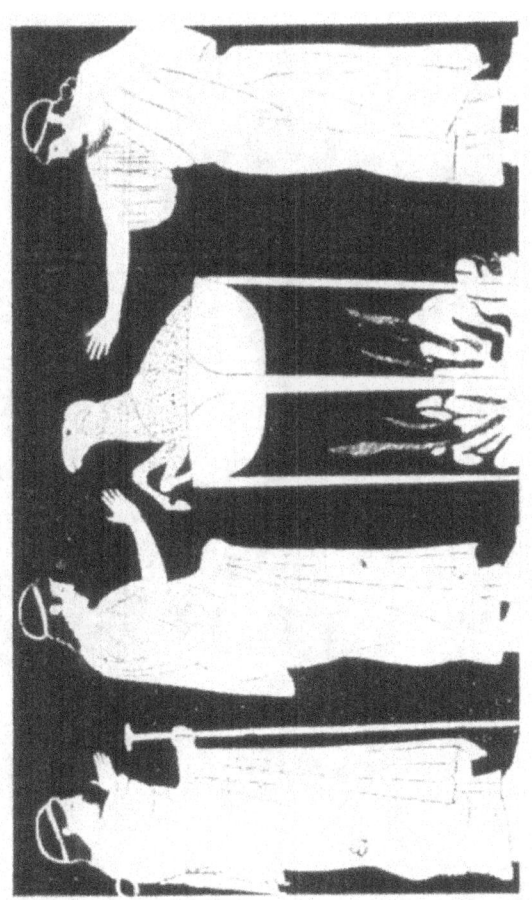

Mus. /Lit. Ref. Munich, Staatliche Antikensammlungen 2408

Refs. LIMC "Pelias" 12* SIDE A; SIDE B

Meyer, pl. 8 (nos. 2 & 3) & pl. 9 (no. 1)

Meyer, pl. 9 (no. 1) SIDE B

Beazley, J.D., Attic Red-Figure Vase-Painters, 2nd edition (Oxford, 1963), 257.8, 258, 1640

Figure No. 084

Character Jason
Episode Rejuvenation

Name
Artifact Hydria
Item Red-figure
Style
Made in Attica
Found
Date 450 B.C.

Artist Villa-Giulia Painter
Details

Mus. /Lit. Ref. Cambridge, Fitz. Mus. GR 12.1917

Refs. LIMC "Peliades" 12*

Meyer, pl. 10 (nos.2 & 3)

Beazley, J.D., Attic Red-Figure Vase-Painters, 2nd edition (Oxford, 1963), 623.66, 1662

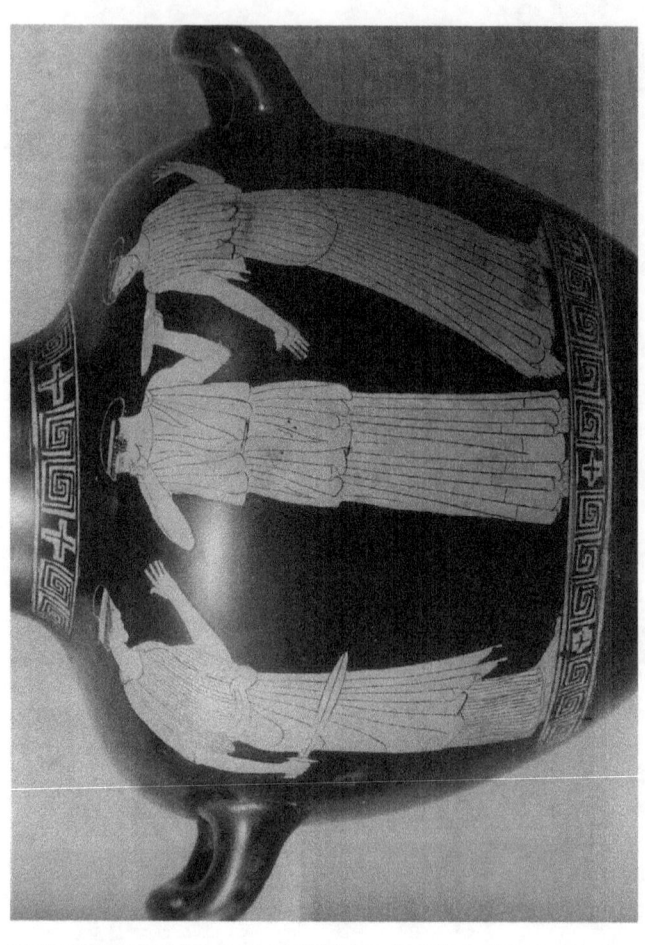

Figure No. 085

Character	Jason
Episode	Rejuvenation
Name	
Artifact	Kylix
Item	Red-figure
Style	
Made in	
Found	
Date	c. 450 B.C.
Artist	Euaion painter
Details	
Mus./Lit. Ref.	Private Collection, Basel
Refs.	Meyer, pl. 11 (no. 1)
	Meyer, pl. 11 (no. 2)
	Meyer, pl. 12 (no. 1)
	LIMC "Peliades" 10*
	LIMC "Pelias" 17

Figure No. 086

Character	Jason
Episode	Rejuvenation
Name	
Artifact	Calyx-krater
Item Style	Red-figure
Made in	Attica
Found	
Date	440 B.C.
Artist	Kleophron painter
Details	Pelias and woman
Mus. /Lit. Ref.	MuM Sonderlisten R (1977) Nr. 63
Refs.	LIMC "Pelias" 18*
	Meyer, pl. 13 (no. 1)

Character Jason
Episode Rejuvenation

Name
Artifact Kylix
Item Red-figure
Style
Made in Attica
Found
Date 440 B.C.

Artist
Details Pelias

Mus. Rome, Vatican, Museums 16538
/Lit.
Ref.

Refs. LIMC "Pelias" 21*

Meyer, pl. 12 (no. 2) [drawing]

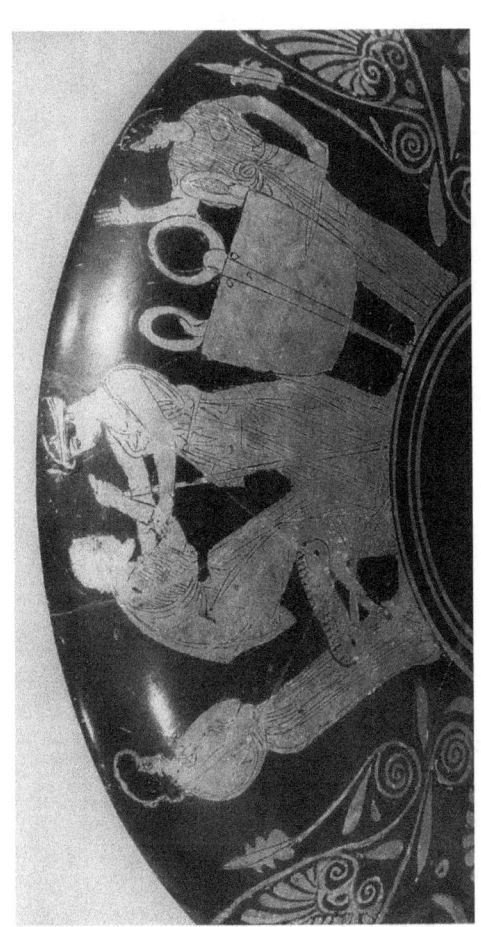

Character Jason

Episode Rejuvenation

Name

Artifact Pyxis

Item red figure
Style

Made in Attica

Found Eretria

Date 430 B.C.

Artist Painter of Hiedelberg 209

Details Rejuvenation of Pelias

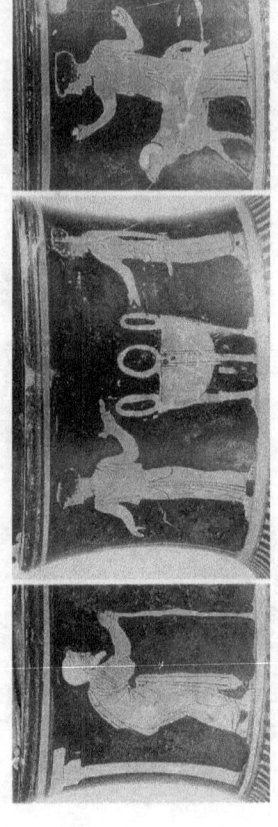

Mus. Paris, Louvre CA 636
/Lit.
Ref.

Refs. LIMC "Pelias" 19*

Meyer, pl. 13 (no. 2)

Beazley, J.D., Attic Red-Figure Vase-
Painters, 2nd edition (Oxford, 1963), 1289.25

Figure No. 089

Character	Jason
Episode	Rejuvenation
Name	
Artifact	Relief
Item	
Style	
Made in	
Found	
Date	420-410 B.C.
Artist	
Details	
Mus.	Berlin
/Lit.	
Ref.	
Refs.	Meyer, pl. 14 (no. 1)

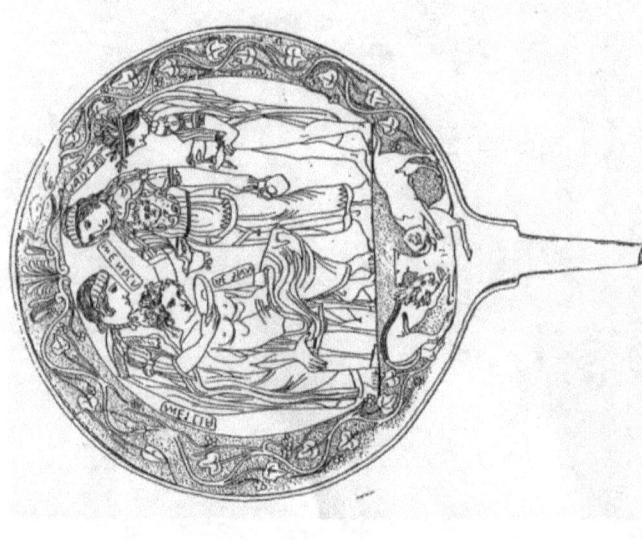

Character	Jason
Episode	Rejuvenation
Name	
Artifact	Hand-mirror
Item Style	Bronze
Made in	Etruscan
Found	Talamone
Date	370-360 B.C.
Artist	
Details	Rejuvenation of Jason?

Mus. /Lit. Ref.	London, British Museum GR 1906.6-18.1
Refs.	Neils, J., pp. 190-5; image- pp. 191 fig.17.1
	LIMC "Iason" 63*
	Meyer, pl. 26 (no. 12)

Character	Jason
Episode	Rejuvenation
Name	
Artifact	Hand mirror
Item Style	Bronze
Made in	Etruscan
Found	
Date	325-300 B.C.
Artist	
Details	Rejuvenation of Jason. 4th century.
Mus. /Lit. Ref.	Paris, Cab. Med. 1329
Refs.	Neils, J., pp. 190-5; image- pp. 191 fig.17.2
	LIMC "Iason" 64*
	Meyer, pl. 17 (no. 2)

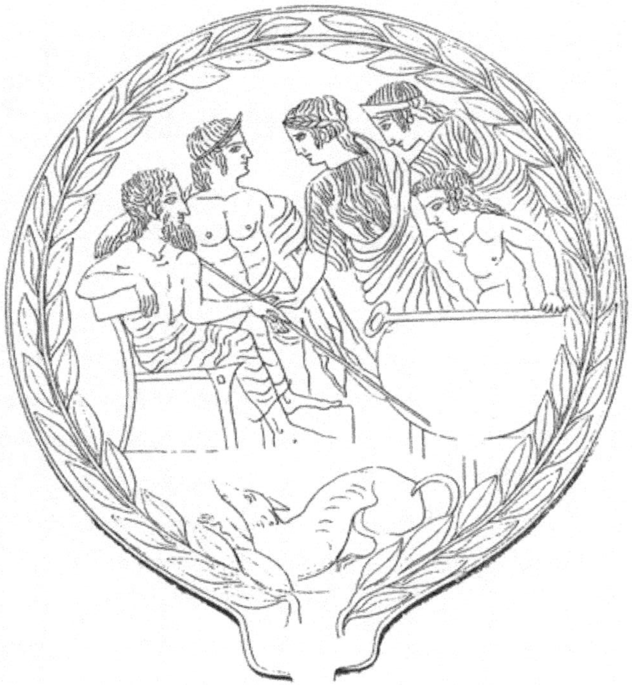

Character Jason
Episode Talos

Name
Artifact Column krater
Item Style Red-figure
Made in Chiusi
Found Chiusi
Date 500-475 B.C.

Artist
Details Two youths with swords (Dioskouroi) attacking a third man (Talos?). Third man attacks with a rock.

Mus. /Lit. Ref. Private Collection, Chiusi

Refs. LIMC "Talos" 7

Figure No. 094

Character Jason
Episode Talos

Name

Artifact Column krater

Item Red-figure
Style

Made in Attica

Found Montesarchio (ancient Caudium)

Date 450-425 B.C.

Artist Unattributed (compared to Orpheus P.)

Details Talos falls back and is supported by the Dioskouroi. Youth (Jason?) kneels in front of Talos and attempts to remove nail from heel; assisted by Thanatos. Medea stands holding a bowl.

Mus. Benevento, Mus. del Sannio
/Lit.
Ref.

Refs. Lesky (1973), pp. 1115-19 figs. 1

Lesky (1973), pp. 1115-19 figs. 2

LIMC "Talos" 6

LIMC "Iason" 55

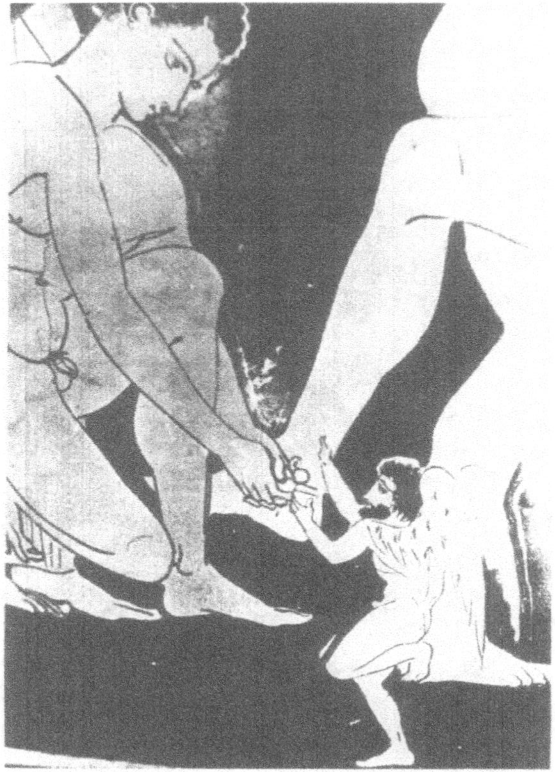

Character	Jason
Episode	Talos
Name	
Artifact	Bronze mirror
Item Style	Relief
Made in Found	Rome
Date	420 B.C.
Artist	
Details	Talos (?) with two Boreadai (?). Silen's head between legs of Talos.
Mus. /Lit. Ref.	Staatliche Museen zu Berlin-Preußischer Kulturbesitz, Antikensammlung Inv. 30480 (mirror)
Refs.	LIMC "Boreadai 44"** LIMC "Talos" 10

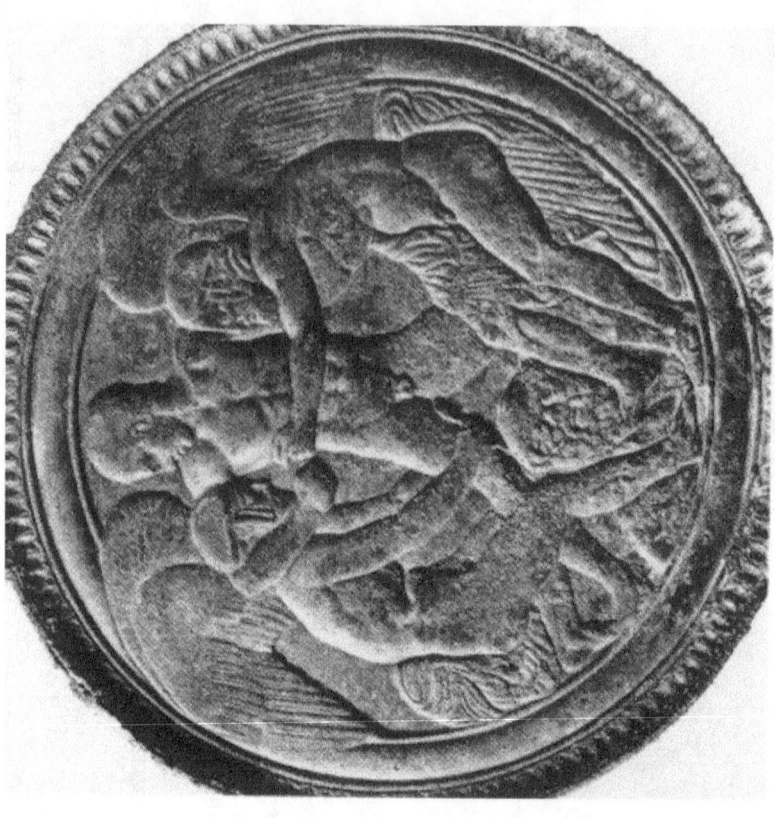

Figure No. 095

Character	Jason
Episode	Talos
Name	
Artifact	Volute krater
Item Style	Red-figure
Made in	Attica
Found	Ruvo
Date	400 B.C.
Artist	Talos Painter
Details	Death of Talos
Mus. /Lit. Ref.	Ruvo, Mus. Jatta. J 1501
Refs.	Carpenter, T.H., fig. 279
	Meyer, pl. 20 (no. 1)
	3: Lesky (1973), pp. 1115-19 figs. 2
	LIMC "Talos" 4*
	LIMC "Iason" 56

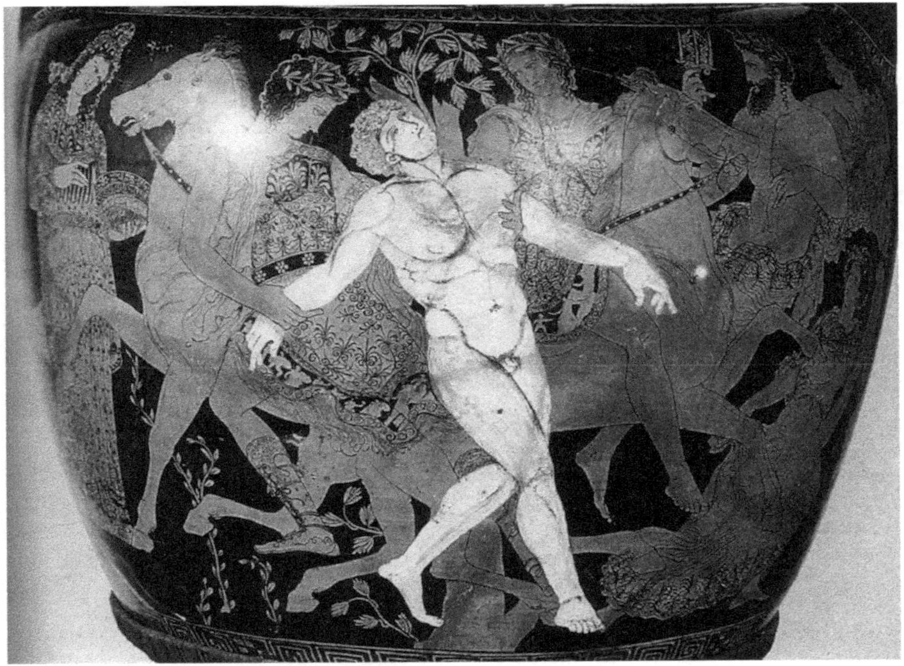

Character Jason
Episode Talos

Name
Artifact Krater
Item
Style Fragment
Made in
Found Spina
Date 400 B.C.

Artist
Details

Mus. Ferrara, Mus. Naz. 3092
/Lit.
Ref.

Refs. LIMC "Talos" 5*

LIMC "Thanatos" 30

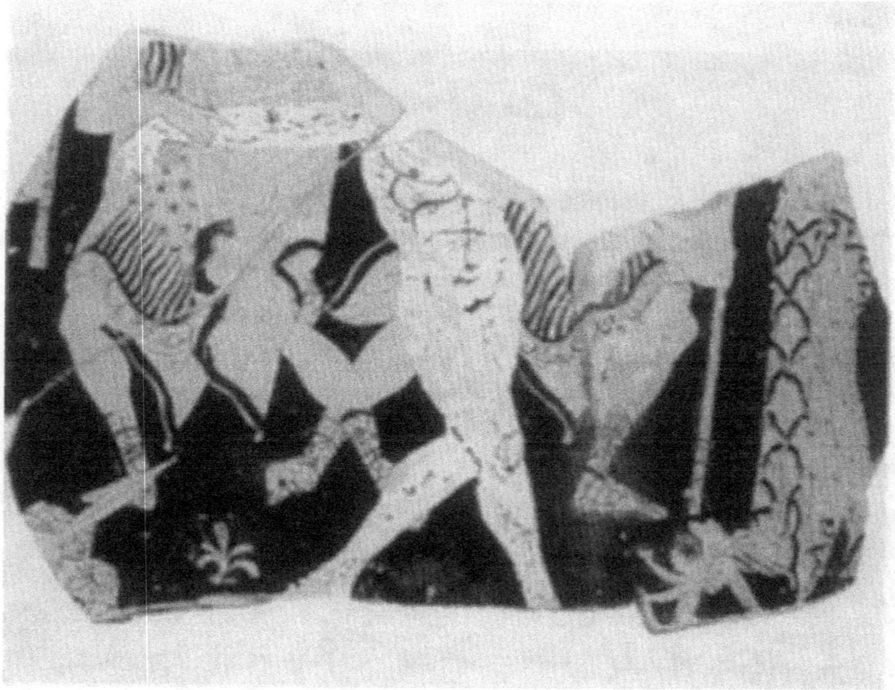

Character	Herakles
Episode	Fleece
Name	
Artifact	Volute-krater
Item Style	Red-figure
Made in Found	Apulia
Date	350-340 B.C.
Artist	Close to Lycurgus Painter
Details	Herakles attacks serpent

Mus. /Lit. Ref.

Refs. LIMC "Argonautai" 21*

LIMC "Herakles" 2796

LIMC "Iason" 39

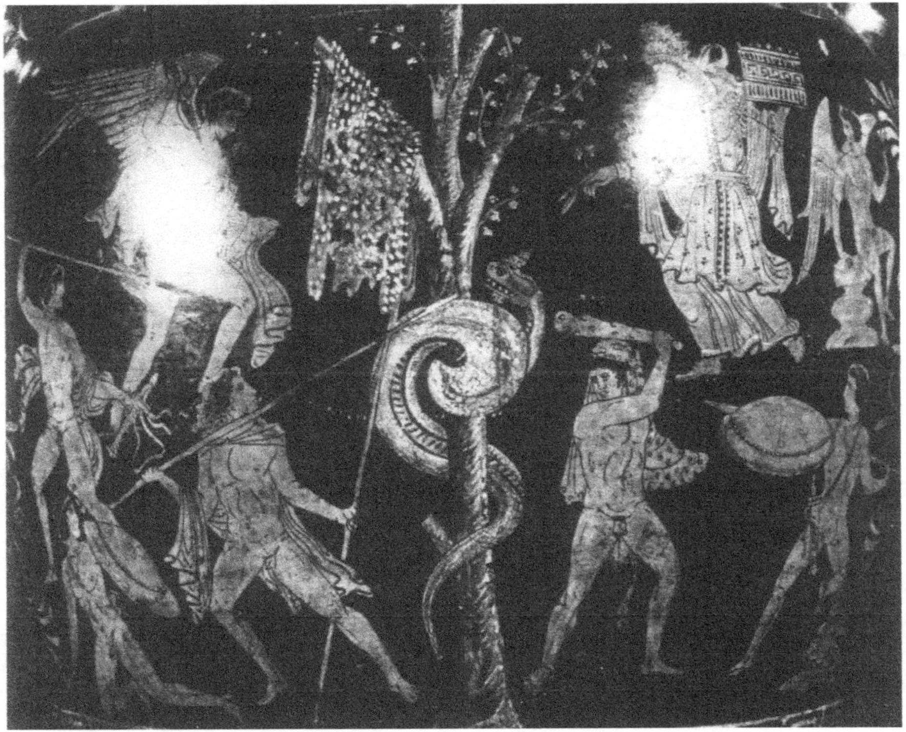

Character	Perseus
Episode	Andromeda & Ketos
Name	
Artifact	Amphora fragment
Item Style	Black-figure
Made in	Korinth
Found	Cervetri
Date	560 B.C. 575-550 B.C. (LIMC)
Artist	
Details	Perseus attacks ketos; Andromeda stands behind. Rocks (?) beneath Perseus. Characters named. Perseus has winged boots, petasos, kibisis; throws rocks at ketos.
Mus. /Lit. Ref.	Berlin, Staatl. Mus. F 1652
Refs.	Carpenter, fig. 158 LIMC "Andromeda" 1* Schefold, K, 44b Woodward, J., fig. 9 a & b LIMC "Perseus" 187

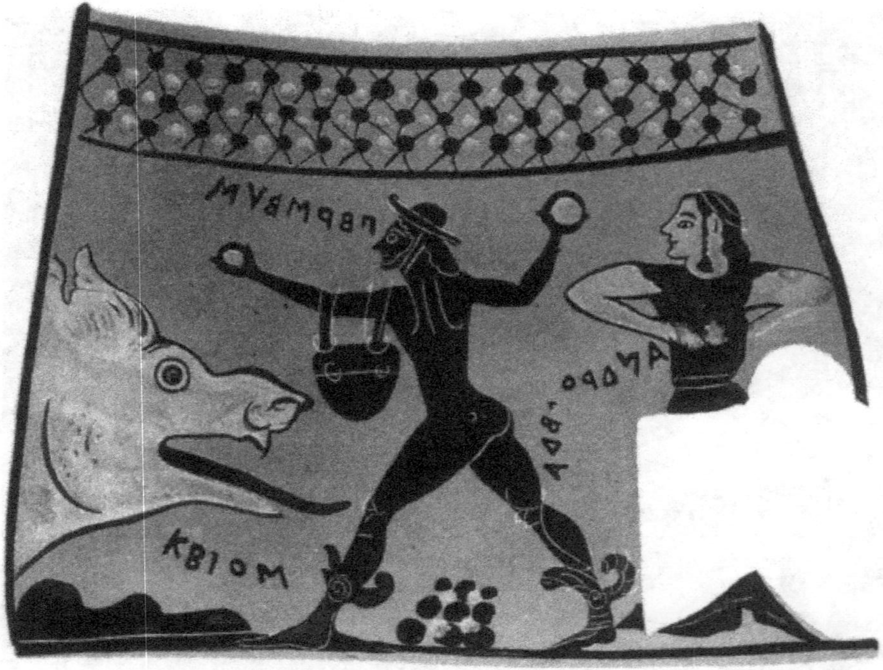

Figure No. 099

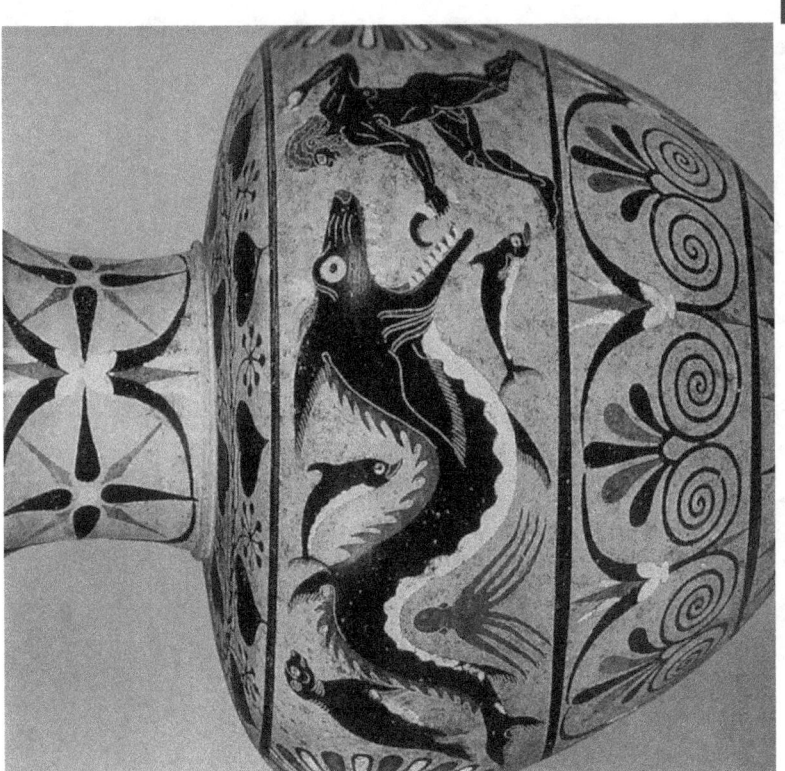

Character Perseus
Episode Andromeda & Ketos

Name
Artifact Hydria
Item
Style Black-figure
Made in Caeretan vessel
Found
Date 530 B.C.

Artist
Details Perseus (?) approaches ketos with
curved harpe; also identified as Herakles

Mus.
/Lit. Kusnacht, Hirschmann, Hemelrijk # 29
Ref.

Refs. *The Oxford History of Classical Art*, (ed.)
Boardman, fig. 71

Boardman (1998), fig. 496

LIMC Perseus 188*

Character	Perseus
Episode	Fleeing Gorgons
Name	
Artifact	Louterion or bowl fragment
Item Style	Black-figure
Made in	Attica
Found	Aegina
Date	610-600 B.C. 620- Schefold
Artist	Nettos Painter
Details	Perseus (beard, short chiton, cap, winged boots, kibisis, sword) and Athena. Perseus and Athena (both named) flee. Hermes (?) foot to left. See also fig. 39
Mus. /Lit. Ref.	Berlin, Staatl. Mus. F 1682 (lost)
Refs.	LIMC "Perseus" 152* LIMC "Athena" 6* Schefold, K, 44a Woodward, fig. 4a-b Henle, J., fig. 46

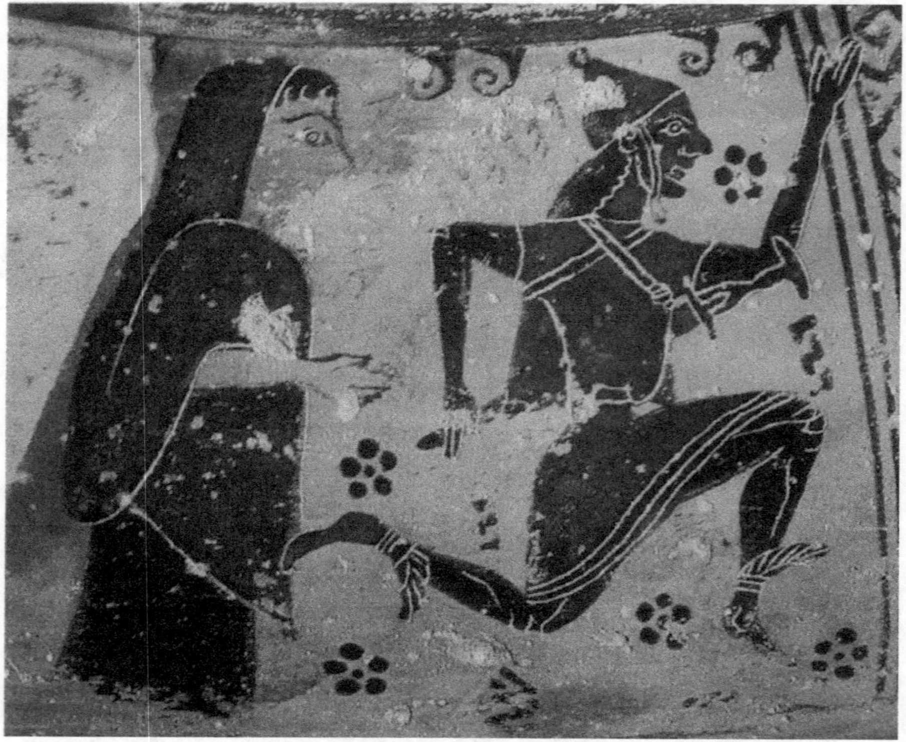

Figure No. 101

Character	Perseus
Episode	Fleeing Gorgons
Name	
Artifact	Dinos
Item Style	Black-figure
Made in	Attica
Found	Vulci
Date	570-560 B.C. 600-580 B.C. (LIMC Athena 7*) 590 B.C. LIMC Gorgo, G. 314*
Artist	Gorgon Painter
Details	Perseus, Athena and Hermes flee the Gorgons
Mus. /Lit. Ref.	Paris, Louvre E 874
Refs.	Biers, fig. 12
	LIMC "Athena" 7*
	Schefold, K, 45
	LIMC "Gorgo, Gorgones" 314*
	Woodward, fig. 6a-c

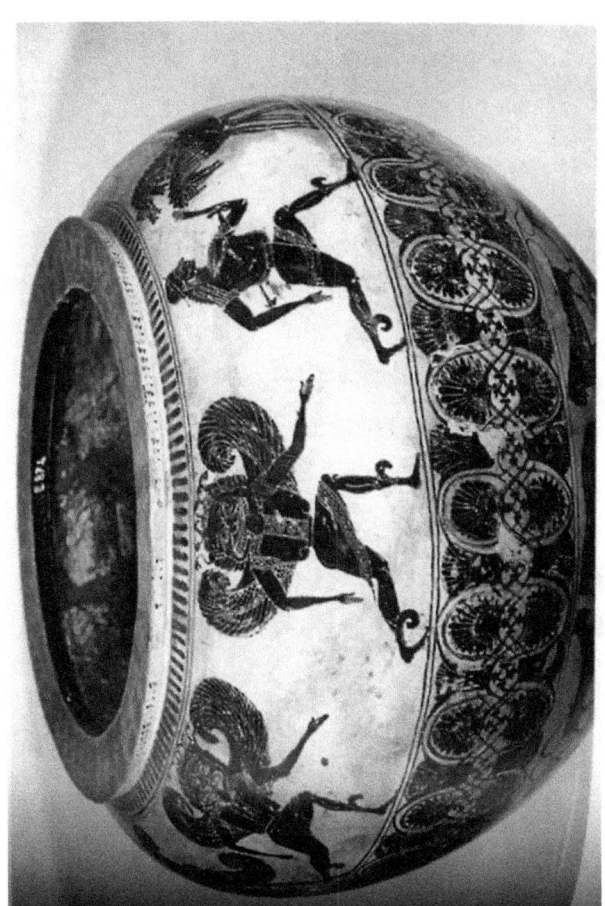

Figure No. 102

Character Perseus
Episode Graiai

Name
Artifact Column krater
Item Style Red-figure
Made in Attica
Found Pisticci, Lucania
Date 460 B.C.

Artist
Details Three Graiai. There is a simple line drawn for their eyes, indicating blindness.

Note: On the other side of the vase is Perseus, Hermes and Poseidon. fig. 187

Mus. /Lit. Ref. Metaponto, Antiquarium 20.145

Refs. LIMC "Graiai" 1*

Oakley, fig. 2

Oakley, fig. 4

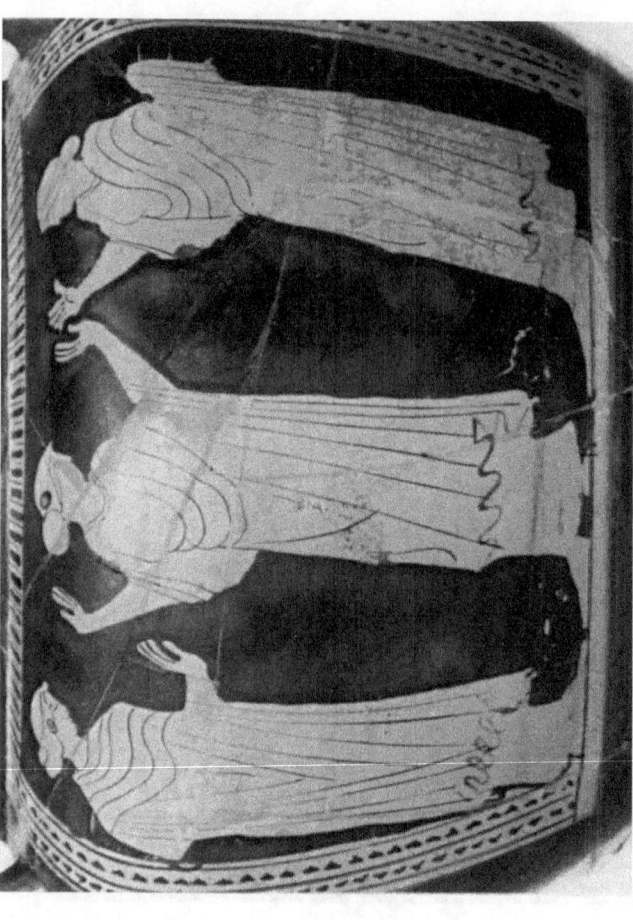

Figure No. 103

Character	Perseus
Episode	Graiai
Name	
Artifact	Pyxis cover
Item Style	Red-figure
Made in	Attica
Found	
Date	450-425 B.C.
Artist	
Details	Perseus attempts to take eye from Graiai as they pass it between them. Athena, Hermes and Poseidon all appear. Perseus with cap, winged shoes, short chiton, mantle & spears.
Mus. /Lit. Ref.	National Archaeological Museum, Athens 1291 (CC 1956)
Refs.	LIMC "Graiai" 2*
	Woodward, fig. 27a & b
	Schefold & Jung, fig. 119
	LIMC "Perseus" 89
	LIMC "Hermes" 482

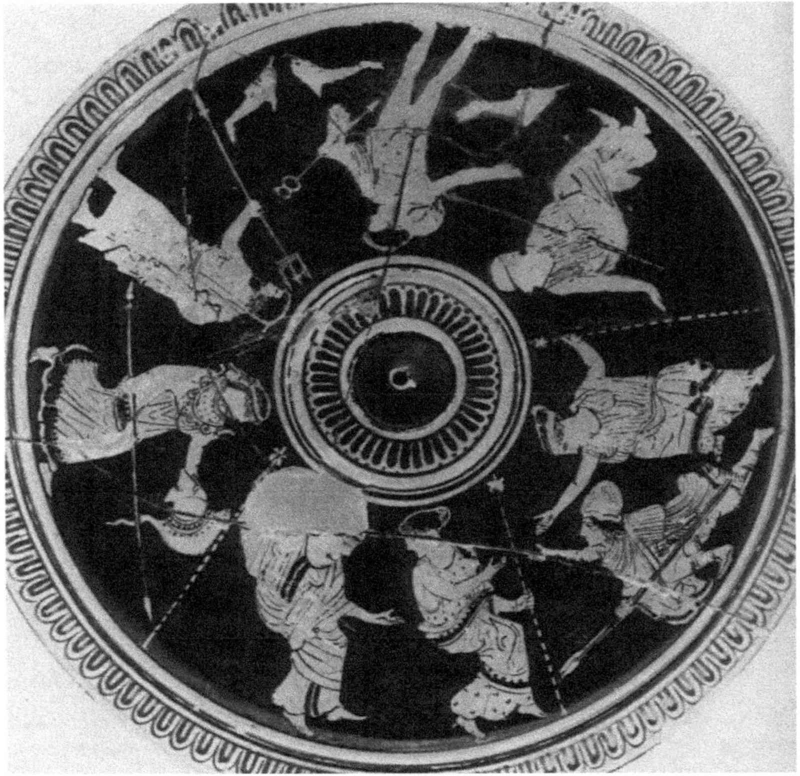

Character	Perseus
Episode	Graiai
Name	
Artifact	Pyxis cover fragment
Item	
Style	Red-figure
Made in	Attica
Found	Brauron
Date	440-430 B.C.
Artist	
Details	Perseus with winged shoes, chlamys, harpe and kibisis; Gorgones

Mus. /Lit. Ref. Brauron, Mus. 282 (A49)

Refs. LIMC "Perseus" 104*

LIMC "Gorgo, Gorgones" 302

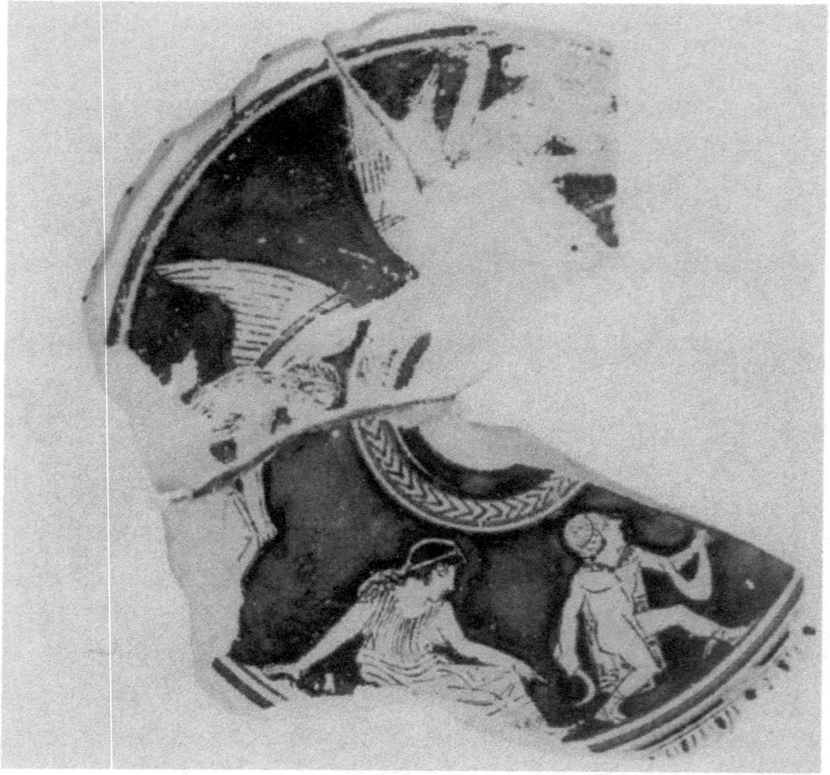

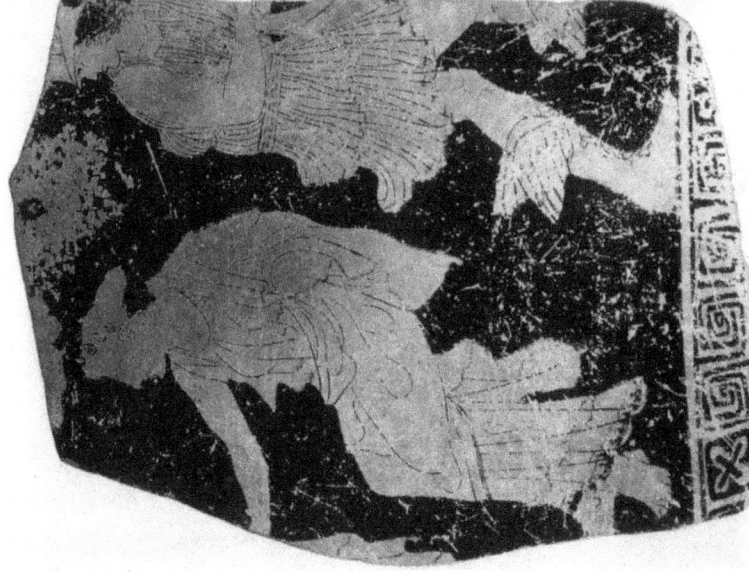

Character Perseus
Episode Graiai

Name
Artifact Krater fragment
Item Red-figure
Style
Made in Attica
Found Delos
Date 430-425 B.C.

Artist Phiale Painter
Details Perseus and the Graiai. Perseus wears short chiton, winged cap and winged boots. Possibly a seconc Graiai to left?

Mus. Delos Museum, B 7263
/Lit.
Ref.

Refs. Carpenter, T.H., fig. 147

LIMC "Graiai" 3*

Schefold & Jung, fig. 118

Oakley, J., fig. 7

Figure No. 106

Character	Perseus
Episode	Receiving gifts
Name	
Artifact	Relief plaque
Item Style	Bronze
Made in	Sparta, Temple of Athena
Found	Now lost
Date	560-540 B.C.
Artist	Gitiades
Details	"...Nymphs bestowing upon Perseus...a cap and the shoes...."
Mus. /Lit. Ref.	Literature: Pausanias 3.17.3
Refs.	LIMC "Perseus" 96

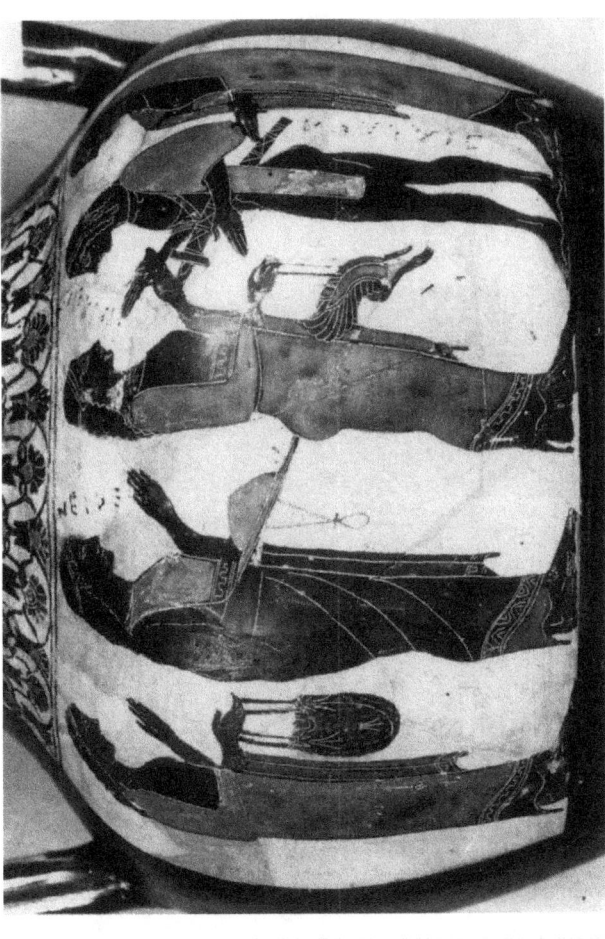

Character	Perseus
Episode	Receiving gifts
Name	
Artifact	Amphora
Item Style	Black-figure
Made in	Chalchis
Found	Cervetri
Date	540 B.C. 520 B.C. (LIMC Athena 508)
Artist	Inscription Painter
Details	Perseus (named) receives gifts from the nymphs (inscribed Neides); winged shoes, hat & kibisis Image restored
Mus. /Lit. Ref.	London, British Museum B 155
Refs.	Osborne, R., fig 55 Carpenter, T.H., fig. 148 (restored) Boardman (1998), fig. 470 LIMC "Perseus" 88* Woodward, J., fig. 12a

Figure No. 108

Character	Perseus
Episode	Receiving gifts
Name	
Artifact	Loutrophoros
Item Style	Black-figure
Made in	Attica
Found	Sanctuary of the Nmyphs, Athens
Date	530 B.C.
Artist	
Details	Perseus receives gifts from the Nymphs.
Mus. /Lit. Ref.	Athens, Fethive Djami NA 57-Aa-274
Refs.	LIMC "Perseus" 87

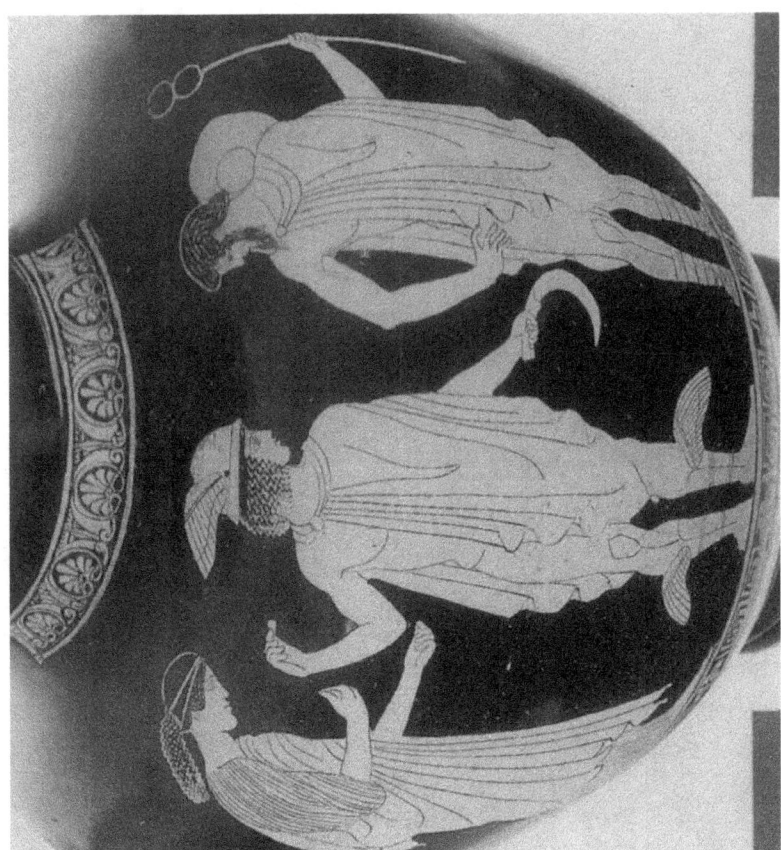

Character Perseus
Episode Receiving gifts

Name
Artifact Hydria
Item Red-figure
Style
Made in Attica
Found
Date 450 B.C.

Artist Villa Giulia Painter
Details Perseus, Hermes and a woman. Perseus with winged cap, winged shoes, harpe and chlamys.

Mus. Edinburgh, Nat. Mus. 1872.23.11
/Lit.
Ref.

Refs. LIMC "Perseus" 91*

Schauenburg, K., Tafel 6.2

Figure No. 110

www.ingramcontent.com/pod-product-compliance
Lightning Source LLC
Chambersburg PA
CBHW071401170526
45165CB00001B/135